Mrs. Tsenhor

Mrs. Tsenhor

A Female Entrepreneur
in Ancient Egypt

Koenraad Donker van Heel

The American University in Cairo Press
Cairo New York

This paperback edition published in 2015 by
The American University in Cairo Press
113 Sharia Kasr el Aini, Cairo, Egypt
420 Fifth Avenue, New York, NY 10018
www.aucpress.com

Exclusive distribution outside Egypt and North America by I.B.Tauris & Co Ltd., 6 Salem
Road, London, W2 4BU

Dar el Kutub No. 4969/14
ISBN 978 977 416 677 8

Dar el Kutub Cataloging-in-Publication Data

Donker van Heel, Koenraad
        Mrs Tsenhor: A female entrepreneur in ancient Egypt—Cairo: The American
    University in Cairo Press, 2015
        p.   cm.
        ISBN: 978 977 416 677 8
        Women—Egypt—History—To 332 B.C.
        Egypt—History—To 332 B.C
        305.40932

1 2 3 4 5   19 18 17 16 15

Designed by Andrea El-Akshar
Printed in Egypt

Contents

Illustrations

Tables

The Tsenhor Papyri

Concordance between the publication numbers in *Les papyrus démotiques de Tsenhor: Les archives privées d'une femme égyptienne du temps de Darius Ier* (Leuven: Peeters, 1994) and the museum inventory numbers.

INV. NR.	P. TSENHOR	P. TSENHOR	INV. NR.
P. Bibl. Nat. 216	5	1	P. Louvre E 10935
P. Bibl. Nat. 217	6	2	P. Vienna KM 3853
P. Bibl. Nat. 223	8	3	P. BM EA 10120A
P. BM EA 10120A	3	4	P. BM EA 10120B
P. BM EA 10120B	4	5	P. Bibl. Nat. 216
P. Louvre AF 9761	15	6	P. Bibl. Nat. 217
P. Louvre E 3231A	14	7	P. Turin 2122
P. Louvre E 7128	10	8	P. Bibl. Nat. 223
P. Louvre E 10935	1	9	P. Turin 2123
P. Turin 2122	7	10	P. Louvre E 7128
P. Turin 2123	9	11	P. Turin 2124
P. Turin 2124	11	12	P. Turin 2125
P. Turin 2125	12	13	P. Turin 2126
P. Turin 2126	13	14	P. Louvre E 3231A
P. Turin 2127	16	15	P. Louvre AF 9761
P. Turin 2128	17	16	P. Turin 2127
P. Vienna KM 3853	2	17	P. Turin 2128

Preface

Once again, this book was not primarily written for my colleagues, even though Egyptologists, demotists, and (legal) historians may think something of it and even use it to their advantage. But they are not my intended audience. I want this to be a book for everyone.

The year 2012 was a strange but wonderful one, in which I was invited to rejoin Leiden University as a lecturer in demotic and abnormal hieratic—the latter part of the job description obviously coming from me—with ancient Egyptian law thrown in for good measure. This was too good an opportunity to miss, especially since it combines wonderfully well with the commercial work from which I make my income. All I have to do now is to get used again to the constraints imposed by life in academia.

My ambition, however, remains to write about ancient Egypt in a language that people can understand and relate to. This book is the natural sequel to *Djekhy & Son: Doing Business in Ancient Egypt* (2012), which was republished as a paperback in 2013. It seeks to explore the life of an ancient Egyptian woman living in the reign of the Persian pharaoh Darius I and, by proxy, the lives of common women in ancient Egypt in general. That is also why I included many known and, more importantly, not so known hieratic, demotic, Greek, and Coptic sources in which mostly ordinary women appear, in an attempt to show that the ancient Egyptian woman was in fact very different from her Middle Eastern and Greek counterparts. This book really aims to modify the picture most people have of ancient Egyptian women, which is far too often based on the lives of famous queens such as Hatshepsut, Nefertiti, Ahmose Nefertari, and, yes, Cleopatra (who was anything but an Egyptian woman).

Since the main character of this book lived through the reigns of Amasis II, Psamtik III, Cambyses II, Darius I, and perhaps even Psamtik IV, it felt appropriate to embed her story in the slightly larger picture— however fragmentary and kaleidoscopic—of Egypt under Persian rule. For reasons that may not be obvious to some, the choice was made to maintain this approach in the treatment of the sources that tell us about the life of our ancient Egyptian girl next door. Although this anecdotal report may repel some, a purely chronological approach would have led to a much more boring story. Anyway, this is not a book for the lazy reader.

The main character of this book is called Tsenhor, who was a business-woman in her own right. She came from the same social circles as Djekhy and his son Iturech, and she undoubtedly knew the latter. So once again this is a book about people like you and me.

The papers left to us by Mrs. Tsenhor were first published in *Les papyrus démotiques de Tsenhor: Les archives privées d'une femme égyptienne du temps de Darius Ier* (Leuven: Peeters, 1994), the magnum opus by the Dutch demotist and legal historian Pieter Willem Pestman. However, this book only addressed a tiny audience within the scientific community. It also sold Mrs. Tsenhor short. The exciting story of her life is something that should be shared with all. That is why I decided to tell it for her.

It was only when the manuscript of this book was in its final stages— that awkward moment at which most manuscripts are relegated to the drawer for an indefinite period of time—that I learned of the existence of Terry Wilfong's *Women of Jeme: Lives in a Coptic Town in Late Antique Egypt* (Ann Arbor, MI: University of Michigan Press, 2002). Terry's book (he sent me a copy right away) provided me with unknown—well, to me at least—fascinating material about common Egyptian women living in the same neighborhood in which Tsenhor had spent her days more than a thousand years earlier, displaying much of the same independent spirit. It also filled me with new energy, becoming an additional source of inspiration overnight, and the reader is reminded that wherever some of the Coptic material is incorporated in the chapters below, it is entirely Terry's work, not mine.

Maren Goecke-Bauer—my dearest pal from Deir al-Medina days that have long since been left behind—was more or less forced by me to write a book when she was still a student. She kindly repaid the favor by more or less forcing me to finish this one, just because she wanted to read the manuscript. Her persistent encouragement came right in time, so that we can now actually say that sometimes writing books—just like life itself—hinges on people telling you to shut up and get to work. Maren also kindly selected the plate on the cover. She is now herself working on a new book about Deir al-Medina. Go get 'em, girl!

Thank you both very, very much for giving me the kick in the pants needed to bring this project to a close. I owe you both one. A big one.

When in the spring of 2012 I looked at the cover of *Djekhy & Son*, the first book I wrote for the American University in Cairo Press, it suddenly dawned on me that my late dad—although he probably would never have said it—would have been a proud father, indeed. Finally some return for the love, effort, and money he invested in me. Still, the dedicatee of this book is clear. To all the Tsenhors in this world. And to people who still believe in magic.

The symbols used in the translations are as follows:

[...]	Papyrus is damaged or broken off
< ... >	Omission by the Egyptian scribe
{ ... }	Superfluous words
(...)	Translator's remark

Acknowledgments

Once again, many people gave willingly of their precious time and energy just to help me out, filling me with a sense of awe and gratitude. The word to describe this feeling has not been invented yet. And a simple thank you is not enough.

Guillemette Andreu, the present director of the Department of Egyptian Antiquities of the Louvre, kindly allowed me to use O. IFAO 2892 from Vandier d'Abbadie, *Catalogue des ostraca figurés de Deir el-Médineh, Nos. 2734 à 3053*, DFIFAO 1959. Elisabeth David and Marc Etienne of the Louvre happily cleared up the fog surrounding the acquisition of early demotic P. Louvre E 3231A–C. Eugene Cruz-Uribe, formerly of the Department of History at Northern Arizona University, who was the first to publish P. Louvre E 3231B and C, readily shared with me his view on whether these papyri do or do not belong to the Tsenhor papers (they do).

Günter Vittmann, the foremost expert in abnormal hieratic texts today, graciously allowed me to reproduce his facsimile of the Late Period inscription of Petosiris son of Wenamun in this book.

Susanna Moser, then of the University of Pisa, and François Tonic, historian and editor in chief of *Pharaon Magazine*, gave me the exact leads I needed to familiarize myself with the tomb of Pabasa (TT 279), saving me much extra effort.

Friends and colleagues from the Netherlands also chipped in. Huub Pragt of egyptologie.nl—who is an expert on how to make ancient Egypt accessible to a larger audience—kindly read the entire manuscript and gave valuable tips on the way the material should be presented. The maps prepared by Hans Schoens for *Djekhy & Son* (2012) were so good that the decision was made to reuse them in this book. Jurgen van Oostenrijk graciously put his Master's thesis on Late Period *ushabti*s at my disposal, providing a direct and very clear inspiration for the subchapter "Four Hundred and One Little Workers." Cisca Hoogendijk, a Greek papyrologist and my nearest and dearest colleague at the Papyrologisch Instituut in Leiden, had to choose between reading my manuscript and a holiday in Sicily. Although the latter sadly won the day, she did contribute (well, some) to the subchapter "The Days on Which Tsenhor Did Not Work." My former editor at the Economische Voorlichtings Dienst in The Hague, Karin Hakkenberg van Gaasbeek, agreed to read the manuscript with her typical editor's eye. Although other commitments precluded her from doing this, the intention was there, which is enough for me. Paulien Retèl, publications manager at the Allard Pierson Museum (Amsterdam), is one of those rare people who can tell you exactly what makes a book tick, prompting the remark by one of my reviewers that it was very smart of me to include her, because "an ex-girlfriend will surely be very critical of the way you write about women." And yes, she liked the manuscript.

Janet Johnson of the Oriental Institute in Chicago—fellow demotist and one of the gender studies specialists whose work no one can afford to miss—did read the whole manuscript, even though she was severely pressed for time (as usual), pointing out to me two very important truths that I had missed completely.

Damien Agut of the French National Center for Scientific Research (Archéologies et Sciences de l'Antiquité) is a specialist on the Persian period in Egypt, as well as a demotist who can see the humor of many things, including my manuscript. This may be because he is a Gascon, just like d'Artagnan. He kindly checked the sections on Persian history and, perhaps more importantly, provided me with the idea for the Gascon farewell at the end of this book. And that is just right.

Bahar Landsberger from Münster University, my former student in demotic, abnormal hieratic, and ancient Egyptian law in Leiden, gladly took up the challenge of critically reading the manuscript. At present she is preparing a dissertation on the famous Siut trial that is also described in this book, clearing up one crucial reading problem in my manuscript in the process. I expect to hear great things about her in the future.

Neil Hewison, Nadia Naqib, and Johanna Baboukis of the American University in Cairo Press are much thanked for turning my manuscript into a book and seeing it through to publication with their usual efficiency. Special thanks are reserved for my wonderful copyeditor

Jasmina Brankovic, who managed to improve the manuscript with only minimal interventions. Pure magic if you ask me. Randi Danforth, formerly of the AUC Press, always believed that one day Tsenhor would receive her own little monument. So here it is!

Apart from Terry and Maren, whose essential contributions have already been mentioned in the Preface (they also thoroughly checked the manuscript), there is one other person who has put his indelible mark on this book. My friend Cary Martin of University College London, who happens to be a demotist, once again—and despite many other engagements—agreed to check the English of the manuscript. Linking a keen eye for demotic and style with his vast knowledge of the Late Period, it is probably his dry wit that makes being reviewed by him such a pleasure. Thank you all very, very much!

And yes, all remaining errors, blunders, and mistakes are mine, no one else's.

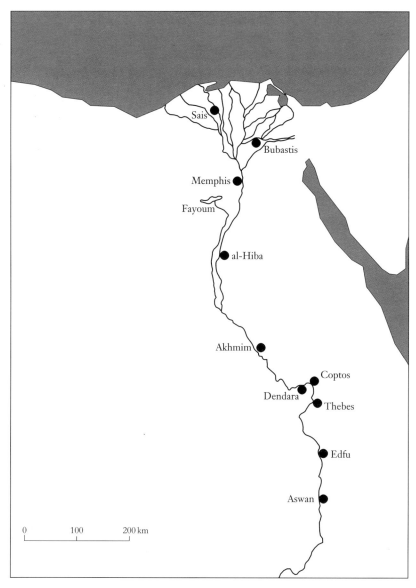

Figure 1. Ancient Egypt in the sixth century BCE [Courtesy Hans Schoens]

Chronology

Twenty-sixth Saite Dynasty

Necho I	672–664
Psamtik I	664–610
Necho II	610–595
Psamtik II	595–589
Apries	589–570
Amasis	570–526
Psamtik III	526–525

Twenty-seventh Persian Dynasty

Cambyses II	525–522
Darius I	521–486
Xerxes I	486–466
Artaxerxes I	465–424
Darius II	424–404

All regnal years are BCE. They are taken from John Baines and Jaromir Malek, *Atlas of Ancient Egypt* (New York: Facts on File, 1983).

1

People

The Family

If Tsenhor were alive today, she would be wearing jeans, driving a pickup, and enjoying a beer with the boys. Instead she was born around 550 BCE in the city of Thebes (Karnak), in the deep south of Egypt. From the papers she left behind—now kept in the Bibliothèque Nationale (Paris), the British Museum, the Louvre, the Museo Egizio (Turin), and the Kunsthistorisches Museum (Vienna)—a picture emerges of a woman who had firm control over her own life. One assumes that this happened with the full support of her second husband, Psenese, who fathered two of her children. Just like Djekhy and Iturech—the main characters in *Djekhy & Son: Doing Business in Ancient Egypt* (Cairo: American University in Cairo Press, 2012)—Tsenhor was a choachyte, a funerary service provider who was hired to bring offerings to the deceased who were buried in the necropolis on the west bank of the Nile. By this we mean that Tsenhor did the work herself. In P. Turin 2127 from 491 BCE her eldest (half-)brother Nesamunhotep allots to her one-quarter of the income of a choachyte in return for her funerary services, presumably because she was a partner in the family business together with Nesamunhotep and two of her other (half-)brothers, Inaros and Burekhef. By that time, Tsenhor may already have been sixty years old, which was ancient in Late Period Egypt.

To you (Tsenhor) belongs a quarter of the bread of the choachyte and any other things that will be given to us as an offering for the mouth of the *kalasirian* (policeman) of the nome Nespaser son of Teos and his children. You will perform the service of a choachyte for its quarter in accordance with their needs at any time.

1

If it had not been for P. Turin 2125, in which the same man allots a part of their father's house to Tsenhor, we probably would never have known that they were related. In this contract from 506 BCE Nesamunhotep refers to himself as "son of Petemin, whose mother is Tays," while addressing his sister as "Mrs. Tsenhor daughter of Nesmin, whose mother is Ruru." It is only in the first line of the actual contract that their relationship becomes clear: "I have given to you a large space of the house of Nesmin, our father."

Ten years earlier, in P. Bibl. Nat. 217 from March 517 BCE, Tsenhor allots half of her inheritance to her baby daughter Ruru, who was named after her grandmother (this was a popular custom), showing that she herself owned part of the income of a choachyte established by her father Petemin (or Nesmin):

> To you (Ruru) belongs half of what I (Tsenhor) own in the field, the temple, and the city, namely houses, field, slaves, silver, copper, clothing, *it* grain, emmer, ox, donkey, tomb in the mountain, and anything else on earth, as well as half of my share that comes to me in the name of the choachyte of the valley Nesmin son of Khausenwesir, my father, and (in the name of) Mrs. Ruru daughter of the choachyte of the valley Petemin, whose mother is Taydy, my mother. To you belongs half of my share that comes to me in the names of my mother and father mentioned above and in the names of their father and mother. To you belongs (half of) what is rightfully mine, in their name.

Ruru eventually followed in her mother's footsteps. In September or October 497 BCE she herself closed a deal with a high official from the temple of Amun in Karnak to provide funerary offerings to a Mrs. Tadyipwer in return for four *arura*s of land, which was slightly over a hectare (P. Louvre E 3231A).

The other papyri left by Tsenhor also show that she was a businesswoman in her own right. In 516 BCE she bought a slave (P. Bibl. Nat. 223), and in 512 BCE, together with her second husband Psenese, she acquired a house or building site in the Theban necropolis (P. Turin 2123). Above, it was seen how Tsenhor (in P. Turin 2127 from 491 BCE) was appointed as a choachyte for one-quarter of the income connected with the funerary services to be performed for the family of a policeman. Since she had three brothers, dividing their parental home into equal parts in 506 BCE (P. Turin 2125), it seems that the four siblings may have continued the funerary services business of their father Petemin as a single company. Although the members of the family were mere choachytes, belonging to the lower middle class, in some of the contracts—maybe because they were standing in a notary office (not an everyday experience)—they call themselves "choachyte of the valley (the Assasif)," "choachyte of the necropolis of Djeme," and "choachyte of the west of Thebes," as if to underline the solemnity of the occasion. Most Egyptians would probably never have owned a written contract in their entire lives.

Then there was the land, eleven *arura*s that we know of, almost three hectares. These had been acquired by Tsenhor's father in 556 BCE (P. Louvre E 10935) in return for his funerary services for a woman also called Tsenhor. The papers collected by 'our' Tsenhor tell us that she and her brothers were also engaged in the cultivation of this land. In P. Turin 2124 from 507 BCE we see her (half-)brother Burekhef ('He does not know') pay another man for the use of the cow he had leased for plowing the land. In view of the Turin inventory number—P. Turin 2122 up to and including 2128 are all papers connected to Tsenhor—we may be certain that this contract made out for Burekhef was originally part of Tsenhor's archive. In 487 BCE we see Tsenhor's son Ituru exchange cows with a cattle-keeper (P. Turin 2128). If Tsenhor was still alive at this time, she would have been sixty-three.

To the eleven *arura*s of family land we can add the four *arura*s acquired by her daughter in 497 BCE (P. Louvre E 3231A). If both her father and her daughter acquired land in return for their services, it is hardly likely that a keen businesswoman such as Tsenhor would not have acquired land on her own, so the family probably owned more land than we know of (she did have two husbands). Some believe that the eleven *arura*s acquired by Tsenhor's father were owned by her exclusively, but she could actually have co-owned and cultivated these fields together with her three (half-)brothers.

But where did Tsenhor come from? Her father Petemin ('Whom Min has given') was also called Nesmin ('Belonging to Min') and married at least twice in his life. His first wife was an otherwise unknown Mrs. Tays, who bore him a son called Nesamunhotep, or Amunhotep for short. Petemin was to have two more sons who survived childhood, playing a minor role in some of the papers left by Tsenhor. They were called Inaros and Burekhef, but we do not know their mother's name.

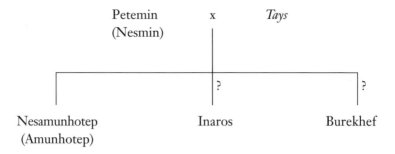

The names of the women are in italics.

Petemin's second marriage was to a choachyte's daughter called Ituru, or Ruru for short, who gave birth to our Tsenhor ('The sister of Horus') around 550 BCE. She was probably named after Petemin's best-paying customer, the deceased Mrs. Tsenhor, whose son had endowed the family with eleven *arura*s of fields. It is difficult to believe that Tsenhor would have been the only surviving girl in this household, but the sources are silent on this point.

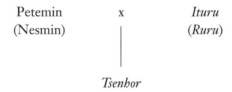

If we assume that Petemin (Nesmin) was in his early twenties when he concluded this deal about the eleven *arura*s in 556 BCE, he may have lived well into his seventies. Only in 506 BCE did Tsenhor and her (half-) brothers divide the house he once owned (P. Turin 2125), although it is equally possible that Petemin died much earlier and that the eldest brother Nesamunhotep managed the estate for some years before the formal decision was made to split up the house. This would include the writing of at least three new title deeds for Tsenhor and her (half-) brothers Inaros and Burekhef and maybe even three more in which the siblings promise their eldest brother not to claim some other part of the house in the future. In any case, as the ancient Egyptians were a very practical people, when the siblings divided the house, the scribe—no doubt wise through experience—specifically mentioned that the staircase would remain in communal use. The clause about the right of way was not a standard clause, although it does occur more often going into the Coptic period.

Perhaps in 535 BCE Tsenhor married for the first time, to a Mr. Inaros, presumably also a choachyte. They had one son that we know of, Peteamunhotep. In March 517 BCE Tsenhor, now about thirty-three years old, allotted half of her parental inheritance to her son (P. Bibl. Nat. 216). The other half went to Peteamunhotep's baby half-sister Ruru from Tsenhor's second marriage, in a contract that was drawn up the same day (P. Bibl. Nat. 217). After this, nothing is heard about Peteamunhotep again, and some Egyptologists believe that he died in his early youth.

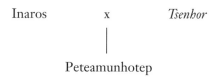

Inaros   x   *Tsenhor*

Peteamunhotep

This day in March 517 BCE was to be a special day in Tsenhor's life. Apart from the division of her inheritance between Peteamunhotep and Ruru, she also concluded a marital property arrangement with her second husband, the choachyte Psenese son of Heryrem (P. BM EA 10120A). On the same day, in a separate contract, the latter also formally recognized the rights of his daughter Ruru to his inheritance (P. BM EA 10120B). This is strange, because normally the husband would designate his heirs in the marital property arrangement itself, thus guaranteeing his wife that the children from their marriage would be the future heirs to his property. We do not know what happened to Tsenhor's first husband Inaros. He may have died, but the couple could equally well have divorced, which was a rather simple and common procedure in Late Period Egypt. A man could *khâa*, 'repudiate,' his wife and compensate her financially if she had been a faithful wife, and a woman could just as easily decide to *shem*, 'go away,' as long as the obligations laid down in a written marital property arrangement, or dictated by customary law, were observed and the wife had not been unfaithful.

As will be seen later, adultery by men was not exactly approved of, although the reasons for this seem to have been practical rather than ethical. For women, adultery was a much bigger problem. There is, for instance, P. BM EA 10416, also known as P. Salt 1821/131, which is dated to the late Twentieth Dynasty, about 550 years before Tsenhor was born. This text of 23.5 x 22 cm, with eleven lines on the recto (front) and thirteen on the verso (back), is a letter that clearly deals with an affair between a married man and an unmarried woman, which was not exactly approved of by some immediate relatives. The text was published by the famous Deir al-Medina expert Jac J. "Jack" Janssen, my first and most beloved teacher in Egyptology, at a time when his own marriage had gone wrong and people were pointing fingers at him for no reason. P. BM EA 10416 was an intelligent reply, at the same time showing that the maxims about adultery that we encounter in, for instance, the demotic teachings of Ankhsheshonqy (about which we will hear more below) are often mistaken by mainstream Egyptology for 'the' Egyptian outlook on life—which of course they were not. This could happen in real life and it probably was not an accident:

Your people were on the move, their old and young, both men and women, in the evening. They left saying: "We will beat her up together with her people." [It] was the steward who told them: "But why are you going [to the house] of my scribe to beat up my people? She will not be there." And he withstood them and told them: "Is it your man who will be found there? My envoy told me: 'Him whom we will find we will beat up.' So please tell me." This he said to them, and they answered back at him: "He has been sleeping with that woman for eight full months until this day, although he is not (her) husband. Were he her husband, would he not have sworn this oath about this (?) woman?"

Since this is a letter the content is, as ever, rather obscure, but it seems clear that the brave steward managed to repel an angry mob intent on blood, preferably the blood of the woman having an affair. It continues with a piece of advice that could have been given yesterday: "Why did you receive him to sleep with him repeatedly? [Are you] look-ing for partners to argue with? (. . .) If the heart of that man is after you, then let [him] enter the court together with his wife and let [him] swear an oath and return to your house." Apparently, if the adulterous man were to file for divorce in the *qenbet* (local court of law) and then wrap things up financially, things would calm down almost immediately. If not, village justice would be theirs.

In ancient Egyptian marriage there were three kinds of property, although further subdivisions were possible (see "When Old Age Sets In" below): the property of the husband, the property of the wife (which was often at least partly managed by the husband during their marriage), and the property the couple acquired together during their marriage. If they divorced, the wife stood to receive the property she brought into the marriage as well as one-third of the joint property. As will be seen later, just like today, a divorce would often involve a nasty financial backlash.

Some time after 517 BCE Tsenhor and her husband Psenese had a son, who was named Ituru. Since Tsenhor's mother had been called Ituru and Ruru for short, it seems that both children of Psenese and Tsenhor were named after her mother, once again proof—admittedly totally inconclusive—that she may have been a woman used to having things her own way.

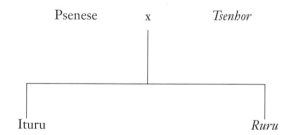

Psenese came from a family of choachytes, meaning that he was a member of the Association of Theban Choachytes, of which some records written between 542 and 538 BCE have come down to us (P. Louvre E 7840). Since both his elder brother Rery and his father Heryrem are mentioned in these records alongside Iturech of the family business of Djekhy & Son—whereas he himself is not—one takes it that he had not reached the age of sixteen in 538 BCE, which is believed to be the age at which the sons of choachytes were expected to enter the Association of Theban Choachytes. This would set Psenese's date of birth at approximately 553 BCE, meaning that he was the same age as Tsenhor.

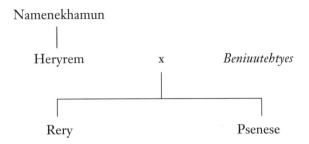

Although the subtitle of the scientific edition of Tsenhor's papers, *Les archives privées d'une femme égyptienne du temps de Darius Ier*, suggests that her papers form a proper archive, it is actually a dossier, a collection of papers connected to an event or person, that was assembled in modern times.

The first we hear of Psenese is when his elder brother Rery allots to him half the inheritance of their parents that had apparently been managed by him as long as Psenese was still too young. This happened sometime between 530 and 526 BCE (P. Vienna KM 3853). Slightly less than ten years later, in March 517 BCE, we see him married to Tsenhor, who would have been slightly over thirty by then. This was not exactly the ideal age for a woman to marry, so maybe Psenese had lost his wife, just as Tsenhor had lost her husband. Or maybe—and we should never exclude this—their hearts met somewhere in the Theban necropolis, right in time.

In March 517 BCE the couple visited the temple to have four official contracts made, probably all on the same day: (1) P. BM EA 10120A, a marital property arrangement between Psenese and Tsenhor; (2) P. BM EA 10120B, in which Psenese promises an equal part of his inheritance to his daughter Ruru according to the number of children he will have; (3) P. Bibl. Nat. 216, in which Tsenhor promises half of her inheritance to her son from her first marriage, to Peteamunhotep, and (4) P. Bibl. Nat. 217, where she does the same for her daughter Ruru from her marriage with Psenese. These children, a boy and a girl, would be treated equally through their entire lives. In Egypt, 2,500 years ago.

Five years later, in 512 BCE, Psenese presents his wife with half of a house, or a building site, somewhere in the Theban necropolis on the west bank of the Nile (P. Turin 2123). This share really becomes Tsenhor's own property. Half is much more than the one-third of the communal property a wife could expect to get out of a marriage, so one wonders why her husband gave her half. Then again, Tsenhor was thus obliged to pay half the cost of their future building activities. Two years later Psenese acquires another plot—perhaps even a house that may be in ruins—right next to the first (P. Louvre E 7128).

In 498 BCE Psenese decides to have a new will written for his daughter Ruru and his son Ituru. Each will receive half of all he owns. In the previous will written for Ruru about nineteen years earlier (P. BM 10120B), Psenese had allotted her a share in accordance with the number of children he would have, so we may take it that Ruru and Ituru were the couple's only surviving children. It is believed that Psenese died soon afterward, because in 494 BCE Tsenhor, accompanied by her eldest brother Nesamunhotep—or Amunhotep for short—wrapped up some business concluded between Psenese and a Mr. Djedamuniufankh nine years earlier (P. Louvre AF 9761). These men must have been friends because Djedamuniufankh was one of the witnesses of the second will made by Psenese for Ruru a few years earlier.

We see their daughter Ruru contracting her first client on her own in 497 BCE (P. Louvre 3231A), which makes perfect sense, because both Psenese and Tsenhor were now too old to do much physical work. Surprisingly, two additional contracts were found with this papyrus, both of which seem to mention Psenese, but their relationship with Tsenhor's other papers is contested (P. Louvre E 3231B and C). In 497 BCE Tsenhor herself receives one-quarter of the choachytes' income connected to the tomb of a policeman and his family from her eldest brother Amunhotep in return for one-quarter of the choachytes' services at the tomb. The fact that Tsenhor receives a quarter suggests that this was revenue that came from the inheritance of their father Nesmin. The day-to-day work would of course be done by Ruru and her brother Ituru.

This may all look much like a normal, uneventful life, but we are dealing here with an Egyptian woman in the sixth and fifth centuries BCE who owned houses and land, worked in the necropolis as a professional choachyte, and most probably did more business of which we are unaware. As for her life being uneventful, we can be sure that Tsenhor buried some of her children during her lifetime and that she would reserve a special prayer for them when she made her weekly round in the Theban necropolis. In fact, what we have here is an unprecedented and privileged peek into the life of an ancient Egyptian girl next door that will never make it into the official history books.

If we list the documents left to us by Tsenhor in chronological order and combine these with the major events in her life, the following picture emerges.

Table 1. A summary of Tsenhor's life

YEAR BCE	PAPYRUS	EVENT
556	Louvre E 10935	Tsenhor's father Nesmin (Petemin) receives eleven *aruras* as an endowment from the deceased Mrs. Tsenhor. She apparently gave her name to Nesmin's daughter who was yet to be born.
Around 550		Tsenhor is born.
530–526	Vienna KM 3853	Psenese, the future second husband of Tsenhor, receives his share of the parental inheritance from his eldest brother Rery.
before 517		Tsenhor marries the choachyte Inaros (mentioned by name in P. Bibl. Nat. 216) and gives birth to a son, Peteamunhotep.
517	BM EA 10120A	Tsenhor's second husband, the choachyte Psenese, has a contract drawn up for her to arrange the marital property.
517	BM EA 10120B	Tsenhor's second husband, the choachyte Psenese, acknowledges their baby daughter Ruru as his rightful heir.
517	Bibl. Nat. 216	Tsenhor acknowledges her eldest son Peteamunhotep from her first marriage as her rightful heir.
517	Bibl. Nat. 217	Tsenhor acknowledges her baby daughter Ruru from her second marriage as her rightful heir.
after 517		Tsenhor's son Peteamunhotep presumably dies.
517–516	Bibl. Nat. 223	Tsenhor buys a slave boy.
512	Turin 2123	Tsenhor's second husband Psenese gives her the title to one-half of a house or building plot.

510	Louvre E 7128	Tsenhor's second husband Psenese buys a plot adjacent to the site co-owned with her (mentioned in P. Turin 2123).
507	Turin 2124	Tsenhor's (half-)brother Burekhef compensates a cattle-keeper for the use of an ox to work the land, presumably the eleven *aruras* acquired by their father Nesmin (Petemin) in 556 BCE (P. Louvre E 10935) that is now co-owned by Tsenhor and her three (half-)brothers.
about 506		Tsenhor's father Nesmin (Petemin) dies (?).
506	Turin 2125	Tsenhor's (half-)brother Nesamunhotep allots to her part of a building that was acquired by their father Nesmin (Petemin).
498	Turin 2126	Tsenhor's second husband, the choachyte Psenese, allots half of his inheritance to their daughter Ruru (the other half goes to her brother Ituru).
498–494		Tsenhor's husband Psenese dies.
497	Louvre E 3231A	An official of Amun hires Tsenhor's daughter Ruru as a choachyte.
497	Louvre E 3231B	Official memo ordering someone to let Psenese (?) work some fields.
497	Louvre E 3231C	Official memo explaining in detail the issue mentioned in P. Louvre E 3231B.
494	Louvre AF 9761	Tsenhor wraps up the business that her deceased husband Psenese concluded in 503 BCE, assisted by her (half-)brother Nesamunhotep.
491	Turin 2127	Tsenhor's eldest (half-)brother Nesamunhotep, now calling himself Amunhotep, allots to her one-quarter of the choachytes' services to be performed for the family of a policeman.
487	Turin 2128	Tsenhor's son Ituru exchanges an ox with a cattle-keeper.
after 490 (?)		Tsenhor dies.

Mummies as a Source of Income

The ancient Egyptians believed in life after death. There were many ways to achieve this. The body would be preserved through mummification, *ushabtis* (small statues of workers) were installed in the tomb to do the work on the fields in the hereafter, and—if family members were not able or willing to do so themselves—choachytes or water-pourers made sure the deceased were nourished with food and drink. One other typical Late Period strategy was to put up one's own statue in the local temple—so that people would have to make sure that the right name would be on the statue—and in this way take part in the daily offerings to the gods. There were many ways to get a life after death and it seems the ancient Egyptians knew them all.

Apart from mentioning a few mummies by name, the choachytes' papers from the Saite and Persian periods are generally sketchy when it comes to the actual number of clients they served. To get a proper idea of the number of mummies that could be stashed away in the tombs in the Theban necropolis, we may look at a bilingual sale—demotic and Greek—recorded in three papyri that are now kept in Berlin and Leiden. These mummies, or rather the right to the income derived from them, were sold on 30 January 136 BCE by a woman called Taese daughter of Psenamun and Taese—the demotic scribe neatly added that she was thirty-three years old and of average height with a honey-colored complexion—to a relative through marriage, a Mrs. Shakhepery daughter of Amunhotep and Tahedja. Taese was married to Wennefer son of Hor, who was actually her uncle, because he was her mother's brother, and Shakhepery was married to Hor son of Hor, who was a brother of Wennefer. Choachytes liked to marry among themselves. Ancient Egyptian family relations had a tendency to quickly become very complicated.

Two of the contracts were written in demotic and one in Greek (all recently published by the British papyrologists Rachel Mairs and Cary Martin). The two demotic contracts were both needed to complete a legal sale in Ptolemaic Egypt. The first was a 'contract against silver,' a document of sale recording that the seller had been paid (P. Berlin 5507). To complete the sale a so-called cession or 'contract of being far' was required, in which the seller stated that he—or in this case she—no longer had any claim on the object sold, nor did anyone else in the world (P. Berlin 3098). The Greek contract (P. Leiden 413) is a translation of the demotic document of sale that may have been used for some official business with the Greek authorities or perhaps even in a court case. But this is not what interests us here. What we want to know is how many mummies a single female choachyte from the Ptolemaic period could possess, and presumably also service each week. The papers from both Djekhy & Son and Tsenhor, from the earlier Saite and Persian periods, are not very specific on this subject, but P. Berlin 5507 and 3098 from the Ptolemaic period certainly are (the numbers in square brackets were added by me). Shakhepery will receive:

[1] The tomb of Heriu the builder, [2] the tomb of Psenkhonsu son of Payna, [3] the tomb of Hor son of Abeq, [4] the tomb of Kephalon the smith, [5] the tomb of Hor son of Nesmin and the exalted Petekhonsu the blessed one, [6] the tomb of Panouphis the blessed one, [7] the tomb of Amunhotep son of Thotirtais, [8] half of the tomb of Paheb son of Nakhtnebef, [9] half of the tomb of Nesnebay, the man from Apis, [10] half of the tomb of Heriu the carpenter, [11] one-third of the tomb of Ammonios, [12] half of the tomb of the land-measurers, [13] half of the tomb of Psenmin son of Paret, [14] half of the tomb of Khaapis, [15] half of the tomb of Pahor the *pastophoros* (shrine-bearer) of Amun, [16] one-third of the tomb of the people from Philae, [17] half of the tomb of Hetepbastet the blessed one, [18] half of the people of Amunhotep the builder, [19] half of the people of Paymut, [20] half of the people of Patem son of Psenkhonsu, [21] half of the people of Paimy the fisherman and his blessed one, [22] half of the people of Peteanubis the dyer, [23] half of the people of Petosiris son of Pahema and his children, [24] half of Pakhnum son of Amunhotep and Tsen-amun, his sister, [25] half of the people of Amunhotep the smith, [26] half of Pasha, [27] half of Wesirptah the beekeeper, [28] half of Lysimachos, [29] half of Payu the *isionomos*, [30] half of the children of Wedjarenes, [31] half of Hewen, the smith from Qus, [32] half of Apollonios, the man from Thebes, [33] half of Peteamun, the man from Pay, [34] half of Merinher the fisherman, [35] half of the exalted Payu, the blessed one and (the people) who rest with him, and [36] one-third of Psenamun the doctor.

This adds up to no fewer than thirty-six tombs or groups of people (and their children). To some mummies she admittedly only possessed half or even one-third of the rights. In view of the enormous number of mummies that were sometimes stashed away in tombs, Shakhepery probably had done a good deal. It looks almost like a monopoly, but there were more choachytes in Thebes in this period and one supposes there were always plenty of mummies to go around. The supply obviously never stopped. Also, the Association of Theban Choachytes saw to it that the rules of competition were upheld. Crowded tombs must have been the rule all over Egypt. In the Memphite tomb of the famous general Horemheb, who would one day become king himself, for instance, a British–Dutch excavation team found the remains of at least sixty-six individuals from the first century BCE. Finds of more than a hundred intrusive burials are really not uncommon. So it seems the choachytes of Late Period Egypt and their like used tombs wherever they could find them, although in most cases we do not know who actually owned these tombs.

The sheer number of mummies tended by a single female choachyte does, however, raise one serious question. The Theban choachytes were obliged to bring funerary offerings for every ten-day week (or decade) and most probably on important festival days. If we assume that Shakhepery had at least 150 additional mummies to care for—and probably more in view of the many children who would die in infancy and the mummies that already belonged to her family's portfolio—and that the absolute minimal funerary service per individual mummy would take her five minutes, taking personal care of all her deceased new 'clients' would add up to twelve and a half hours, assuming that she would be able to perform 150 five-minute ceremonies in a row, which is not very likely. And if she were not pregnant, which was uncommon for a woman in ancient Egypt, or old, at least one week per month she probably could not perform any religious services because she would be ritually unclean. The most sensible thing to do—and the ancient Egyptians were highly practical—would be to hold collective services for all the occupants of a single tomb, which would narrow the time needed to service all her new 'clients' down to 36 x 5 minutes, or three hours at the very least. But then she would also have to walk from tomb to tomb, carrying water and probably bread and incense, too. From the very few pictures we have of choachytes at work, such as stela Cairo CG 22022, it appears that they used a carrying pole slung over their shoulder, with a jug on either side, just as Egyptian farmers do today. But all this work would take time and, especially if it was a hot summer day, a lot of effort. From a purely logistical point of view, one would expect Tsenhor to bring a donkey (or a slave) to carry the equipment, but that is one of those questions that is not often asked in Egyptology: was there any regulation about donkeys—an animal associated with the god Seth—in the necropolis? Probably not, but still. The documentary papyri from ancient Egypt often tell us what people did, but very seldom how they did it.

A similar state of affairs must have existed at Memphis, the other famous findspot for documents left by funerary service providers (although there is actually one contract suggesting that choachytes were also active in nearby Hawara). Does this mean that choachytes were confined to these three sites? Probably not. The ancient Egyptians had more than one expression for 'to make a libation,' one being *iry qebeh*, and indeed there were people calling themselves *qebeh*, or 'libationer,' leaving us to wonder whether they did the work of the choachytes. Cary Martin recently published a number of important contracts from the Memphite necropolis in his *Demotic Papyri from the Memphite Necropolis* (Turnhout: Brepols, 2009) that inform us how these people from Memphis conducted their business.

In P. Leiden I 379 from regnal year 29 of Ptolemy II (February–March 256 BCE) the choachyte Petosiris meticulously describes the share of their father's inheritance that will accrue to his sister Tetimuthes, which is one-quarter. She probably had already been given a dowry by her parents when she married, assuming that she was married. Her other brother receives one-third and the rest goes to Petosiris, who also takes it upon himself to look after their mother, who is still alive.

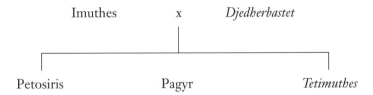

The names of the women are in italics.

After describing the many family members who contributed to Tetimuthes' inheritance—their father, paternal grandfather, paternal grandmother, and a whole list of people who were relatives of some sort—Petosiris specifies the tombs and endowments involved. Tetimuthes stands to receive the current and future income from one-quarter of (the numbers in square brackets were added by me):

[1] the two *ka* tombs that are cut into the mountain whose entrances open toward the east, their vacant plots in front of them, and the ten storerooms in them, which are in the southern part of the necropolis in Memphis (*description of neighboring plots*), [2] the tomb which is built and roofed containing nine storerooms, which is in the southern part of the necropolis in Memphis (*description of neighboring plots*), [3] the tomb which is built and roofed, which is in the southern part of the necropolis in Memphis (*description of neighboring plots*), [4] the *ka* tomb of the choachyte Phchoiphis son of Teos, which is in the possession of his children (*description of neighboring plots*), [5] the tomb called 'the tomb of Tamekhy,' together with its storerooms, which is in the southern part of the necropolis in Memphis (*description of neighboring plots*), [6] the tomb called 'the tomb of Atum' (*description of neighboring plots*), [7] the yard called 'the yard of Pamen son of Psenhapy,' [8] the mummies acquired by Pawya son of Paapis, [9] the village of revenue the Land of Mooring in the district of Memphis, [10] (any) person above in the temple of the village of revenue the Land of Mooring in the district of Memphis, and [11] the people of the district of Memphis or any person entering them (the tombs mentioned) in their name (the ancestors of Tetimuthes specified earlier in the contract who formerly had a right to the income from the mummies inside the tombs, which right was now inherited by Tetimuthes).

The scribes who assisted the Memphite funerary workers left very little to chance, which often resulted in exhaustive lists of mummies and endowments. This makes sense, as there was money involved. In P. Leiden I 380A, written on 28 July 64 BCE (also published by Martin), the god's seal-bearer Djedherbes, who worked in a line of business similar to that of the choachytes, describes the mummy collection in the Memphite necropolis sold by him to a colleague, which came from the former endowment of his grandfather. Once again the scribe made sure that no category was missed. There is no mention of tombs or individual people, just categories, and there were lots of them:

My one-sixth share of their priests, their scribes, their *pastophoroi*, their brewers, their merchants, their farmers, their soldiers, their blessed ones, their men of Nut, their dancers, their men of Anubis, their servants of the ibises, their servants of the falcons, their water-carriers, their gum-makers, their temple officials, and their town officials, and my one-sixth share of their husbands, their women, their parents-in-law, their siblings, their children, their male servants, their female servants.

One presumes that being a choachyte for such a diverse collection of people involved a lot of administration. With mummies coming in every day, the choachytes would have to keep a tab on those that entered the necropolis, for which a small tax also had to be paid to the overseer of the necropolis. From P. Louvre E 7840, which belongs to the records of the Theban Association of Choachytes written between 542 and 538 BCE, we know that the overseer of the necropolis attended the meetings held by the Theban choachytes. We also know that these overseers often wrote contracts for them, so one almost sees—and this is speculation—choachytes visiting the office of the overseer of the necropolis somewhere on the west bank of the Nile once a week to have a chat and to check or report on the mummies that had gone to the necropolis in the previous week. It sounds profane, but to these people mummies were merchandise. In fact, we may have to flex our brains a little bit more in order to try and imagine what such a necropolis was like. Was it a quiet and slightly eerie place, or—and we borrow here from the introduction to Martin's edition of the Leiden demotic papyri, quoting from an article by Amir Taheri in *The Times* of 28 August 2004—did it bustle with life?

Death is the centre of life here. Tens of thousands of grave-diggers, undertakers, masters of funeral ceremonies, tomb watchers, givers of prayers for the dead, intercessors, (sacred book) reciters, mediums for communication with the departed, and so on make up the bulk of the workforce.

Even though Taheri described what he saw in 2004 in the city of the dead in Najaf (Iraq), the image he creates may actually be very close to Tsenhor's working environment.

Did the Choachytes Keep Mummies at Home?
After the physical embalming process the mummy would be wrapped up. In an embalming workshop (see "The Good House" below), more than one mummy would be processed at the same time. It even happened in

the Ptolemaic period that the Theban choachytes stashed mummies in a house on the east bank before they ferried them over to the necropolis on the other side of the Nile, meaning that the mummies simply had to wait.

The house owned by choachytes on the east bank—they seem to have lived on the west bank in and around Djeme (Medinet Habu)—had come into their possession after the southern uprising in the reign of Ptolemy V (205–180 BCE). Greeks were no longer wanted in the Theban area, so the Greek owner of the house, an army man called Ptolemy, was forced to go south in 205 BCE. But Ptolemy had a son, Hermias, who wanted the house back. The only problem was that in the meantime—apparently his father had not reclaimed the house in the eighty years after his evacuation—it had been bought by a number of Theban choachytes. Between 126 and 117 BCE Hermias, who must have been a very old man by then, made many visits to Thebes to reclaim the house of his father. Apparently he had heard the choachytes had rebuilt the property and were now living there.

The first thing Hermias did was to approach the choachytes directly, but they told him that they had bought the house from a woman called Luba, so Hermias filed a petition against her. In court Luba suddenly had acute memory loss, stating that she never actually had a claim to the property. Case closed? Not by a long way. Intent on getting the choachytes to admit that they were not the rightful owners, Hermias, himself an army commander, made frequent visits to Thebes, but each time he tried to drag the choachytes into court they somehow magically disappeared. After one of many more hearings the *strategos* (the governor of the nome, who also had military power) ordered the chief of police to evict the choachytes and to restore the rights of Hermias. But the moment he went south again they simply returned and squatted in the house.

In the years that followed, Hermias filed many petitions with the authorities, but each time the choachytes simply refused to appear in court and went into hiding, and then returned to the house the moment Hermias went south. In 119 BCE Hermias suddenly added a new element to his accusation: the choachytes were not just squatting in the house but also were using it to store dead bodies. Not in the least impressed, the choachytes hired a Greek lawyer aptly called Deinon ('Terrifying'). Apparently he managed to produce a document stating that there had already been a court case concerning the house, which the choachytes had won. In any case, Hermias had to return home empty-handed.

Two years later, in 117 BCE, Hermias tried again. This time he filed a petition with the *epistates* (district official) Demetrios, who immediately summoned the choachytes to appear before him. Not surprisingly, nobody showed up. It is as if the choachytes knew that the highest Greek authorities would not remain in Thebes for long stretches at a time (they often went on tours of inspection), so if they just managed to stay out of their way long enough they would eventually give up. Another effort to corner them therefore had failed.

But in the end something happened. In the winter of 117 BCE Hermias once more pointed out to the authorities that there were dead people all over the premises, and this time the choachytes did show up. However, in court it turned out that Hermias was not able to prove beyond doubt that his father had been the original owner of the property. The choachytes won the case and continued happily stashing their mummies there for many years after. Whether keeping mummies at the house was standard practice with the Theban choachytes is unknown. Tsenhor did own a house on the western bank of the Nile, conveniently located next to an embalmer's workshop (P. Turin 2123 and P. Louvre E 7128).

But how did the choachytes tell the mummies apart? From the outside they all more or less look the same, and this is why the choachytes used wooden mummy labels. Often containing a pious wish about the *ba* of the deceased becoming a faithful follower of Osiris and the name of the deceased, these labels would be strapped to the mummy. Some of the more profane-looking labels seem to have been used for identification purposes only. This may have had to do with a regional practice.

The collection of the Papyrologisch Instituut in Leiden keeps a very interesting mummy label from the Hermonthite region (inventory number V. 3). It is actually a bit of a mix of an identification label and a memo. It is relatively large, namely 16.4 x 7.4 cm (see fig. 2). On it, some official wrote an instruction to a Mr. Tutu about the mummy to which the label was attached. In this case one has to assume—or rather hope—that the label was written first and then attached to the mummy, although one should probably not be too surprised to see experienced mortuary workers using mummies as writing boards every now and then.

The text itself is short and businesslike, showing little concern for the well-being of the eternal soul of the mummy that we find on other labels. This was business:

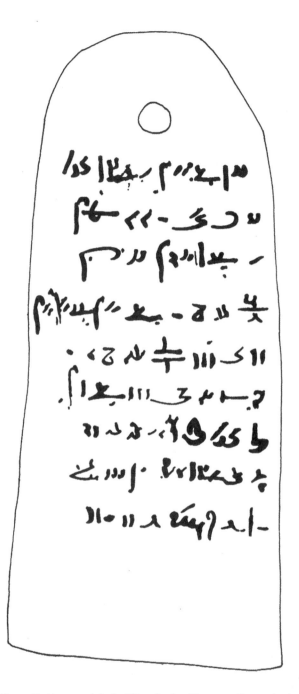

Figure 2. Mummy label of Tanefershy [Courtesy Papyrologisch Instituut]

Petosiris son of Wedjahor is the one who says to Tutu son of Imuthes, the manager of the secret of Osiris-Buchis: "Make a burial for Tanefershy daughter of Hor, her mother being Nebetwedja." Written in regnal year 15, fourth month of the *peret* season, day 6 (1 April 15 BCE).

At some point the mummy of Tanefershy would have been moved across the Nile by boat. Either she was first stashed away at a choachytes' waiting station on the west bank or she went straight to her burial place. In that case she was probably accompanied by a choachyte, other professionals who would be needed for a proper burial—for instance, someone who could do an 'opening of the mouth' ceremony at the tomb and professional mourners (with Tsenhor moonlighting?), all costing money—and presumably some of her (Tanefershy's) relatives.

To handle things as efficiently as possible, a choachyte would probably ship mummies a few at a time. On the west bank he or she would report to the overseer of the necropolis, who managed the incoming traffic and had to be paid a tax for bringing in a new mummy. It is also possible that this rather offensive detail would be taken care of afterward, when the family had gone home. The choachyte would pay the tax and receive a receipt. O. Cairo TR 12470 is such a receipt from 253–252 BCE, which was regnal year 33 of Ptolemy II:

Heriu son of Petesematawy is the one who says to Amunhotep son of Parety: "You have given me the one-half kite as the silver (money) for the overseer of the necropolis in the name of the (deceased) Horwennefer son of Amunhotep, whom you have brought into the necropolis." In the writing of N.N. in regnal year 33, second month of the *akhet* season, last day.

What makes these tiny memos interesting is that they tell us how things operated in the necropolis, although it is not certain that the way it is described above is really the way things went. Tsenhor and Psenese did have their own house in the necropolis area that could have served as a waiting station for mummies, and we have to presume that their parents had also acquired some real estate during their working lives. We know that these temporary facilities existed. This is not exactly a scene we will ever see depicted on tomb walls: mummies in transit, stacked somewhere in the house awaiting their final destination.

But we have to return to Mrs. Tanefershy. Her mummy was now delivered, and the tax was paid. So what came next? One assumes this would be the burial, but sometimes mummies were simply forgotten—left on the quay, so to speak.

During a number of restoration excavations near the royal tombs KV (Valley of the Kings) 16 and 17 in 1999–2001, two tiny and seemingly insignificant demotic ostraca were found, which were published by the American demotists Eugene Cruz-Uribe and Steven Vinson. Tiny maybe, but they are actually highly significant because they inform us about the actual process of proper mummy handling—customer services long before the term was invented—and of the fact that someone in the necropolis (probably its overseer) was really keeping tabs on things, such as mummies lying around unattended.

Both ostraca deal with the same master of secrets, whose name cannot be read with confidence. He failed to give a proper burial to the deceased entrusted to him on two separate occasions. One of the memos is dated to New Year's Day in regnal year 30 of either Amasis II (reigned 570–526 BCE) or Darius I (reigned 521–486 BCE), so in this case the culprit may perhaps be excused. But the accusation that the mummies had been sold short only minutes before they could enjoy eternal life in the hereafter is there, although we do not know to whom these memos were addressed. The message in VOK (Valley of the Kings) Demotic Ostracon 2 is as factual as it is terse, and it looks timeless in the sense that there will always be bureaucrats putting the blame on others for clogging up the machine:

> N.N., the master of secrets, has not buried Tawa daughter of Panakhetu yet. But I have not put up any obstacle for her. In the writing of Pasheramunip in regnal year 30, fourth month of the *shemu* season, day 24.

Now these would also be the sort of events that Tsenhor would encounter in everyday life. Taking mummies to the necropolis, paying the tax to the overseer, and then, over dinner, asking her husband: "How was your day today? Mummy delivered at the tomb all right?"

"Uh-oh (I thought *you* would do that)."

The Persian Administration

When Egypt was conquered by the Persians in 525 BCE, Tsenhor was probably well into her twenties. The Persians were used to ruling foreign lands, and they knew the best way to do this was to leave the bulk of the administration intact and to appoint trusted Persian officials to key positions. Egypt had now become a satrapy—the Persian Empire counted twenty under Darius I—but life in Thebes probably continued as usual, although not for everyone. The office of the high priestess of Amun or divine adoratrice, a position that had been reserved for Nitocris II, the daughter of King Amasis (reigned 570–526 BCE), was abolished, never to be resumed again.

But apart from the dating formula in the contracts mentioning Pharaoh Darius, there is no apparent trace of the Persian occupation to be found in the papers left by Tsenhor. We do not know, therefore, what she may have thought about the regime change—if she gave it any thought at all—but we do know that, just like his predecessor Cambyses II, Darius was quick to adopt his own royal titulary in Egyptian, and we may assume he also spent some time in his study working out how the ancient Egyptian pantheon worked. With considerable success. Darius not only has gone down in history as one of Egypt's great law-givers, he also was revered as a god in some parts of Egypt, which was no mean feat for a non-Egyptian.

The Berlin Museum keeps a small limestone stela of 29 x 19 cm (inventory number 7493) that is believed to come from the Fayoum. The stela is very crudely cut, and in the upper register we see—below the familiar winged sun disk with cobra heads—a falcon god. There is a bald-headed Egyptian dressed in a loincloth kneeling in front of him, the man who dedicated this stela. The caption to the left of the falcon clearly reads, "The Good God, Lord of the Two Lands, Darius."

An Egyptian man venerating the Persian pharaoh Darius as a god. Right. According to the Greek historian Diodorus Siculus, who lived between around 90 and 30 BCE, Darius was so anxious to demonstrate his piety toward the Egyptian gods—and the former kings of Egypt—that even during his reign the Egyptians started to call him a god, turning him into an object of veneration well beyond the usual reverence paid to Pharaoh (*Bibliotheca Historica* I 95.5). But the ancient Egyptians maintained a very subtle balance even in the status of the gods. The real gods were called *netjer aâ*, 'the Great God,' whereas the king would be referred to as the *netjer nefer*, 'the Good God.' So, St. Berlin 7493 is not real proof that Darius was revered as a god. But as a good pharaoh, yes.

On a daily basis the administration was the responsibility of the Persian governor, or satrap, who was generally a member of the royal family. He collected the taxes, acted as the highest judicial authority, and maintained stability and security. This included stationing garrisons at strategic points such as Memphis and, in the south, Elephantine. From a number of demotic papyri found by German archaeologists on the island of Elephantine at the beginning of the twentieth century we know that the satrap—on behalf of King Darius—even had a say in the appointment of temple officials. Before we go into this, however, we must first look at another early demotic papyrus found on Elephantine by the German excavation team. It is now kept in Berlin under inventory number P. Berlin 13572. It was written on 6 June 492 BCE:

> Naneferibraemakhet greets Nes[khnum]pamet, the *lesonis*. Oh, may Ra cause his lifetime to be long! You have satisfied my heart with the one-fourth of the silver about which you wrote to Inkhy to give them to me. You have (now) given them to me. My heart is satisfied with them. I will cause Inkhy to be far from you concerning them. If I do not cause him to be far from you I will give you five (deben, about 450 grams) of silver, without citing any legal document on earth with you. In the writing of Naneferibraemakhet son of Pakhar in regnal year 30 second month of the *peret* season, day 15.

The letter, which is actually a cross between a letter and a receipt, was signed directly below the main text by four witnesses. We learn nothing from it, apart from the fact that someone has been paid and that the sender of the letter is satisfied with it. But the importance of this letter lies in the date—6 June 492 BCE—and the fact that it was written to the financial manager *(lesonis)* of the temple of Khnum, a Mr. Neskhnumpa-met. We know this man from a very famous correspondence between the priests of Khnum and the Persian satrap Pherendates himself.

Among demotists, these letters—two papyri now kept in Berlin—are known as the Pherendates correspondence and have sparked much debate on the chain of events. The first text is P. Berlin 13540, a letter from Pherendates to the priests of Khnum that was written on 21 April 492 BCE. The letter shows considerable influence from Aramaic, the lingua franca of the day. One assumes there was an Aramaic original that was copied into demotic so that the priests could understand it. The Aramaic influences—for instance, new paragraphs starting with the curious phrase 'at this moment' that was copied by the demotic copyist—have not been included in the translation below:

Pherendates, to whom Egypt has been entrusted, says to all the priests of Khnum, Lord of Elephantine. Pherendates is the one who says: there are *wab* priests that the first chief brought before me at an earlier occasion, saying: "Cause them to be made *lesonis*." However, one of the abovementioned *wab* priests had fled, and an order was given to look for him. Another was a servant of another man. It is not fitting to make these kinds of men *lesonis*. The *wab* priest who is suitable to be made *lesonis* will be a great man and (then) it will happen that I will cause him to carry out his task (?), there being nothing that he has let become a failure, a person who will be selected according to what Pharaoh Darius has ordered. This kind of person is suitable to be made *lesonis*. The *wab* priest chosen to be made *lesonis* will be like this: the person who will be chosen must be brought forward according to what Pharaoh Darius has ordered. As for the *wab* priest who has let something become a failure or who is the servant of another man, do not let these kinds of persons be brought forward to be made *lesonis*. Let it be known to you. Satibar is aware of this order. In the writing of Apries in regnal year 30, fourth month of the *akhet* season, day 29.

But the residence of the satrap was conveniently far away in Memphis and the priests of Khnum were apparently not in a mood to be rushed. P. Berlin 13539, which was also found on Elephantine, is probably the early demotic copy of a draft of the Aramaic original that was sent back to the satrap. It is dated to 25 December 492 BCE, so about eight months after Pherendates sent his letter. In view of the precise instructions given by him, the answer sent by the Egyptian priests from Elephantine was a slap in the face. The matter-of-factness of P. Berlin 13539, completely ignoring the instructions of the satrap and consequently also a decree by Darius himself, acts as an insult:

Message from the priests of the Great Khnum, Lord of Elephantine, before Pherendates to whom Egypt has been entrusted. We pray for Pherendates before Khnum, the Great God. Oh, may Khnum cause his lifetime to be long! It happened in regnal year 30, fourth month of the *peret* season, that it was time to succeed the *lesonis*. We have removed (from office) Petekhnum son of Haaibra, who was the *lesonis*. We have caused Neskhnumpamet son of Horkheb to succeed him as the *lesonis*. We have agreed that he will act as the *lesonis*. He will cause burnt offerings to be carried and made before Khnum. In the writing of Nespamet son of Neshor, the overseer of (sacred) clothing in regnal year 3[1], first month of the *akhet* season, day 2.

To recapitulate: On 21 April 492 BCE, the satrap Pherendates wrote to the priests of Khnum about the appointment of the new financial manager of the temple domain (P. Berlin 13540). On 25 December 492 BCE, the priests wrote back that they had elected Neskhnumpamet and that the actual appointment had taken place somewhere in July or August of 492 BCE. We also have the letter P. Berlin 13572 quoted above. This was written on 6 June 492 BCE, and clearly refers to Neskhnumpamet as the *lesonis*, weeks before the date he was appointed that is mentioned in P. Berlin 13539. In fact, there is even a letter by Ravaka, the Persian garrison commander of Syene (Aswan), to the *lesonis* Neskhnumpamet dated to 7 May 492 BCE (P. Berlin 23584), which is earlier still.[1] It therefore seems the priests of Khnum had decided not only to insult the satrap and ignore a decree by King Darius but also to secretly appoint Neskhnumpamet to office several months before the actual time had come to elect a *lesonis*, which was July or August 492 BCE. Then they waited some months before they sent word to Pherendates to inform him of their unilateral decision, even though he had instructed them that appointments like these should take place in accordance with the decree by Darius.

The fact that there was a Persian garrison a stone's throw away from the temple of Khnum suggests either that the priests of Khnum liked to live dangerously or that something in P. Berlin 13539 and 13540 had been read the wrong way ever since the papyri were first published by the brilliant German demotist Wilhelm Spiegelberg in 1928. In fact, the regnal year in which Neskhnumpamet was elected is not 30 (P. Berlin 13539), as was previously believed, but 29. Also, the date on which P. Berlin 13539 was written is probably not regnal year 3[1], first month of the *akhet* season, day [1]4, but regnal year 30, first month of the *akhet* season, day 2 (or perhaps 4).

This discovery was made by the French demotist Michel Chauveau, who convincingly showed why the figure that had always been read as 30 was actually an intricate ligature of the numbers 20 and 9. In that case, the chain of events in the Pherendates correspondence suddenly starts to make perfect sense:

- Neskhnumpamet is appointed as the new *lesonis* between 22 July and 23 August 493 BCE (P. Berlin 13539).

- The priests of Khnum inform Pherendates, the satrap of Egypt residing in Memphis, on 25 December 493 BCE (P. Berlin 13539).
- The satrap sends an answer to the priests of Khnum in Elephantine on 21 April 492 BCE (P. Berlin 13540).
- Neskhnumpamet is in office, receiving P. Berlin 23584 and 13572 on 7 May 492 BCE, and 6 (or perhaps 7) June 492 BCE, respectively.

In the end, one is left to conclude that what looked like a rather volatile conflict between the Persian satrap and the Egyptian priests of Khnum far away in southern Elephantine is actually based on a misreading of some of the essential dates in the Pherendates correspondence.

The letters also prove that Darius I took an active interest in the internal affairs of Egypt. In fact, according to the verso of the so-called Demotic Chronicle (P. Bibl. Nat. 215), he even decreed that all the laws of Egypt up to and including regnal year 44 of Amasis had to be collected and recorded in both demotic and Aramaic. The aim was of course to allow the Persian authorities in Egypt to govern the country according to native law. The German demotist Sandra Lippert—who published an extremely useful survey of the ancient legal sources from the Old Kingdom (2575–2134 BCE) up to and including the Roman period under the misleadingly modest title *Einführung in die altägyptische Rechtsgeschichte* (Berlin: LIT Verlag, 2008)—thinks that legal manuals such as the famous Ptolemaic P. Mattha (around 250 BCE) are actually later copies of this Persian original (which in turn may, however, also go back to an even earlier original by one of the native law-givers). It is a very smart and attractive proposal.

P. Carlsberg 236, written in early Ptolemaic demotic, is a mere fragment of 16.6 x 13.3 cm. The content makes it clear that it comes from a text similar to P. Mattha, and the striking thing is that this fragment was once part of a column numbered "44." One is naturally inclined to think that this number refers to the original column, but what if it is actually regnal year 44 of Amasis? That would be sensational. Unfortunately, it is probably just the column header.

Apart from public and legal order, the Persian occupation of Egypt required some military presence.

An Outpost at Elephantine

One of the best—or at least most entertaining—sources on Egypt under Persian rule is the account written by Herodotus, the Greek journalist and historian from Halicarnassus (now Bodrum in Turkey), who lived around 485–425 BCE. He traveled across Egypt, picking up all kinds of stories that paint a colorful and most valuable picture of Egypt in the fifth century BCE. He also wrote about the garrison on the island of Elephantine that guarded the southernmost border of Egypt. Even though for more than 160 kilometers to the south there was nothing but the Nubian desert, there was always, as the Twenty-fifth Kushite Dynasty had not been forgotten, a need to remain vigilant. Elephantine was also the place through which all trade to and from the interior of Africa passed. Its Egyptian name was Yb, which was also the word for ivory. According to Herodotus, garrisons were stationed at Elephantine, Marea, and Daphnai (or Pelusium) already in the reign of Psamtik I (664–610 BCE) to keep in check the Ethiopians in the south, the Libyans in the west, and the Arabs and Assyrians in the east. In the reign of Darius I the garrisons at Daphnai and Elephantine were still in place. The Persians established another garrison at Memphis near the palace of Apries (who ruled Egypt from 589 to 570 BCE), where the British archaeologist William Flinders Petrie—one of the first modern archaeologists and the father of Egyptian archaeology—found some large armories, although some of the material found there could equally well belong to the second period of Persian occupation that was ended by Alexander the Great. What is typical of these early archaeological reports is that rather than providing the necessary details on the numbers, dimensions, precise findspots, and materials used—as archaeologists do today—Petrie still preferred to show off by citing some classical authors to illustrate his point. Petrie's *The Palace of Apries (Memphis II)* (London: School of Archaeology in Egypt, University College, 1909) had this to say:

> Probably of the Persian age is the large quantity of scale armour. Herodotos mentions the Persians wearing "sleeved breastplates with iron scales like those of a fish" (VII, 61); and, much later, Ammianus describes that "they had plates of iron closely fitting over every limb" (XXIV, ii, 10), they "were covered from head to foot with thin plates of iron like the feathers of a bird" (XXIV, iv, 15), "this armour of theirs being singularly adapted to all the inflections of the body" (XXIV, vii, 8); and "all the troops were clothed in steel, in such a way that their bodies were covered with strong plates, so that the hard joints of the armour fitted every limb of their bodies" (XXV, i, 12).

As will be seen later, after he had conquered Egypt, Cambyses (see "Mad King or Just a Bad Hair Day?" below) decided to push on southward and attack Nubia as well, although it is believed that this was a slightly more modest operation than reported by Herodotus. This expedition was a disaster—as was a previous expedition to the west—and one is left wondering whether the Persian soldiers were really expected to march fifty to sixty kilometers a day wearing this full body armor in the stifling heat, each separate metal plate acting as a perfect heat conductor. Probably yes. But we have to return to the garrisons of Late Period Egypt.

Herodotus writes that during the reign of Psamtik I these garrisons were stationed at their posts for three years without relief. Not very happy with their situation, the soldiers of the Elephantine garrison decided to go AWOL and start a new life somewhere to the south. Apparently Psamtik I went after them, and when he found them he implored them not to abandon the gods of their own country. One of the soldiers pointed at his penis—his own, one assumes—saying that wherever that went, that would be the place where he would have a wife and children. Since this sounds like what a soldier would still say today, the story is probably true. But if it is true, why was the soldier not killed on the spot? We must assume that Psamtik I did not travel alone and that these men were—for all intents and purposes—deserters liable to the death penalty. So why did this soldier get away with his insult? The only explanation that comes to mind is that Psamtik I desperately needed these fighting men—who had been left by the government in the farthest possible outpost of Egypt— and that he was not really in a position to order these men to return. In other words, he may simply have been outnumbered.

According to Herodotus, even Amasis himself, when he was still a general (and something of a party animal), once displayed very similar barracks humor when an envoy sent by King Apries—against whom Amasis had been plotting for some time—begged him to come to his senses and remain loyal to him (the king). Sitting on his horse, Amasis simply lifted one leg and farted, telling the envoy that he could take this answer back to Apries. Not very pleased with the result, Apries had the envoy's nose and ears cut off, which greatly diminished what was left of his popularity. The rest is history. Pretty soon, so was Apries.

In the Persian period, Elephantine and Syene (Aswan) housed Jewish and Aramaic garrisons and some authors believe that the Jews were actually the descendants of the troops that left for Nubia in the reign of

Psamtik I, more or less suggesting that this Jewish garrison may have been in place as early as 650 BCE (which, however, remains to be proved). Unfortunately the Aramaic Elephantine papyri are all dated to the fifth century BCE,[2] so the Jewish and Aramaic settlement on Elephantine may well have been founded only after the destruction of the temple of Jerusalem by the Babylonians in 586 BCE. The Second Book of Kings 25:26 and Jeremiah 41:14–18 both specifically mention army commanders—or guerrilla fighters—fleeing to Egypt. There may perhaps even have been Jewish mercenaries fighting in the Nubian campaign of Psamtik II in 592 BCE, although the king's inscription at Abu Simbel only mentions Phoenicians, Carians, Ionians, and Rhodians. On Elephantine the Jews had their own temple and some of them observed Shabbat and Passover.

Others were obviously less strict. There is the famous case of the financial manager of the Jewish temple, Ananiah son of Azaria, who married an Egyptian slave woman called Tamut, and, although their marriage was legal, Tamut was actually still owned by a Mr. Meshullam son of Zaccur. Not an ideal situation, but there are parallels with some Egyptian legal sources. The main protagonist in the Adoption Papyrus (written around 1090 BCE), the woman Naunefer, owned a slave girl who was married to her (Naunefer's) younger brother (see "Why Not Simply Adopt Your Wife?" below). This slave girl was actually the result of a sexual deal between her husband and a slave woman—apparently Naunefer could not have children—after which she adopted both the girl and her younger brother (as well as the slave girl's other siblings). This was apparently completely legitimate, although this legal procedure is only known from this papyrus. To top it all, Naunefer's own husband had adopted his wife as his daughter so that she would inherit all his property.

In the end the Jewish temple on Elephantine was sacked in 410 BCE by an Egyptian mob, although we do not know exactly why. However, Elephantine was the seat of the temple of Khnum, a ram-headed god, and, if the Jewish offerings to Yahweh included rams, this would probably not have gone down well with the local population. Soon after the temple—believed by some to have been the temporary hiding place for the Ark of the Covenant on its way to Ethiopia—was destroyed, all traces of the Jewish garrison disappeared. Some say they emigrated to Nubia and that their remote descendants are the so-called Falashas who remigrated en masse to Israel in the twentieth century. Maybe, maybe not. But probably not.

2

Earth and Water:
Nesmin, 556 BCE

How Tsenhor Got Her Name
10 March–8 April 556 BCE (P. Louvre E 10935)

There is something strange about P. Louvre E 10935, the contract that
made the Theban choachyte Nesmin son of Khausenwesir—whose daughter Tsenhor would be born a few years later—a true landowner overnight
(although the family probably already had some land). The fields given to
him, or rather paid to him, by a man called Psamtikmenekh son of Horwedja
measured eleven *arura*s, or the size of about five and a half soccer fields.
Ten *arura*s could be used to grow crops and the additional *arura* consisted
of paths and bushes. The most likely reason for this appears to be fiscal,
because landowners would only be taxed for their productive farm land.
Ten *arura*s would produce an annual harvest of about eight thousand liters
of grain, which would have been more than enough to support an extended
family. Psamtikmenekh's fields actually measured twenty-two *arura*s, but
he kept eleven *arura*s for himself. The other eleven *arura*s now owned by
the choachyte Nesmin formed a mortuary foundation for Psamtikmenekh's
mother, Mrs. Tsenhor. The proceeds of this foundation were—in theory—
destined to maintain Tsenhor's funerary cult, but in practice Nesmin would
probably be at liberty to do with the fields as he pleased. It is not very
likely that Psamtikmenekh expected Nesmin to bring his mother Tsenhor
a twenty-something-liter grain offering each day of the week.

The contract was signed at the bottom by the scribe Hor son of Ankh-
wennefer, as well as by Psamtikmenekh himself and his son, a god's father
called Teos. The latter had to authorize this deal, because the eleven
*arura*s given to Nesmin were part of his paternal inheritance. He could of

31

course have refused to sign and seen his father strike him from the will. Teos probably had very little choice:

> Regnal year 15, third month of the *akhet* season under Pharaoh l.p.h. Amasis l.p.h. Psamtikmenekh son of Horwedja, whose mother is Tsenhor, has said to the choachyte of the west of Thebes Nesmin son of Khausenwesir, whose mother is Shepbastet: "I have given to you these ten *arura*s of high and free fields as a (mortuary) foundation for the mouth of Mrs. Tsenhor, my mother, as well as one additional *arura*, makes a total of eleven *arura*s of fields, which are in the Domain of Amun in the district of Coptos, in the west, forming part of twenty-two *arura*s of fields, which are on the Island (?) of Amun to the west of the canal called Patinis, which I bought from Sen son of Iufau, the master of mysteries, whose mother is Kepeshaese in regnal year 14, first month of the *shemu* season."

From other sources we know that the fields described as being "in the Domain of Amun in the district of Coptos, in the west," were located in a rural area known as The Stable of the Milk Can of Amun, which was also used for grazing Amun's cattle, cows actually branded with the mark of a milk can. The canal called Patinis was a well-known landmark in the Ptolemaic period, several centuries later. It is frequently mentioned in the Ptolemaic demotic papyri published by the Italian demotist Giuseppe Botti, in his *L'archivio demotico da Deir el-Medineh* (Florence: F. le Monnier, 1967). It ran from south to north on the west bank of the Nile, near the desert. The canal was bordered by a dike called *ta amet en Paten*, 'the mud rampart of Patinis.' This canal was also called *pa mu en Peraâ*, 'the water of Pharaoh,' and for this reason some Egyptologists believe that Patinis was some sort of royal canal. But maybe this was simply a way to denote a public waterway that could be used by all, just as the public street in demotic contracts is called *pa myt en Peraâ*, 'the road of Pharaoh.'

What then is so strange about this contract? Two things. First, P. Louvre E 10935 lists the entire buying history of these twenty-two *arura*s between the date of the contract itself, 556 BCE, and 628 BCE. During this period the field changed owner several times. Second, the contract was signed on the back by an extraordinary number of witnesses, namely seventeen, which is one witness in excess of the usual sixteen. The seventeenth witness, the scribe of the Domain of Amun in the district of

Coptos Wennefer son of Horwedja, was actually the previous owner of the fields. He had sold them to a Mr. Sen in regnal year 14, second month of the *shemu* season of Amasis, and then Sen *immediately* resold them—no doubt on the same day—to Psamtikmenekh, who also happened to be a son of Horwedja.

It is our contention that Psamtikmenekh and Wennefer were actually brothers. Wennefer's son Horwedja was to become a scribe of the Domain of Amun in the district of Coptos himself, appearing in a number of tax receipts from the archive of Djekhy & Son (P. Louvre E 7842, 7835, 7838, and 7834, all written between 540 and 536 BCE; see *Djekhy & Son*). In three instances these receipts were also signed by one of the witnesses in P. Louvre E 10935, namely Neswennefer son of Sobekemhat, who was some kind of administrator of the Domain of Amun in the district of Coptos.

The former title deeds to the field—four, to be precise—were in the office of the scribe Hor when P. Louvre E 10935 was drawn up:

- From Petosiris for his daughter Nitocris: regnal year 37, fourth month of the *peret* season under Psamtik I (628 BCE)
- From Neskhonsu for Horwedja (Wennefer's and probably also Psamtikmenekh's father): regnal year 3, second month of the *peret* season under Apries (587 BCE)
- From Wennefer for Sen: regnal year 14, first month of the *shemu* season under Amasis (557 BCE)
- From Sen for Psamtikmenekh: regnal year 14, first month of the *shemu* season under Amasis (557 BCE)

Even though Psamtikmenekh stated that he had given the title deeds to Nesmin, this was probably only symbolic, because Nesmin now had his own title deed for the eleven *aruras* (P. Louvre E 10935). The other title deeds all referred to the twenty-two *aruras* as a whole, not to the eleven now owned by Nesmin. They must have been kept by Psamtikmenekh, and maybe this is exactly why the scribe listed these previous contracts. If there was ever going to be a court case in which someone would produce these former title deeds, Nesmin would have conclusive proof that his eleven *aruras* had been taken out of the twenty-two *aruras* listed in them.

An additional reason to list the previous title deeds may have been that these fields had once been owned by some of the most powerful people in Thebes. Any member of one of these powerful families—an ambitious descendant of one of the people mentioned in these earlier contracts smelling easy money and trying to intimidate Nesmin—would now have a hard time proving in court that these fields were actually his (this of course happened).

The singers of the interior of Amun formed the court of the divine adoratrice, a.k.a. the god's wife of Amun, the consort of Amun of Thebes and highest priestess in the land. In 556 BCE the divine adoratrice was Princess Ankhnesneferibra, a daughter of Psamtik II (reigned 595–589 BCE). She held this office from 586 to 525 BCE, when the Persians invaded and terminated the office altogether. Just like the divine adoratrice, the singers of the interior of Amun remained virgins (although some say they did not), adopting their own successors who would then receive a new name, which was often the name of a famous divine adoratrice. The singer of the interior of Amun Nitocris had been adopted by the singer of the interior of Amun Mehywesekhy, who in turn was a daughter of the governor of Thebes and servant of the divine adoratrice Pabasa son of Petebastet (see "A Tomb in the Assasif" below). At the time the earliest title deed was written, the divine adoratrice was Nitocris I, a daughter of Psamtik I, who was to be succeeded by Ankhnesneferibra. Nitocris had been parachuted into this high post to help tighten the grip of the Saite rulers in Lower Egypt on the independent clergy of Amun in Thebes.

P. Louvre E 10935 is an early demotic contract. Early demotic was the administrative script developed in Lower Egypt from the northern late cursive hieratic. As the Saite period progressed and the administrative reforms initiated by the Saite kings started to gain a foothold in the south of Egypt, early demotic gradually made its way to Thebes. Within a few decades it replaced the Theban administrative script developed from the local late cursive hieratic. The southern script is infamous for its tendency to abbreviate and condense administrative hieratic to the extent that—apart from a few specialists—there is no Egyptologist who can actually read it, and even fewer publish in this field. It is called abnormal hieratic for a reason. Abnormal hieratic borders on cryptography, something that might have been designed in a dream by Salvador Dalí on LSD, 2,500 years ago.

There are many differences between early demotic and abnormal hieratic. For one thing, abnormal hieratic contracts generally mention the day on which they were written—thus continuing the Ramesside scribal tradition from which the script was derived. If in P. Louvre E 10935 the scribe refers to one of the earlier title deeds as being written in regnal year 3, second month of the *peret* season, day 18 under Apries (who reigned 589–570 BCE), we can (almost) be sure that this title deed was written in abnormal hieratic. However, one of the other former title deeds is said to be from regnal year 37, fourth month of the *peret* season under Psamtik I (who reigned 664–610 BCE). Apparently this contract does not mention a day date, or the early demotic scribe of P. Louvre E 10935 forgot to copy it. Does this mean it was written in early demotic? This seems hardly likely. With very few exceptions,[1] the contracts from the reign of Psamtik I that we have are all written in the southern local script, abnormal hieratic. This contract from regnal year 37 dealt with twenty-two *arura*s in the direct vicinity of Thebes, so we may assume it was also written in abnormal hieratic. Typical: as soon as you establish a rule, you stumble on the one exception. And actually it is not even the one exception, because there are other examples dating back to the reign of Taharqa that also do not have a day date (for example, P. BM EA 10906 and 10907).

The scribe of P. Louvre E 10935 then lists the buying history of the fields that Nesmin—the future father of Tsenhor—will receive:

> (These are the fields) which he (Sen son of Iufau) bought from the scribe of the Domain of Amun Wennefer son of Horwedja son of Wennefer, whose mother is Khonsupaysarebty, in regnal year 14, first month of the *shemu* season.
>
> (These are the fields) which formerly belonged to the scribe of the Domain of Amun in the district of Coptos Horwedja son of Wennefer, whose mother is Heryes, his father, and which he (Horwedja) had bought from the scribe and servant of the royal palace Neskhonsu son of Pakhery, whose mother is Neithiyty, which came in the name of the singer of the interior of Amun Nitocris daughter of the god's father Petosiris son of Wenamun, the adopted daughter of the singer of the interior of Amun Mehywesekhy daughter of the governor of Thebes and servant of the divine adoratrice Pabasa son of Petebastet in regnal year 3, second month of the *peret* season, day 18 under Pharaoh l.p.h. Apries l.p.h., true of voice, which formerly belonged to the god's father Petosiris son of Wenamun, her father, and which he (Petosiris) had given to her (Nitocris) in her contract of . . . in regnal year 37, fourth month of the *peret* season under Pharaoh l.p.h. Psamtik l.p.h., true of voice.

This completes the buying history of the fields. Psamtikmenekh then proceeds to tell Nesmin that he has given these fields as a mortuary foundation for his own mother Tsenhor, but the actual compensation for this—the eternal mortuary services to be performed by Nesmin and his children, and his children's children, and so forth—is not explicitly mentioned:

> I have given you these eleven *arura*s of fields—forming part of twenty-two *arura*s of fields—as a (mortuary) foundation for Mrs. Tsenhor, my mother, the south of which being the (other) eleven *arura*s, the remainder of the twenty-two *arura*s described above as well as the bushes, their north being the waste (?) field of Heryrem son of Khonsuyres, their west the desert, and their east the canal of Patinis.

At this point, the procedure follows the symbolic transfer of the former title deeds. Maybe this was a physical act to accompany Psamtikmenekh's official statement, after which Nesmin handed them back to Psamtikmenekh, which was then duly noted and recorded by the scribe:

> I have given you these four contracts, to wit: the contract which the scribe of the Domain of Amun in the district of Coptos Wennefer son of Horwedja gave to the master of the mysteries Sen son of Iufau, two contracts, the contract which the scribe of the Domain of Amun Wennefer son of Horwedja, whose mother is Khonsupaysarebty, made for Sen son of Iufau, the master of the mysteries, one contract, and the contract that Sen son of Iufau, the master of the mysteries, whose mother is Kepeshaese, made for me, one contract, which makes up the total. They are yours, your abovementioned eleven *arura*s of fields. I have donated them to you as a (mortuary) foundation for the mouth of Mrs. Tsenhor, my mother.

In 587 BCE Horwedja, the father of the previous seller Wennefer (and of the declaring party Psamtikmenekh here in P. Louvre E 10935), bought a piece of land of twenty-two *arura*s in the Domain of Amun in the district of Coptos. At the end of the seventh century BCE these were in the possession of a god's father Petosiris son of Wenamun (whom we will meet below). He transferred them to his daughter Nitocris, a singer of the interior of Amun, so someone belonging to the elite. Nitocris died before 587 BCE and the land was passed on to a man called Neskhonsu son of Pakhar, a scribe and servant of the royal palace who may have acted as the agent of Nitocris. Neskhonsu then sold the land to Horwedja in 587 BCE. Thirty years later, in 557 BCE, it was sold by Horwedja's son Wennefer to the master of the mystery Sen son of Iufau. Sen then immediately sold it to Psamtikmenekh, who could very well have been Wennefer's brother.

So, did Psamtikmenekh actually buy back the family property to donate half of it afterward? Did the entire field serve as security for a loan? One could assume that his brother—that is, if our assumption is correct—Wennefer had taken a loan. He then had a preliminary contract of sale drawn up that was given to Sen as security for the loan. When he could not pay, the field reverted to Sen and Wennefer's brother had to come to the rescue. It makes sense, but it is still only speculation. This of course did not matter to the choachyte Nesmin, the future father of our Tsenhor. All he was interested in were these eleven *aruras* of land securing a comfortable life for him and his family:

> No man on earth will be able to exercise authority over them except you (Nesmin) from regnal year 15, third month of the *akhet* season onward, forever and ever. The one who will come to you—any man on earth including me—and give you whatever silver or grain that will enter your heart, your eleven *aruras* mentioned above will still be yours forever and ever.
> In the writing of Hor son of Ankhwennefer.
> In the writing of Psamtikmenekh son of Horwedja, whose mother is Tsenhor, in person.
> In the writing of the god's father Teos son of Psamtikmenekh, in person.

One of the questions remaining is whether Nesmin would really name his daughter Tsenhor after the deceased Mrs. Tsenhor who had been entrusted to his care. The contract would guarantee a steady annual income for the rest of his life, so yes, probably so. The singers of the interior of Amun were mostly renamed after a famous divine adoratrice, an institution that guaranteed they would not have any material worries for the rest of their lives. Closer to home we may look, for instance, at seventeenth-century Maria Tesselschade Roemersdochter Visser, a famous woman poet from the Dutch Golden Age. She was born in 1594 and was named by her father after a shipwreck near the island of Texel—Tesselschade meaning 'damage at Texel'—that had cost him a fortune. If people named their children after a business catastrophe in the seventeenth century AD, why not name them after a major benefactor in the sixth century BCE, someone who had changed the family fortune for good? Was the Theban choachyte Nesmin already considering his baby daughter's future career as a choachyte when she was born? One would very much like to think that this was so.

What Happened to the Rest?

Between 10 March and 8 April 556 BCE, so on or near the same date as our P. Louvre E 10935, another papyrus was written by a scribe in Thebes. This is now kept in the Musée du Cinquantenaire in Brussels under the inventory number E 6031. The text was first published in *Corpus Papyrorum Aegypti* (1885–1902), in which Eugène Revillout and August Eisenlohr presented a number of papyri from the archive of Djekhy & Son for the first time, also including the Brussels papyrus. It had been bought by Revillout at a public auction in Paris in 1901. It so happens that P. Louvre E 10935 was also acquired at a public auction in Paris in 1901, so through some incredible coincidence both papyri may actually have been put up for sale at the very same auction, which would be remarkable indeed.

The Brussels papyrus was subsequently published by Wilhelm Spiegelberg, who by then was already starting to eclipse Revillout's fame. As Spiegelberg soon found out, this papyrus contained the almost identical autograph subscriptions by seven people who apparently were not used to writing regularly, meaning that he could not decipher the entire text, nor can we today. While sadly noting that P. Brussels E 6031 probably belonged to our P. Louvre E 10935, Spiegelberg did not miss the opportunity to put another smear on Revillout's reputation as a demotist.

These are the signatures of the seven witnesses who were present when the contract was closed, a contract which, if I am not mistaken, is known as the Louvre papyrus published by Revillout as nr. 25 in his *Corpus Papyrorum* (our P. Louvre E 10935), but unfortunately in a photograph of such bad quality that the details of the text cannot be read, so that one may conclude that the translation by the author was only guessed at.

Since P. Brussels E 6031 was written in the same month as P. Louvre E 10935 and also dealt with eleven *aruras*—likewise setting one *arura* aside as land that could not be worked, so that the new owner would avoid having to pay harvest tax on it—this was a logical conclusion that was even shared by as brilliant a scholar as Jan Quaegebeur, the Flemish Egyptologist (and demotist) who was to die tragically long before his time. However, the witnesses from P. Brussels E 6031 each started their own short statement on a new line, suggesting that this text was once attached to the side or to the bottom of a contract now lost. A very similar case is the abnormal hieratic document P. Louvre E 7849 from the archive of Djekhy & Son. The original contract was kept in the Louvre under the inventory number E 7849, but the unrecognized witness subscriptions—summarizing the content of the original contract at the bottom of the text—were for a long time kept separately as P. Louvre E 7857A + B, to be reunited only in recent times.

But P. Louvre E 10935 was already signed at the bottom of the contract by the scribe, the donating party, and his son, and then there were also the seventeen witnesses on the back, meaning that for this reason alone the Brussels papyrus cannot belong to P. Louvre E 10935 proper. One way out of this dilemma would be to assume that this other, now lost, contract, of which probably only the lower half is left—namely the witness subscriptions contained in P. Brussels E 6031—dealt with the other eleven *arura*s kept by Psamtikmenekh.

The God's Father Petosiris Son of Wenamun

The fields that were given, or rather sold in advance, to Tsenhor's father, the choachyte Nesmin, to provide funerary offerings for the donator's mother, also called Tsenhor, belonged to the Theban elite. Demotic contracts only seldom mention people from the top, but in this case we can actually see whether some of the people mentioned in P. Louvre E 10935 have left any traces behind. And they have.

One of the former owners of the twenty-two *arura*s was the god's father Petosiris son of Wenamun. As the German demotist Günter Vittmann has noted, this same man is mentioned in the abnormal hieratic documents P. Turin 2120 and 2121. These show that Petosiris was high up in the hierarchy, being a chief of priests and fourth prophet of Osiris, Horus, and Isis in Abydos, which he apparently combined with some priesthoods of Amun and Amunrasonter in Thebes, as well as being a governor of Thebes (he originally came from Abydos). One assumes with Vittmann that his daughter Nitocris received the field—half of which was donated in P. Louvre E 10935 to 'our' Nesmin—on the occasion of her adoption by a singer of the interior of Amun.

But life is full of surprises. Not long after Vittmann published his findings, he happened to visit the Badisches Landesmuseum in Karlsruhe, where he saw two limestone blocks together measuring 28.4 x 92.4 cm (see fig. 3). These came from the former collection of the German consul in Cairo, Carl August Reinhardt (1856–1903), with about five hundred other ancient Egyptian objects. The heavily damaged relief, which is believed to come from the necropolis of Abydos, shows Petosiris offering to his deceased parents, the priest of Osiris Wenamun son of Basa and Mutirdis. In between them is an offering table with the usual offerings and a text showing the standard *hetep di nesu* ('an offering that the king provides') offering formula that had been in use for thousands of years:

> An offering that the king provides for Osiris [. . .], Lord of Abydos,
> in all his places (of worship), [so that he may give a funerary offering
> of a thousand bread and beer and] all good and pure things for the *ka*
> of [the *wab* priest of Osiris] Wenamun, true of voice, and his wife, the
> lady of the house [Mutirdis, true of voice].

Figure 3. Petosiris son of Wenamun [Courtesy Günter Vittmann]

The caption above the figure of Petosiris, who probably died between 620 and 618 BCE, simply states, "Their son, the priest of Amun, Petosiris, true of voice." This means that Petosiris was dead, too. The epithet 'true of voice' refers to the passage through the underworld, where the deceased first had to make a declaration about his behavior during his lifetime. This was the so-called Negative Confession, Spell 125, of the Book of the Dead. In other words, the Petosiris shown on the relief from Karlsruhe is Petosiris in the afterlife, where he continues to take care of the needs of his parents, whereas in reality this task was probably relegated to the likes of Tsenhor.

But Petosiris is not the only dignitary mentioned in connection with Nesmin's—and later Tsenhor's—fields from P. Louvre E 10935. There was also the governor of Thebes and servant of the divine adoratrice, Pabasa son of Petebastet. And we actually know where his tomb lies.

A Tomb in the Assasif

The tomb of Pabasa—who is mentioned by name in P. Louvre E 10935—can still be visited in the Assasif today (TT 279). It is located near the entrance to the temple of Hatshepsut at Deir al-Bahari. The Assasif was a popular burial ground among the elite of the Twenty-fifth and Twenty-sixth Dynasties, and we may be sure that on her way to work Tsenhor regularly passed some of these tombs. Maybe she was even aware of the connection between the tomb owner Pabasa and the eleven *aruras* acquired by her father Nesmin. And if she was, one would like to imagine that she would say a short prayer in passing, even though Pabasa was not one of her clients. The demotic contracts often do not tell us what we would most like to know.

The massive stone coffin of Pabasa was found in situ by the famous collector Giovanni d'Athanasi (1798–1854), or Demetrio Papandriopoulos as he was known to his friends, during one of his excavations in ancient Thebes in or after 1817. D'Athanasi sold it to Alexander, Duke of Hamilton some time before 1834. The coffin was then presented to the Glasgow Museum in 1922, where it received the inventory number 1922.86. It is now on permanent display in the Kelvingrove Art Gallery and Museum. Between 1916 and 1919, TT 279 was surveyed and partly excavated by a team from the Metropolitan Museum of Art but, apart from a few pages in the *MMA Bulletin*, never properly published. The excavators did, however, find a granite offering table made for Pabasa near the tomb, and this was allocated to the museum when the finds were divided between the excavators and the Egyptian authorities (MMA inv. nr. 22.3.2). Smaller items belonging to Pabasa's tomb keep surfacing on the antiquities market to this day. The tomb is still in excellent condition, owing to the restoration work undertaken by an Egyptian team in the 1980s. In recent years an Italian team has been carrying out some epigraphic work there. A full publication has yet to appear, however.

The Late Period elite tombs in the Assasif all shared a number of characteristic features. There was always a mud-brick superstructure decorated with so-called funerary cones showing the titles and name of the deceased. These cones were inserted into the walls, the inscription facing outward. The superstructure was mostly oriented from east to west. In Pabasa's tomb, the cult room was actually oriented from south to north, but this was probably done because of a lack of space; the Assasif was a very popular burial ground. A ramp in the superstructure gave access to a sun court located deep inside the rock, surrounded by decorated pillars. In it was an offering table for the tomb owner. In some Late Period tombs clear traces of trees and plants can be found, showing that at least some sun courts were designed as gardens. If there was one place where we would expect a choachyte to do his work, this court may have been it. However, the sun court also gave access to various other rooms, such as a subterranean cult room containing an image of Osiris. From there a shaft led to the actual burial chamber. This cult room would be another likely location for making libations.

So, would a choachyte do his or her work in the sun court representing the world of the living—literally touched by Ra, as it were—or in the shade in the cult room in the presence of Osiris? We have no way of knowing. But the latter guess seems best.

3
Love and Death:
Psenese, Tsenhor, Ruru, and
Peteamunhotep, 530–517 BCE

Dividing an Inheritance
September 530–526 BCE (P. Vienna KM 3853)

Somewhere between September 530 and September 526 BCE, the choachyte Rery son of Heryrem had a contract written for his younger brother Psenese. Within a few years the latter would become the second husband of 'our' Tsenhor. We do not know the exact year because the papyrus is badly damaged on the right, so that the date is lost (demotic is written from right to left). It could be any year between 41 and 44, which was the last regnal year of Amasis. P. Vienna KM 3853 is a rather large papyrus of 19.5 x 76.5 cm, thus underlining the solemnity of the occasion, because through this contract Rery ceded half of their parental heritage—apparently he was the eldest son—to his brother Psenese. One takes it that both their father and mother had died.

According to the official records of the Theban choachytes—P. Louvre E 7840 col. IV *l.* 6—their father Heryrem son of Namenekhamun attended the New Year's meeting of their association in regnal year 29 of Amasis (542 BCE). He was still present at another meeting in the birth month of the patron deity Amunhotep son of Hapu in the same year, where—oddly enough—he is mentioned twice in a single column listing thirteen members of the association (col. III *l.* 7 and 10). The last mention of Heryrem is in 541 BCE (col. VIII *l.* 10), and P. Vienna KM 3853 tells us that he died before 530 BCE. Since his son Rery is also mentioned three times in the choachytes' records—cols. II *l.* 10, III *l.* 8 (right after the mention of his father, meaning that they probably saw the scribe together), and IV *l.* 9, all from 542 BCE—and

Psenese is conspicuously absent from P. Louvre E 7840, Rery was probably the eldest brother.

Like every early demotic papyrus at this time, P. Vienna KM 3853 was published by the French pioneer demotist Eugène Revillout on more than one occasion, but in this particular case the *editio princeps*—or at least partly so—was done by his Austrian pupil Jakob Krall in 1884, no doubt to the dismay of Revillout, who had a vindictive nature and a tendency to stake publishing claims. It was probably Krall who tipped off Revillout about the purchase of the archive of Djekhy & Son in Karnak in the winter of 1884–85 by August Eisenlohr (Krall was there when Eisenlohr bought the papyri), and one wonders whether he did this to patch up his relationship with Revillout. In any case, in the introduction to the *Corpus Papyrorum Aegypti* (1885–1902) that he published together with Eisenlohr, Revillout had the following to say about Krall's publication of P. Vienna KM 3853:

> As for my former student Krall, to whom I liberally gave many private and free lessons in my own study before the official establishment of my courses at the École du Louvre, he has published under his own name, after his return to Vienna, the notes taken during my classes on an archaic contract which is very fragmented and from Vienna, that I had studied during my 1878 mission and which I had meticulously rearranged. However, his work remains incomplete, because the eye of the master did not intervene to correct the mistakes and faults as a result of badly taken notes by his student. The true explanation of this document therefore still waited to be published and one will find it in my book.

And that was Eugène Revillout on a good day. P. Vienna KM 3853 would still have to wait decades before it was properly published, first by the Italian Egyptologist Sergio Pernigotti in 1971, and then by Pieter Willem Pestman in *Les papyrus démotiques de Tsenhor* (1994).

This is a straightforward contract:

> Regnal year 40 + x, first month of the *shemu* season under Pharaoh l.p.h. Amasis l.p.h. The choachyte of the valley Rery son of Heryrem, whose mother is Beniuutehtyes, has said to the choachyte of the valley Psenese son of Heryrem, whose mother is Beniuutehtyes, his brother:

"To you belongs half of all that I own and will acquire, and also half of all that belongs to the choachyte of the valley Heryrem, our father, and half of all that belongs to Mrs. Beniuutehtyes, our mother, namely field, houses, slaves, bread of the temple, bread of Osiris, tomb in the necropolis, and any other thing on earth.

"Half belongs to you and half belongs to me. I will not be able to take them back from you, never unto eternity. But if I take back from you the half shares described above, I will give you one deben of silver of the Treasury of Thebes, in silver bars, being 9 2/3 1/6 1/10 1/30 1/60 1/60 silver kite from the Treasury, being one deben of silver of the Treasury of Thebes again, whereas the half share described above will still be yours."

In the writing of Petehor son of Petosiris.

Rery allots to Psenese—who was now probably between twenty-three and twenty-seven years old—half of the possessions of their father Heryrem and their mother Beniuutehtyes, meaning that (part of) the inheritance would remain undivided and that Psenese had the right to half of the income from this inheritance. It is strange that there were apparently only two children left in this household to divide the inheritance, but it was to be the same situation when Tsenhor's husband divided his inheritance shortly before he died (P. Turin 2126 from 498 BCE).

In addition, Rery starts by saying that half of what he *himself* owns and will acquire will also accrue to Psenese. This is strange, unless of course the property mentioned by Rery had in fact been acquired by managing the parental estate, meaning that these new possessions were direct returns from the family estate. According to Egyptian law, Rery's own property would be divided between his wife and his children. Rery's brothers and sisters would only become involved if Rery had no children.

Little did both men know that in Persia Cambyses had ascended to the throne and was now on his way to becoming their new king. Shortly after the coronation of Psamtik III in 526 BCE, the son of King Amasis, rain fell in Thebes. This happened very rarely, and people thought it was not a good omen.

Mad King or Just a Bad Hair Day?

Cambyses—who was actually the second Persian king by that name—has gone down in history as the mad king who affronted the ancient Egyptian gods, killing the holy Apis bull, desecrating the mummy of Amasis, and in general wreaking havoc. But his reputation may actually be based on malicious rumors spread by discontented native priests that were amplified in the Greek tradition (which had every reason to be anti-Persian).

Cambyses II was a son of Cyrus the Great. He ruled the Persian Empire between 530 and 522 BCE, during which time he was also to decide the fate of Egypt as an independent state. In the spring of 525 BCE (or perhaps slightly earlier), his army went on the attack, routing the Egyptian army under Psamtik III at Pelusium in the eastern delta, some say because he had been insulted by King Amasis. It seems Cambyses had asked Amasis to give him his daughter to marry, but Amasis had instead sent Neithiyty, a daughter of Apries, whose throne he had usurped. Neithiyty, not amused by this turn of events, persuaded Cambyses to attack Egypt and punish Amasis. It is, however, not very easy to fit this in chronologically. Since Apries was killed after he had been decisively beaten by Amasis in 567 BCE—or even in the last battle they fought—for Neithiyty to have been a daughter of Apries means she would have had to be born in 566 BCE at the latest. Amasis died in 526 BCE.

So when exactly did Cambyses ask Amasis to send a daughter of his? Cambyses only became king of Persia in 530 BCE. By then Neithiyty would have been at least thirty-six years old. The people at the Persian court would have considered her to be really old and wrinkled. One can imagine that in that case Cambyses may have felt slighted by Amasis, expecting a young Egyptian princess and receiving an aging woman instead. Whatever the truth, in August 525 BCE Cambyses conquered Egypt.

Although the verso of the Demotic Chronicle (P. Bibl. Nat. 215) suggests that Cambyses did interfere in some way with the financial system of the temples—which usually means that a king tries to steal money from the divine domain by redirecting it to his own—at the beginning of his reign Cambyses was apparently still paying homage to the native gods. When he visited the temple of the goddess Neith in Sais, the town that had seen the rise of the Twenty-sixth Dynasty, he lay prostrate before her. The source for this story is the controversial autobiography of the Egyptian official Wedjahorresne, who is believed by some to have been a traitor and a collaborator, although the evidence seems to point in quite another direction. Besides, if the Persian king who had just conquered Wedjahorresne's country appointed him (an Egyptian) to some unpopular post, would it really have been possible for him to decline politely without losing his head? Another very intriguing possibility is that Wedjahorresne was actually a has-been whose glory days were under Amasis but who had been sidetracked under Psamtik III (he lost most of his titles in this king's reign), which made him a perfect tool for the Persian government.[1]

The question of the alleged piety of Cambyses must, however, wait for a moment, because right after the conquest of Egypt Cambyses still had an appetite for more territory. He first sent an army to the west, but according to Herodotus this was surprised by a sandstorm and perished. Then Cambyses sent an army to the south to conquer Nubia. This latter expedition, again according to Herodotus, met with little success. It seems Cambyses had sent his men on their way with insufficient supplies (most wars are lost because of bad logistics), so that he had to withdraw in the end, having lost a large part of his army. One would very much like to imagine Tsenhor, who would be about twenty-five years old by now, standing among the crowds of Egyptians, impassively watching the defeated Persian army retreat through Thebes on its way back to Memphis.

If we now pick up the story as it is told by Herodotus—and the reader is reminded that at times Herodotus can be more of a journalist recording gossip than a fully reliable historical source—when Cambyses arrived in Memphis, he saw that the Egyptians were all celebrating. This did not go down well after his ill-fated expedition against Nubia, so Cambyses sent for the authorities and asked them why the people of Memphis were rejoicing when last time he was there they had done nothing of the sort. Surely the only reason for this celebration could be his misfortune? The Memphite authorities told the king that the holy Apis bull had appeared once again, something that happened only rarely, and that this explained the festivities. Cambyses would hear none of this and had them all summarily executed. He then summoned the local priests, asking them the same question, and they replied as the authorities had done. So then— allegedly—Cambyses told the priests to bring the holy Apis, which they did. As the story goes, Cambyses then struck the animal in the thigh with his dagger, mocking the priests for producing a god that turned out to be as vulnerable as any other mortal creature. The animal was left to die in the temple and those who were found still celebrating the advent of the new Apis were killed.

After this, it is reported, Cambyses became totally mad. He started out by sending a courtier to Susa to murder his own brother Smerdis, who he believed was after his throne, and then he killed his sister, who was also his wife. There is, however, some doubt whether these events really unfolded the way they were described by Herodotus.

When Cambyses was crowned king of Babylonia, before he invaded Egypt, he brought a divine statue to a local temple to honor the indigenous gods. The only problem was that Cambyses and his men wanted to do this fully armed, and, when it was pointed out to him that this was not allowed, he reportedly at once took off his armor so as not to offend the Babylonian gods and his new subjects. The Persian system of administration hinged on relatively benevolent rule that gave the people from whatever country had been subjugated the freedom to worship their own gods. This was a sensible policy because it enabled the Persians to rule their vast empire with only limited garrisons at strategic points.

The information provided by Herodotus about the murder of the Apis is also at odds with ancient Egyptian sources. These were first collected about eighty years ago by the French Egyptologist Georges Posener in *La première domination perse en Égypte* (Cairo: Institut Français d'Archéologie Orientale, 1936).

An Apis did die in Cambyses' sixth regnal year, which would be 524 BCE, because he counted his years as king of Egypt from the moment he ascended the throne in Persia in 530 BCE. The dead bulls would be buried in the Serapeum near Memphis, often accompanied by a stela mentioning the salient facts of the bull's life, such as date of birth, coronation as Apis, death, and funeral. Stelae were also left by pious believers, so that when the French archaeologist Auguste Mariette excavated the Serapeum in 1853, he found hundreds of them, which were shipped to the Louvre. One of these is St. Louvre 354, which at one time was also known under the inventory numbers SN 83 and 407. This much-battered stela shows that an Apis bull was buried with full honors in year 6 of Cambyses.

The stela portrays the king kneeling before the Apis and the inscription clearly states that Cambyses himself provided this final resting place. The Apis had been embalmed, dressed, and adorned with amulets and jewels of precious materials, all according to the king's orders. But there is more, because the actual sarcophagus that was used to bury the dead Apis, of which Herodotus wrote that it was buried in secret by the Egyptian priests, is still there. The British Egyptologist Battiscombe Gunn—who first tried his luck as a banker, an engineer, and a journalist, to finally become one of the more remarkable Egyptologists England has ever seen—published a short account in 1926 in the *Annales du Service des*

Antiquités Égyptiennes after he saw the grey garnite sarcophagus in situ in the Serapeum. According to him, the inscription on the coffin showed many traces of hasty work. Not the most exquisite workmanship:

> The signs, which have an average height of 5 cm., are spaced out in a somewhat inept way; the cutting is rough and for the most part very shallow, making the reading rather difficult.

The sarcophagus had not been moved to one of the alcoves, as one might expect, but appears to have been simply left on a bed of sand to block one of the four old entrances to the Serapeum. Is this then proof of the assertion by Herodotus that the Memphite priests secretly buried the Apis after it had been killed by Cambyses in a mad rage? In that case, how do we explain stela Louvre 354, which clearly states that Cambyses himself ordered—and arranged—the burial? And what should we make of the inscription on the sarcophagus itself? This again is very precise:

> Horus, Uniter of the Two Lands, King of Upper and Lower Egypt Mesutyra, Son of Ra, Cambyses, may he live forever. He made a monument for his father Apis-Osiris, a great sarcophagus of granite, which the King of Upper and Lower Egypt Mesutyra, Son of Ra, Cambyses has made, given all life, enduring and domination, all health and joy, appearing as King of Upper and Lower Egypt, forever.

Even if the workmanship of the sarcophagus is below standard, this—as well as the strange location of the coffin—is hardly sufficient proof of a secret and hasty burial. Also, given the fact that Cambyses is mentioned on the coffin with his full titulary, claiming that he commissioned this sarcophagus would be the last thing one would expect the Memphite priests to have done if he had really murdered the Apis. Surely nobody in his right mind would have dared to use the king's name on the Apis sarcophagus if the very same king had killed the Apis in a mad rage only shortly before. So it seems that the account of Herodotus could do with some slight revisions here and there. And this is not all.

Cambyses was also said—once again by Herodotus—to have desecrated the body of Amasis, who was buried in Sais in a beautiful stone tomb. The moment Cambyses entered Amasis' palace, he reportedly ordered some of his men to take out the body of his enemy to have it whipped, stabbed, and robbed of its hair. But apparently the mummified body of Amasis would not come apart, so that in the end Cambyses had it burned. If there is any truth in the story of Amasis sending Neithiyty, the daughter of Apries, to Persia to marry Cambyses instead of one of his own daughters, this would go a long way toward explaining why Cambyses acted the way he did. But ultimately the conquest of Egypt by the Persians appears to have been the result of a cunning plan by an Egyptian eye doctor who had been sent to the Persian court by Amasis against his will, leaving his family behind. He grew very close to the Persian king and, when he decided that the time for payback had arrived, he suggested to Cambyses to ask Amasis for the hand of his daughter. The rest is history, or maybe just a good story. There may have been some Persian spin doctor at work here somewhere, trying to legitimize Cambyses' claim to the Egyptian throne.

Some even believe that Herodotus may have heard a garbled version of the life of Wedjahorresne, who was serving as a doctor at the Persian court for some time and—if the evidence is interpreted correctly—may also have been the object of veneration at Memphis. How this came about we will see later.

There may well have been a time of great distress in Egypt shortly after it was conquered by the Persians—which is also referred to in the inscription by Wedjahorresne (see below)—but in the sixth century BCE, looting, rape, and pillage were accepted by-products of modern warfare. Likewise, the execution of Psamtik III, who had apparently plotted to get his throne back, along with two thousand highly placed persons, was not just a Persian act of atrocity but also an effective way to eliminate the people most likely to organize future resistance. In any case, something bad seems to have happened shortly after the Persian conquest.

We know, for instance, that the funerary equipment of some of the close relatives of Amasis was badly damaged, and this must have happened after the invasion of the Persians. Among the items proving the *damnatio memoriae* of Amasis and his relatives allegedly carried out by order of Cambyses are two beautiful sarcophagi now in the Hermitage in St. Petersburg. They are anthropomorphic—following the shape of the human body—and made of black greywacke. They were apparently found in tomb LG 83 in Giza in the nineteenth century and once contained the bodies of Queen Nakhtbasteru ('Bastet has power over them') and the prince and overseer of the army Amasis (inventory numbers ДВ767 and 766, respectively). They were the wife and son of King Amasis II. Although the two sarcophagi have still not been published scientifically, we do have an insightful preliminary report by the Russian Egyptologist Andrey Bolshakov. The pages below draw heavily on his findings. Bolshakov investigated the extent and the purpose of all the conscious mutilations of the sarcophagi, presumably undertaken at the time when Egypt was overrun by the Persians under Cambyses. This assumption was voiced by the famous Russian Egyptologist Wladimir Golenishchev (1856–1947), who visited Egypt more than sixty times, building up a vast collection of antiquities that included the Moscow Mathematical Papyrus, the Prophecy of Neferti, and the Story of Wenamun, and—as things often go in Egyptology—his view was generally accepted until someone decided to take a look at the evidence. Bolshakov noticed that the names of the owners had in fact been extremely carefully chiselled away, leaving the theophoric elements in their names intact:

> The unknown vandal acted very sensibly. He destroyed all the signs belonging to the titles of the owners of the sarcophagi and fixed parts of their names. Both names are theophorous—'Iah is born' and 'Bastet is strong against them'—and the signs of the gods' names remain intact.

In other words, the man (probably not a woman) who was hired to eradicate the memory of Nakhtbasteru and Amasis—if the names were no longer present on the coffin, the owner no longer existed, either here or in the afterlife—made sure that he left the theophoric elements in the names of his victims intact, either through fear of the gods or for another reason. Also, the elements that were chiseled off are still visible, if only barely, to the trained eye of an Egyptologist, and presumably also the gods themselves, so that the owners of the coffins retained their passport to the afterlife after all.

The notion that removing people's names and achievements from statues, stelae, and tomb walls was designed to magically destroy their owners' chances in the afterlife is typical mainstream Egyptology. The notion may be correct (and it probably is), but if we look at the famous early demotic P. Rylands 9 from the reign of Darius I (which may be a real draft or copy of a petition to the Persian satrap) describing the eventful lives of Petiese I and his offspring—which was all about the priestly income from the temple of Amun in al-Hiba (they wanted it back and the priests would not give it)—this tells us there could also be more mundane motives. Money, for instance. P. Rylands 9 gives a first-hand account of *damnatio memoriae* the demotic papyrological way, which differs much from the Egyptological way. In col. XVIII *l.* 13ff. we read how one of the Wedjasematawys of the clan of Petiese is forced to flee in the face of the priests of Amun of al-Hiba. This was a wise thing to do, because these priests had already proved that they would not stop at arson and murder to protect their income. As soon as the priests heard Wedjasematawy had fled,

> they went to his house and took all his property and they razed his house and his place in the temple to the ground. They (also) had a stonemason brought and caused him to erase the stela Petiese son of Ituru (Petiese I) had had set up on the stone platform.

Petiese I had managed Upper Egypt on behalf of Psamtik I under the umbrella of the great harbormaster Petiese son of Ankhsheshonq, whose title belies his actual power, which must have equaled that of the earlier vizier. Petiese I was actually one of the people who played a key role in the Saite Restoration. He also appointed just about any clan member he could think of as a priest in the temple of Amun in al-Hiba, thus robbing the local priests of their income. To make sure that people would remember his accomplishments, Petiese I had two stone statues placed in the local temple (just as Wedjahorresne would do several hundred years later) as well as a stela (but apparently there were two) recording all his achievements:

> Then they (the priests) went to the other stela of stone from Elephantine that was in the holy of holies, saying: "We want to have it effaced." But the stonemason said: "I cannot erase it. Only a graniteworker can erase it. My tools would go blunt." Then a priest said: "Leave it. Look, no man can see it. Also he (Petiese I) had it made before he acted as a priest (in al-Hiba) and (even) before the great harbormaster Petiese had written for him a title to the share of a priest of Amun (in al-Hiba). We can withstand him (Wedjasematawy and anyone from the clan of Petiese claiming the income), saying: "Your father was never a priest of Amun (in this temple)." So they left the stela of stone from Elephantine and did not erase it.

In other words, for the priests of al-Hiba the only reason not to erase the granite stela of Petiese—thus granting him a place in the afterlife—was that nobody could see the stela (it was in the holy of holies) and they could actually use it to counter any claim to the priestly income of Petiese I from the temple of al-Hiba (which they wanted for themselves) because this specific stela did not mention it. In fact, one of the priests even hints at the fact that the stela may come in handy if Wedjasematawy or one of his offspring decides to take them to court after all. This interpretation is really a long way away from the accepted view, it is true, but this is what the papyrus tells us, and it is also good thinking. Not quite satisfied with the results, the priests then threw the two statues of Petiese I standing near the entrance to the chapels of Amun and Osiris into the Nile, which also looks more like destroying evidence than a proper *damnatio memoriae*.

So there is possibly rather more to it than meets the eye, and in the case of the St. Petersburg coffins the sheer fact that the mutilation was done so expertly could only mean that it was the work of a born, and perhaps highly literate, Egyptian. Why was that? Was it because the Egyptians hated Amasis, the usurper of the throne, who also had the reputation of being a heavy drinker and a thief? This would be strange. Amasis was actually one of the most successful pharaohs in history. Within a year after his death the country was conquered by the Persians, after the defeat of his son Psamtik III. Somehow it does not seem very likely that the mutilation of the coffins of his wife and son could have taken place in the short space of time between his death and the defeat of Psamtik III. Was it the Persians under Cambyses after all? Even if we discard the colorful report by Herodotus about the atrocities committed by Cambyses, something happened to cause someone up the hierarchy to order the mutilation of the coffins of Nakhtbasteru and Prince Amasis.

The Egyptian Wedjahorresne, who was to rise high up in the Persian administration, does refer to a period of very great distress in Egypt after the conquest by the Persians. But one of the problems we still face is that we do not know when Nakhtbasteru or Prince Amasis died. Did they outlive King Amasis only by a few years, did they commit suicide after the defeat of Psamtik III, or did they linger on for a decade? In that case, the mutilation of their coffins could not have taken place under Cambyses because the owners would either have restored their sarcophagi or, as they were still royalty, simply ordered new ones.

We can say, however, that the papers left by Tsenhor show no apparent break with Egyptian traditions, even if the ruling pharaoh was now the Persian Darius I. But on a micro scale, things did change. P. Vienna KM 3853—in which Rery promises half of the estate of their parents to Tsenhor's future husband Psenese somewhere between 530 and 526 BCE—still makes reference to the Treasury of Thebes. This specific treasury was actually the successor to another treasury, the Treasury of Harsaphes, which is known from the abnormal hieratic contracts. Harsaphes ('Who is on his lake') was the god of Herakleopolis, and when this city rose to prominence in the Twenty-second Libyan Dynasty, the power of the god Harsaphes rose with it. During the Twenty-seventh Persian Dynasty the treasury was moved to Memphis, and that is why some of the documents from Tsenhor's papers (for example, P. BM EA 10120A) refer to the Treasury of Ptah—the main Memphite god—instead of the Treasury of Thebes as in P. Vienna KM 3853, which is from the Twenty-sixth Dynasty. The question of what this reference actually means is still under debate. Was the treasury responsible for the alloy of the precious metals used for payment or did it keep the official weight—such as a kite and a deben (a deben was about 90 grams)—issuing officially calibrated weights to the local authorities? This could well be the case. An Aramaic papyrus from roughly the same period actually mentions these weights of Ptah, and in the Ptolemaic demotic P. Chicago Hawara 6 from 259 BCE, a marital property arrangement, the capital changing hands is somewhat cryptically referred to as "in pieces that are in the Treasury of Ptah," which is presumably the same. Egypt was to become a real money economy only in the Ptolemaic period, although barter probably remained the most popular way to trade things in large parts of the country. In Tsenhor's days value was still expressed in weights of specific precious metals, exactly the way it was done in New Kingdom Deir al-Medina centuries earlier. However, before we return to the little world of Tsenhor in Thebes, we must have a closer look at the life of a man who appears to have played a crucial role in the relations between the Persians and the Egyptian elite, Mr. Wedjahorresne.

Wedjahorresne: A Smart Career Move
Wedjahorresne is mainly known from his naophorous headless basalt statue, which bears his autobiography. He began his career under Amasis and after the defeat of Psamtik III served both Cambyses II and Darius I

with apparently equal loyalty. The statue is now kept in the Museo Gregoriano Egizio in the Vatican (inv. nr. 158 [113]). It is believed that it was placed in the temple of Osiris in Sais at the beginning of the reign of Darius I. Statues like these served a double purpose. They were a votive offering to the god showing that one had done one's religious duty, as well as—yet another—guarantee for a comfortable afterlife.

This double purpose is corroborated by the beginning of the text, which is the typical *hetep di nesu* formula known so well from the Middle Kingdom stelae from Abydos, in which the king presents bread, beer, bulls, and geese to Osiris, from which the *ka* of the deceased is allowed to take a share. Just to make sure, in his inscription Wedjahorresne reminds Osiris—safely tucked away in the naos held by Wedjahorresne—of the fact that he, a god, is being protected by him, a mere mortal:

> O Osiris, Lord of Eternity. The overseer of doctors Wedjahorresne has put his hand upon you to protect you. Let your *ka* order to make everything that is beneficial for him, just as he is keeping your chapel protected forever.

But this is not all we know of this man. Another statue was found at Mit Rahina near ancient Memphis. This statue also bears an inscription by a priest called Minirdis, saying that he restored it 177 years after it had been placed in a sanctuary somewhere in the Memphite region. Some people even believe that in the end Wedjahorresne achieved the status of saint with the power of healing (which of course often happens with saints).

All this is nothing compared to the sensational find made by a Czech archaeological team in nearby Abusir, namely the discovery of Wedjahorresne's tomb. It was excavated between 1980 and 1993, and according to some of the finds—three foundation deposits that were found contained a number of blue-green faience tablets bearing the name of King Amasis and some of the sixty-one demotic inscriptions (inspection marks) inside the tomb mention regnal years 41 and 42—building started only near the end of the reign of Amasis. The mummy of Wedjahorresne was gone, and the tomb turned out to have been robbed in antiquity at least twice, which left about seven thousand pottery shards, a small number of *ushabti*s, and some other intrusive material. Maybe the Abusir tomb was actually a cenotaph—an 'empty tomb' that could be either Wedjahorresne's initial tomb or a monument erected to honor him—meaning that

Wedjahorresne was actually buried in Sais. But if he was, the chances of ever finding him are probably zero, because the ground-water level and modern building activities have destroyed much nondurable material.

The location selected by Wedjahorresne for his tomb was peculiar, near the Old Kingdom cemetery at Abusir, but not too far away from Memphis, where the necropolis was becoming crowded. As far as we know, he was the first Late Period official to make this choice, although soon after more tombs were built in the direct vicinity. The tomb itself—a shaft tomb—appears to have been a Twenty-sixth Dynasty Memphite invention. It consisted of an 8 x 10 m shaft that was up to thirty meters deep. At the bottom a burial chamber was built of limestone, after which the shaft was again filled with sand, apart from a smaller shaft ending in a horizontal vaulted corridor that gave access to the burial chamber. Inside the burial chamber would be a massive limestone sarcophagus protecting an anthropoid inner coffin. Both were still in situ in Wedjahorresne's tomb. The outer coffin, made of Tura limestone, had a length of five meters. The much smaller inner coffin was made of basalt. It seems as if this Memphite innovation was actually simply an upgraded copy of the Old Kingdom *mastaba* tombs that could be found nearby. If so, this would not surprise us. In the Twenty-sixth Dynasty the Egyptians were often inspired by Old Kingdom examples.

Apart from Wedjahorresne's titles—chief of doctors and commander of the foreign mercenaries, or *mer khasut haunebu*, in which *khasut* refers to anything foreign and *haunebu* is believed to be a designation for people from the Aegean (and became the name for an alleged highly secret Nazi flying-saucer project)—a few religious images, and several spells, including Chapter 72 of the Book of the Dead on the inner coffin, there is no extensive tomb decoration, suggesting that the tomb may not have been finished. What we know is that the name and titles of Wedjahorresne were left intact, which suggests that nobody tried to erase them—something one would expect to have happened if he indeed was a collaborator.

The Czech team also found the remains of the ancient 25.5 x 26 m girdle wall of crude stone that would have been lined with white limestone up to a height of two and a half meters. The courtyard inside was paved, and in the middle stood a structure of about 5 x 5 m, although the exact shape is still a matter of conjecture (meaning archaeologists do not know). Apart from several cult items found near the tomb, no indication of any mortuary service was found, but this may simply be a coincidence. Wedjahorresne was not the sort of man who would have been stashed away in one of Tsenhor's tombs to receive a collective weekly libation. He was rich enough to buy a private tomb, and if the Abusir shaft tomb is indeed a cenotaph, he was rich enough to buy two, including the services of a choachyte. But a tomb alone was not enough to guarantee a carefree hereafter in the Late Period, so people started putting up statues of themselves in temples to share in the divine offerings, more or less as a safety measure.

The inscription on Wedjahorresne's Vatican statue—which once stood in the Villa Tivoli as part of the personal collection of Emperor Hadrian—so far is the only Egyptian source telling us about the Persian conquest of Egypt and its immediate aftermath, and the debate about its subject is still far from over among Egyptologists. One of the main questions that keeps returning is whether Wedjahorresne was a collaborator who went over to the Persians. If he was, why were his tomb and statues not destroyed after the Persians were expelled from Egypt? If there is one thing we learn from Egyptian history, it is that the Egyptians had very long memories, and they had a perfect way to ensure that Wedjahorresne's existence would be obliterated from this world and the next: simply destroy all material traces and erase his name and titles wherever they were found. But the Vatican statue is largely intact, apart from the head and part of an arm, and his Abusir tomb was not vandalized, except by tomb robbers.

So maybe the solution lies in the inscription itself, which was described by the British Egyptologist Alan Lloyd as containing "an apologetic dimension designed to excuse Udjahorresnet's policy of co-operation." In other words, Wedjahorresne had a lot to explain to his fellow Egyptians during his own lifetime. To see whether this is true we will have to go through parts of his autobiography, which actually starts beneath his right armpit. Since this autobiography was Wedjahorresne's official legacy to posterity—and of course he would be well aware of this—he made sure that all the details were exactly the way he wanted them to be, more or less in the same way as the rich seventeenth-century Dutch traders from Amsterdam had themselves portrayed by Rembrandt, as the image of perfection (so the big wart on the cheek would not make it into the painting nor into Wedjahorresne's autobiography).

Blessed by Neith the Great, the Mother of God, and blessed by the gods of Sais. The Hereditary Nobleman, Prince and Seal-bearer of the

King of Lower Egypt, Sole Friend, True Acquaintance of the King, who loves him, Scribe, Inspector of the Scribal Council, Overseer of the Scribes of the Great Hall, Manager of the Palace, Overseer of the Royal *Kebenut* Ships under the King of Upper and Lower Egypt Khnumibra (Amasis), Overseer of the Royal *Kebenut* Ships under the King of Upper and Lower Egypt Ankhkara (Psamtik III) Wedjahorresne (. . .).

And these are still only just the titles of the man. In the past *kebenut* ships were believed to be navy ships, hence the widespread notion that Wedjahorresne was an admiral, although in view of later events in his life maybe he was simply an able administrator with a knack for figures and logistics. As far as we know *kebenut* ships were large seagoing ships, which could therefore also have been used for trade with the Aegean. But at this point things start to get interesting:

> The Great Ruler of All Foreign Lands, Cambyses, came to Egypt, the foreigners from all foreign countries being with him. (. . .) His Majesty commissioned me with the office of Chief Doctor, causing me to be next to him as a Friend and Manager of the Palace after I made his titulary in his name of King of Upper and Lower Egypt, (namely) Mesutyra.

In other words, apparently Cambyses, having conquered Egypt and given his troops a rest, had a staff meeting with his closest advisors and most probably also the local Egyptian elite, and then someone at this meeting suggested that the first thing he should do is to become an Egyptian pharaoh, which would make it easier to be accepted by the population. The system was later perfected by the Ptolemies, who combined it with tax reductions and land donations to buy the loyalty of the elite, the Egyptian priests, and the army. And then someone came up with the name of Wedjahorresne? Was he promoted to the position of chief physician to the Persian king and entrusted with the health of the most powerful man in the world, designing a royal titulary along the way? Somehow this does not seem very likely. Ancient Egyptian autobiographies are—just like their modern-day counterparts—notoriously sloppy when it comes to providing us with the details we really would like to know. But perhaps we should accept at face value Wedjahorresne's assertion that he himself instructed Cambyses to save the famous sanctuary of Neith, especially since his statue was put up on display in a temple for all to see and left alone by the temple officials. Neith was the local goddess behind the striking success of the Twenty-sixth Dynasty from Sais.

Something—and now we move on to the left armpit—happened inside this temple complex. People had taken up residence there, and the divine power of Neith had not been enough to prevent it. So Wedjahorresne—now one of the king's confidants—instructed Cambyses that this situation had to be redressed, and suddenly it becomes easy to see where Alan Lloyd's suspicion that he was a collaborator comes from. Who but someone who had thoroughly ingratiated himself with the Persian invaders would have been able to take this matter up directly with the king? But in reality the situation may have been more complex, and one almost senses Wedjahorresne's predicament. The Persian king was obviously aware of his many talents, and he was already in it up to his neck. Refusal was probably not a very healthy option. So the question then becomes whether Wedjahorresne really had any choice. If he had a wife and children—a most effective tool for coercion—one would say probably not. Even if he just valued his own life, the same answer would probably apply.

The autobiography of Wedjahorresne shows that little was wrong with the piety of Cambyses:

> I (Wedjahorresne) petitioned in front of His Majesty, the King of Upper and Lower Egypt Cambyses, about all the foreigners who had established themselves in the temple of Neith in order to drive them out (. . .) and His Majesty ordered the expulsion of all foreigners who had established themselves in the temple of Neith, as well as the destruction of their houses and all their infringements (abominations?) that were in the temple (. . .) and His Majesty ordered that the temple of Neith should be purified and that its entire staff should be restored to it.

Not only that. Cambyses also made sure that offerings were to be given to Neith and that from this moment on all religious festivals were to be celebrated just as they had from time immemorial. The scene described by Wedjahorresne is an age-old motif found throughout Egyptian history, namely of Pharaoh maintaining or restoring *ma'at*, or cosmic order,[2] which was his main task on earth. When Cambyses visited the temple in person—probably to inspect the restoration work set in motion by Wedjahorresne—he paid his respects to Neith, prostrating himself before her, which is not something a mad king would do (well, maybe). And while he was doing this, Wedjahorresne was there to witness it.

Wedjahorresne's autobiography then proceeds with the clauses already familiar to us from the Middle Kingdom Abydos stelae. He fed the poor, upheld the law, and supported his native city and anyone in his family who needed it. All these good deeds, however, did not preclude Cambyses from taking his favorite physician back with him to Persia, and the next section of Wedjahorresne's story shows that he was in Elam when Darius I called him back to Egypt. Darius took an active part in the administration of Egypt, and this time he needed someone to restore the House of Life (*per ankh*) to its former glory. The House of Life was an ancient institution. It was often connected with the temple, although the actual remains of the House of Life in Amarna, the New Kingdom city of Akhenaten, were found next to the royal archives for state correspondence. In essence, the House of Life seems to have been a library, scriptorium, and wise men's residence all in one. One may even surmise that legal manuals such as P. Mattha were written by the scribes of the House of Life. But the House of Life—presumably the one in Sais—had fallen on hard times. And once again one is left to wonder what happened here. Only a few years had gone by between the death of Amasis (526 BCE) and the accession of Darius I (521 BCE). It is difficult to see how the House of Life could have withered away under Amasis. Could it perhaps have suffered war damage or looting (Wedjahorresne does refer to a period of distress in Egypt)? The fact that the House of Life was in ruins had far wider implications than just another library going up in flames. It was the cultural heart of Egypt. Wedjahorresne was asked to restore it:

> I acted in accordance with the order of His Majesty. I provided it with all its scribes from the sons of (eminent) men, there being no children of low-ranking people among them. I put them under the mentorship of all wise men . . . all their works. (. . .) The reason why His Majesty did this was because he recognized the use of this skill for keeping alive people suffering from any disease and to ensure that the names of all the gods, their temples, their offerings, and the conduct of their religious festivals endured forever.

So, through the offices of Wedjahorresne, King Darius—in turn—is also seen to restore *ma'at*, by ordering him to rebuild and restaff the House of Life. Would Wedjahorresne have dared to put up his statue in just any temple, claiming that he had saved the temple of Neith in Sais from ruin and that he had also revived the House of Life, if the Egyptians thought he was a traitor? The more one considers this issue, the more problematic it becomes.

But whatever may be the truth about Wedjahorresne, none of it concerned 'our' Tsenhor in Thebes. Her worries were of a different nature. By now in her mid-thirties, she was either a widow or divorced and had had to bury some of her children. That was not a good prospect. But love was on the way. Right in time.

A Pregnant Widow
29 February–29 March 517 BCE (P. BM EA 10120A)

We do not know how Tsenhor met her second husband Psenese, nor when, but the fact that he was also a choachyte suggests they could even have met in the necropolis. But meet him she did, and from what follows it is clear that they started a household together. In March 517 BCE the couple had no less than four official contracts drawn up by the scribes Teos son of Ip and his son Ip. Teos was a god's father of Montu and chief priest in the fourth phyle—the monthly rotating crew of the temple of Montu—as well as a monthly priest in the second phyle of the same temple. This suggests that these scribes kept office somewhere in the temple and that on this day Tsenhor and Psenese came to the temple of Montu in Karnak, a site that can still be visited today. March probably meant winter, so that the temperature would have been between twenty-two and thirty degrees Celcius. Tsenhor may have had a rough day. Some say she was about to give birth, at the age of thirty-three.

Tsenhor and Psenese had come to the temple of Montu to marry. Or, to be more precise, on this day she and her husband made arrangements about their marital property. The contract between Tsenhor and Psenese is straightforward. Tsenhor had given three deben (about 270 grams) of silver to Psenese, which she would receive back in the case of a divorce—this, by the way, may very well have been a fictitious sum in many cases—apart from one-third of the property she and Psenese would acquire together during their marriage:

Regnal year 5, third month of the *akhet* season under Pharaoh l.p.h. Darius l.p.h. The choachyte of the valley Psenese son of Heryrem, whose mother is Beniuutehtyes, has said to Mrs. Tsenhor daughter of the choachyte of the valley Nesmin, whose mother is Ruru: "You have given to me three (deben) of silver of the Treasury of Ptah, being two deben of silver and 9 2/3 1/6 1/10 1/20 1/60 kite from the Treasury of Ptah, being three (deben) in silver bars again. If I repudiate you as wife or if I hate you, I will give you these three (deben) in silver bars from the Treasury of Ptah mentioned above that you have given me, as well as one-third of all that I will acquire together with you. I will give them to you."

In the writing of the god's father of Montu Lord of Thebes, chief of priests in the fourth phyle and monthly priest in the second phyle in the temple of Montu Lord of Thebes Teos son of Ipy.

This was not the only document written for Tsenhor in March 517 BCE. The approaching birth of her baby daughter Ruru—although some (me, for instance) believe that she had already been born—raised some serious questions about the future of the family, or rather the family property. In ancient Egypt keeping the family property together was just as important as it is in farming communities today. So the scribe Teos and his son Ip were asked to write four contracts.

Table 2. Four contracts on a single day?

Scribe [Contract]	Declaring Party (Party A)	Beneficiary (Party B)	About
Teos son of Ip [P. BM 10120A]	Psenese	His wife Tsenhor	Marital property arrangement
Teos son of Ip [P. BM 10120B]	Psenese	His baby daughter Ruru (and the children born before and after her)	Acknowledgment as heir
Ip son of Teos [P. Bibl. Nat. 216]	Tsenhor	Her eldest son Peteamunhotep from a previous marriage	Acknowledgment as heir
Ip son of Teos [P. Bibl. Nat. 217]	Tsenhor	Her baby daughter Ruru	Acknowledgment as heir

P. BM EA 10120A is not the only contract written on the papyrus measuring 24.5 x 89 cm, which is rather large. To its left we find P. BM EA 10120B, which the same scribe Teos drew up for what was presumably Psenese's first child by Tsenhor, a daughter called Ruru. She may have been named after Tsenhor's own mother, whose full name was Ituru (see, for example, P. Turin 2123), but was called Ruru in daily life. Since the early demotic scribes wrote from right to left, one takes it that Psenese and Tsenhor arranged their marital property first (P. BM EA 10120A) and then the separate contract about the inheritance that Ruru would receive from her father (P. BM EA 10120B). It is, however, difficult to see why the scribe did not simply include a clause about Ruru's right to her father's inheritance in the marital property arrangement itself. This was in fact standard practice in demotic contracts. Mostly this would be a clause like, "To the children you will bear me belongs everything that belongs to me and what I shall acquire," or something similar. Could it be because of Peteamunhotep, Tsenhor's son from a previous marriage, who would inherit from his mother but not from Psenese? We know Peteamunhotep was there on this day as well. Did Psenese want to make absolutely sure that it was Ruru who would inherit from him, and not Tsenhor's son from her first marriage?

Whether Teos wrote both contracts on the same day is a moot point. The handwriting in the contracts shows some differences, suggesting that they were written on two separate occasions (then again, since there was only the one scribe who had to write two contracts in succession, the contracts would always be written on separate occasions, including the inevitable loss of concentration when writing the second contract, resulting in sloppier writing, mistakes, and so forth). Also, one of the witnesses who signed the back of P. BM EA 10120A did not sign the back of P. BM EA 10120B.

This raises the interesting question whether Tsenhor and Psenese really ordered the scribe to cut off an extra large sheet of papyrus to leave room for P. BM EA 10120B—which could easily have been written on a separate sheet as well—so that they could come back after the baby was born. And lived. The same would apply to Tsenhor, because giving birth in ancient Egypt was a life-threatening event. So if she was still pregnant on this day in March 517 BCE, the timing of their visit to the temple—ordering a double-sized papyrus to have a single contract written and then go home—would be very strange.

Above, it was seen how Psenese stated to Tsenhor that she had given him three deben of silver on the occasion of their marriage, which may in reality have been a fictitious sum. In case of divorce she would receive these back. In most of these ancient Egyptian marital property arrangements—often misleadingly called marriage contracts—it is the man who does the talking, but there are some exceptions.

One famous example is P. Libbey (337 BCE), which was written in regnal year 1 of the mysterious King Khababash, who led a revolt against the Persians from Upper Egypt during the Second Persian Occupation. The occupation would ultimately be ended by Alexander the Great in 332 BCE. The legacy of Khababash was not forgotten by the Ptolemies. The Ptolemaic satrap Ptolemy Lagides, who was appointed by Alexander and later became King Ptolemy I, mentions him favorably in the so-called Satrap Stela, which commemorates the restoration of the rights enjoyed by the temple of Buto that had been abolished by the Persians. In P. Libbey, the declarant is a woman called Mrs. Setairetbint, or Thabis for short:

Regnal year 1, third month of the *akhet* season under Pharaoh l.p.h. Khababash. Has said Mrs. Setairetbint daughter of Petehorpakhrat, her mother being Tsenmin, to the *pastophoros* of Amenophis of the west of Thebes (choachyte) Teos son of Iufau, whose mother is Neshorpakhrat: "You have made me wife. You have given me 5 kite of silver making 2½ stater making 5 kite silver again, as my woman's gift. If I repudiate you as husband and if I hate you or love another man, I will give you 2½ kite silver making 1¼ stater making 2½ kite silver again out of this 5 kite silver makes 2½ stater makes 5 kite silver again, that you gave me as my woman's gift, and I will be far from you regarding the one-third of everything and every possession that I will acquire together with you.

"On your day of telling me that you will do, (namely): 'Cause that a copy of the above contract is laid down in another papyrus,' I will cause that it will be laid down. I will include every word above in said contract. I will cause that it is filled with sixteen witnesses and I will give it to you, whereas I will not be able to give you another term on account of it, without citing any legal contract or any word on earth with you."

Although not all the clauses in P. Libbey are fully understood, the message is clear enough. Mrs. Setairetbint was wearing the pants. Marriage in ancient Egypt appears to have been an informal business, and most marriages were probably the result of a simple oral agreement based on unwritten customary laws. People could decide to live together, which was called *hemes irem*, or 'to sit with.' The same expression is found in the Coptic sources from Djeme in the seventh and eighth centuries AD. A couple could also decide to *gereg per*, or 'establish a house,' although one takes it that the parents—or rather the fathers of the families involved— would have to give their permission and of course provide the financial means to start a family.

In the famous Will of Naunakhte (1154 BCE), the female testator explicitly states that she has provided each of her children with a household outfit (see "When Old Age Sets In" below), and this was presumably done the moment they left the house to start their own families. Even the autobiography of Wedjahorresne, seen above, contains a paragraph in which he claims that he helped his closest relatives to start their own household:

> I established the office of a priest for them (his brothers, and perhaps also his sisters) and I gave a fruitful field to them in accordance with the order of His Majesty (Cambyses) forever and ever. I made a beautiful coffin for the one who was without coffin, I fed all their children and I established all their houses.

In ancient Egyptian society, marriage seemed to focus on acquiring property (and keeping it within the family), as can be seen in the relevant documents. At present we have approximately 150 so-called marriage contracts, mostly written in demotic between 600 and 100 BCE. Most of these were made after the marriage itself in order to arrange the matrimonial property, including the designation of heirs.

Very little is known about the formal procedures involved, although the few abnormal hieratic contracts dealing with matrimonial property that are left all mention the son-in-law entering the house of his father-in-law "to make his daughter a wife, namely Mrs. N.N." (for example, P. Louvre E 7846). In fact, and not very surprisingly, this tradition was much older. The act of entering the house of the father-in-law as the prelude to marriage (or cohabitation) already occurs in the New Kingdom sources from Deir al-Medina, and also in the slightly later Adoption Papyrus (P. Ashmolean Museum 1945.96), which was written around 1090 BCE. The son-in-law then made a statement under oath that he would provide for his wife. Abnormal hieratic contracts stated that she would receive a 'gift of a female virgin' if he divorced her, on the condition that she had not slept with another man. In the case of P. Louvre E 7846 this gift comprised two deben of silver (about a hundred and eighty grams) and fifty sacks of emmer corn (four thousand liters). The wife would also receive any profit and accumulation the couple made during their marriage and part of the possessions her husband had inherited from his parents. These possessions are then further specified as "belonging to my children that she has borne me." This may well be the essence of many ancient Egyptian marital property arrangements: the guarantee that the wife would be provided for and that the children would be the heirs to their father's estate. Strangely enough, however, in the few abnormal hieratic marital property arrangements that are left there is no statement about the maintenance of the wife *during* the marriage, which would change with the introduction of demotic in the south of Egypt.

In short, 'marriage' did all kinds of things to a man's property, as it still does today. For instance, if the husband made a so-called contract of maintenance or annuity contract for his wife that guaranteed she and her children would be provided for during and for some time after the marriage, his entire property became security for this contract. This meant he was no longer able to sell his house without the consent of his wife. The annual allowance given by the husband to the wife was called *ak hebes*, or 'food and clothing.'

What also distinguishes the demotic marital property arrangements from their abnormal hieratic counterparts is the range of options from which couples could choose. Basically, they had two real choices. In the first type of contract the man gave his wife a sum of money called the *shep en sehemet*, or 'gift of a woman.' In the Ptolemaic period this sum almost never exceeded three deben (about two hundred and seventy grams) of silver, but then the wife often also received her food and clothing. It is, however, not always clear if she actually received this money right away or only in case of a divorce. This type of contract comes very close to the arrangements made in abnormal hieratic P. Louvre E 7846. In the second type of contract, it was actually the wife who gave a sum of money to her husband. This sum was called *hedj en ir hemet*, meaning 'money to become a wife,' or *sankh*, meaning 'maintenance, endowment, annuity.' When Tsenhor and her husband arranged their marital property in P. BM EA 10120A in 517 BCE, it was Tsenhor who paid money to her husband.

In the Ptolemaic period these written marital property arrangements between husband and wife could become highly intricate. In P. BM EA 10394 (226 BCE) a man called Melas from a mixed Greek–Egyptian marriage promises his wife Tsenbastet—also from a mixed marriage—many things, as any man would do. Following the obligatory dating formula and mention of the parties involved, Melas states:

> I have made you my wife. I have given to you one deben of silver, being five staters, being one deben of silver again, as your gift of a woman. If I repudiate you as a wife, because I hate you or because I desire another woman than you, I will give you two deben of silver, being ten staters, being two deben of silver again, apart from the one deben of silver aforementioned that I gave to you as your gift of a woman, in total three deben of silver, being fifteen staters, being three deben of silver again.

Apart from his promise to pay a fine if he decided to divorce his wife—one deben would buy a cow—Melas also agrees to provide for the eldest son, but the phrase he uses is ambiguous. Is he referring to their eldest son or to his wife's eldest son from a previous marriage? When Tsenhor and Psenese went to the temple of Montu to have their marital property arrangement drawn up in March 517 BCE, along with three contracts to arrange the inheritance of the children, Peteamunhotep, Tsenhor's son from her first marriage, did not receive any such contract from her second husband, because he was not of the same blood. One supposes that in the case of P. BM EA 10394, Melas is referring to his own first-born son: "Your eldest son is my eldest son, the owner of everything I own and will acquire. I will give you one-third of everything I own and will acquire."

The one-third mentioned in these contracts is generally the one-third of the conjugal property the wife would receive if the husband divorced her or if he died. But here, Melas first states that the eldest son will be the future owner of his estate, and continues by saying that when he dies one-third of his property—so apparently not just the conjugal property—will go to his wife Tsenbastet. Lawyers may have had a hard time sorting this one out. Melas then comes up with a detailed list of all the things his wife has brought into the house, including their value. Tsenbastet had brought a very valuable piece of cloth (one deben and six kite), a bronze cup (one and a half kite), a silver necklace (four kite), and two beds (three kite), along with other household goods representing a total value of five deben (about four hundred and fifty grams) of silver. Melas states that he has received these goods and that—although he is allowed to manage or even sell them—their ultimate fate lies with his wife, meaning that these items would become a hot issue in case of a divorce: "If I repudiate you as a wife or if you desire to leave yourself, I will give you your things of a woman aforementioned or their value in silver in accordance with what has been written above."

Melas also promises that he will not stoop so low as to take a temple oath stating that Tsenbastet never brought these goods into the house in the first place. The fact that such a clause was included—it is very rare— suggests that either Melas or Tsenbastet had previously gone through an eventful divorce. P. BM EA 10394 neatly summarizes what was really important to the ancient Egyptian couple: the property rights of both spouses needed to be secured, and this always included the future of the property. And the children. That is why these contracts always contain a clause about the future heirs. The contract made by Tsenhor and Psenese was an exception. They had separate contracts made about their inheritance right after the 'marriage.'

If the contract made by Melas for Tsenbastet appears to be rather generous toward his wife, even including the statement that he would not cause any trouble by taking an oath at the temple (or forcing his wife to do so), other people were less scrupulous. O. BM EA 31940, which was written in 117 or 100 BCE, records the temple oath that a Mrs. Tamin daughter of Kallias—Gelya in demotic—had to take at the dromos of the temple in Djeme. The oath was imposed on her by her husband Patem son of Amunhotep, neatly illustrating what could happen if an ancient Egyptian marriage fell apart. Tamin swears:

> As Amun of the Holy Eight lives, who resides here, and equally all gods who reside here with him. From the moment of sitting (in the) house that I have done with you until today, I have not stolen from you, I have not robbed you, I have not done anything against you in stealth for more than twenty deben.
>
> I have not slept with a man when I was with you.
>
> There is nothing belonging to you in my hand, except for the (household) goods that I had brought to you.

If Mrs. Tamin was prepared to take this oath, her husband, or rather her former husband, would have to leave her alone and take no further legal steps. What happened here? For one thing, the marriage of Patem and his wife had most probably gone wrong and the couple had divorced. As we saw above in P. BM EA 10394, in a normal divorce the wife would receive some money from her husband, the household goods that she had brought into the house or their equivalent in money, and one-third of the property the couple had acquired during their marriage. The fact that Tamin had apparently taken some things with her—the oath seems to imply that she had taken goods valued at over twenty deben—suggests that she was now living somewhere else. But the divorce still required a financial wrap-up, and that was precisely what her husband had been waiting for. He first accused her of having taken more goods than their twenty deben's (1.8 kilos) worth and then said that she had slept around. This was a very clever move because, if his former wife did not disprove the accusation, he would not have to pay her any money or give her one-third of the communal property. It all looks very modern: people fall out of love and then start making each other's lives miserable the only way they can think of, by denying them access to the children or by making a financial claim, just as Patem did about 2,100 years ago. Adultery was legitimate grounds for divorce, as it is today, even though it is only explicitly mentioned in the abnormal hieratic marital property arrangements that went out of use in Thebes around 535 BCE. On closer inspection we see that it was only adultery by the woman that is referred to in these contracts. In the demotic contracts adultery by the wife is no longer mentioned as grounds for divorce. Adultery by men was, however, not approved of, if we are to believe the famous maxims of Ankhsheshonqy (P. BM EA 10508) from the Ptolemaic period, although the original may have been much older:

Col. 8, x + 12:
Do not start a relationship with a woman whose husband is still alive, so that he will not become your enemy.

Col. 21, x + 18–19:
Do not sleep with a woman who has a husband. He who sleeps in a bed with a married woman, his wife will be slept with on the floor.

Col. 23, x + 6–7:
Do not love a woman who has a husband. He who loves a woman who has a husband will be killed on the threshold.

Sadly, these timeless pieces of advice only refer to sleeping with married women, not women in general. Sleeping with a household slave, for instance, would that be tolerated? Probably not by Tsenhor. Also, in Ankhsheshonqy no ethics seem to be involved. These maxims sound like a warning about what may happen if a man sleeps with another man's wife: the betrayed husband will become an enemy or even kill you, or someone else will sleep with your own wife.

For women it was different. Even though they were the equals of men in many respects, adultery by women was evidently seen as a great offense. The abnormal hieratic contracts refer to it as "the great crime that is found in a woman," almost implying that the desire to commit adultery is a natural female disposition that cannot be helped. Interestingly, this ambiguous attitude toward women—probably also the result of the ongoing effort by men to dominate the other sex only to find that this is impossible—is echoed in the Coptic evidence from Djeme in AD 600–800, although how much misogyny actually comes from the ancient Egyptian sources (like Ankhsheshonqy, quoted above) and how much from the Coptic Christian tradition is difficult to say. The Djeme site has produced thousands of mostly Coptic texts that allow a comparison to be made with two other large hoards from Egypt—but only to a limited extent—namely the New Kingdom sources from Deir al-Medina and the demotic (and Greek) sources from later periods. The Coptic evidence includes accounts, lists, letters, receipts, contracts, wills, records of sales, and so forth, apart from literary and religious writings. As we would expect in a region that was literally spotted with monasteries, a considerable share of the written sources comes from monks, who were not the first in line to be well disposed toward women.

One of these monks, called Pisentius, became the bishop of nearby Coptos in AD 599, but when the Persians invaded Egypt in 616 he went to live as a hermit in the tombs in the ancient Theban necropolis near Djeme, where he was kept alive by his followers. Pisentius only returned to Coptos in 632, the year in which he died. His fame spread as far as Ethiopia. In fact, the Ethiopic *Synaxarium* contains a section on the miracles ascribed to this saint. He also wrote a literary treatise, which seems to be a sermon that was regularly delivered by him. Its title leaves little to the imagination: *The Discourse that Apa Pisentius of the Monastery of Tsenti Preached Concerning the Holy Apa Onnophrios, to the Glory of God.* The sermon instructed audiences on how to live a virtuous life, just like the holy Apa Onnophrios had done. In Pisentius' view, this specifically included the women of Djeme. Apparently their behavior left much to be desired. The translation below—and the description of the life of Pisentius above—was taken from Terry Wilfong, *Women of Jeme* (2002):

> Now also to you I write and beseech and to you I command emphatically and in a great instruction in order that no woman at all go outside the door of her house with her head uncovered, nor that she lift her eyes up to the face of any strange man at all. Rather, may you go about on any occasion, O women, with your eyes turned down to the ground, your covering on all sides (of your body) in all propriety. But also, as for your adornment of yourselves, may it become a true measure and a respectability, while you give your hearts at all times to the word of God obediently and you thirst for him at all times. Also, teach your little sons to conduct themselves well and your daughters to love their homes and their husbands. For indeed, the teaching of our fathers is the shepherd of the children into propriety.

The fact that Pisentius had to preach to women to cover their heads and not look at strange men when they went out probably means that the women of Djeme generally did not bother to cover their heads and were wont to notice any fine male specimen wandering around in Djeme, so the question is whether any of them would have paid heed to admonitions by—as so often—a man in a skirt. Also noteworthy is the fine distinction made by Pisentius when it comes to bringing up the children. The girls only needed to be happy in their homes and love their husbands.

That sexual relations in Djeme were loose from time to time becomes clear from the next part of his sermon. What sets this apart from the demotic admonitions by Ankhsheshonqy is that Pisentius makes no distinction between men and women (see *Women of Jeme*):

> Who is it who has hindered you from taking a wife, O man, so that you stop fornicating? Or who is it who has hindered you, O woman, from taking a husband according to the law, so that you do not find an excuse for fornication? If it is not possible for you to exercise self-control, here is pure marriage established for men: take a wife for yourself according to the law, and woman, take a husband for yourself, lest sin take you. Only do not fornicate: for you are wretched,

and you will not be able to bear the punishment. O you who defile your bodies through fornication, whether men or women!

This part of the sermon looks so modern that it could have been delivered today in any house of God around the world. In Pisentius' view there was salvation for those who married according to the law. And then fornication suddenly became sex between a husband and his wife, which was allowed.

Maybe Pisentius—like so many religious men—simply had a problem with women as a source of lust and temptation. In his biography he is seen performing some incredible miracles. In the Sahidic—one of the Coptic dialects—version there is a story about him healing a woman who was suffering from heavy bleeding during her period; fortunately she was allowed to touch his skirt and was promptly healed. In the Bohairic version, however, we see poor Pisentius running away from a number of sick women, covering his head to avoid visual contact. Fortunately someone then had the splendid idea to eat some of the dust from the spot where his right foot had made an imprint, and the women were healed at once.

But now it is time to return to Tsenhor in March 517 BCE. As we saw earlier, the contract made by Psenese for his wife (P. BM EA 10120A) was much simpler than some of the later examples cited above, only referring to the money he had received from his wife. This would be returned if the couple divorced, together with the usual share of the communal property:

> You have given to me three (deben) of silver of the Treasury of Ptah, being two deben of silver and 9 2/3 1/6 1/10 1/20 1/60 kite from the Treasury of Ptah, being three (deben) in silver bars again. If I repudiate you as wife or if I hate you I will give you these three (deben) in silver bars from the Treasury of Ptah mentioned above that you have given me, as well as one-third of all that I will acquire together with you. I will give them to you.

Contrary to most marital property arrangements, this contract does not contain any statement about the money for food and clothing that Tsenhor would receive or anything about future heirs. Yet the inheritance that both Tsenhor and her husband would leave was arranged on the same day in March 517 BCE as their 'marriage' (see "How Many Visits to the Temple of Montu?" below).

Even if nothing is said about any food or clothing that is to be provided by Psenese, it is difficult to see why Tsenhor would have stayed with him for so many years if he had not done so. But what happened if the husband died?

In fact, there is a contract now kept at the Rijksmuseum van Oudheden in Leiden, P. Leiden I 379, in which the inheritance of the father of the family is divided by the eldest son between himself, his younger brother, and his sister. Their mother is still alive. The eldest son receives five-twelfths, his younger brother receives one-third, and their sister receives one-fourth. This may seem unfair, but the eldest son had to perform the mortuary services for their father and look after their mother. As to the quarter received by the sister, she had probably already received a part of her inheritance as a dowry when she married. In the contract their mother publicly authorizes the division of her husband's inheritance—her statement is recorded in the contract—provided the eldest son will give her the food and clothing she is entitled to according to the contract of maintenance her late husband made for her.

So, whenever the girl next door surfaces in ancient Egyptian contracts, she seems very well aware of her rights and ready to act accordingly, a notable case being P. Libbey (337 BCE) discussed above. This contract contains a clause stating that if the couple divorces, the wife reserves the right to return only half of the gift of a woman received from her husband. In other words, she will only give him half of the money back *and* throw him out of the house, in that case forfeiting, however, her claim to the usual one-third of the conjugal property. There were obviously many proud and strong-willed women in ancient Egypt. One of them was living in the city of Asyut in the second century BCE.

A Woman with a Mind of Her Own

In ancient Egypt a marital property agreement between a man and a woman—a contract of maintenance—was a much coveted possession. It guaranteed the woman an income for the rest of her life. To see the impact of such a marital property agreement on family relations we can look at a famous record of a court session held on 22—some say 23—June 170 BCE in Saut, present-day Asyut, in the south of Egypt. This trial record is kept in the British Museum under the inventory number P. BM EA 10591. The papyrus measures 32 x 285 cm. The recto—ten columns of twenty-four to twenty-six lines each, except column X, which has nineteen lines—contains the proceedings of the court session. The verso contains copies of some of the documents that were relevant to the case. It all started with a woman called Khratyankh, who had such a marital property agreement made out for her by a priest called Tutu and derived specific rights from it. Khratyankh filed suit against her brother-in-law, the lector-priest Tufhapy (who was a half-brother of Tutu, from the second marriage of their father). Tufhapy came from a family that was well-to-do, owning real estate in Asyut, some buildings in the necropolis, two vegetable gardens, and about two and a half hectares of arable fields. The family also owned the right to the loaves baked daily for Wepwawet ('The Opener of the Ways'), the local jackal god from Asyut.

P. BM EA 10591 was found with Tufhapy's archive, along with twelve other papyri written in the years up to 169 BCE, although a title deed from 172 BCE (P. BM EA 10575) and the actual trial record refer to various contracts made for the *paterfamilias* Peteatum from 208 BCE onward. Together these papyri tell us exactly why Khratyankh took Tufhapy to court, although she was most probably also acting on behalf of Tufhapy's eldest half-brother Tutu. Tutu came from the first marriage of the lector-priest Peteatum with a Mrs. Tsenese, who received a written marital property agreement that is now lost. They also had a daughter, but she plays no part in the story that is about to unfold.

Tutu married a girl called Khratyankh—the claimant from P. BM EA 10591—and together they had a son called Petewepwawet. In 185 BCE Tutu had a marital property agreement drawn up for her, pledging his entire property as security for her upkeep. We may assume that this security actually consisted of the property owned by Peteatum in Asyut and the necropolis, of which Tutu stood to receive a major part. Khratyankh was now settled for life, or so she thought. But her luck was about to change.

We do not know what happened to her mother-in-law Tsenese, but she either died or Peteatum divorced her. He went to live with another woman called Tawa, probably in 184 BCE or so. To make matters worse, Tawa gave birth to another boy not much later than 183 BCE. He was called Tufhapy. This must have made Peteatum very happy, because on 30 November 181 BCE, he also had a marital property agreement made for Tawa (referred to in the trial record). Since he had made a similar document for his first wife Tsenese before, he could now only pledge one-third of his possessions as security for Tawa's upkeep. His eldest son Tutu—from his first marriage with Tsenese—signed this document to indicate that he agreed to the new arrangement. Why he did this we will never know, but it may have had something to do with the fact that Peteatum had this contract drawn up for his second wife on his deathbed. He could still reserve the right to divide his inheritance as he saw fit, and there was a second son in the family now besides Tutu. If Tutu did not sign, his father could have disinherited him.

In fact, on this same day Peteatum also divided his inheritance. Two-thirds went to Tutu and one-third to Tufhapy (mentioned in the trial record), who was still a very small boy. Tutu signed the contract made for Tufhapy to approve it, so that Tufhapy's future now seemed more secure. Probably on the same day Peteatum allotted one-eighth of a house to his daughter Tetimuthes, who was a full sister of Tufhapy. She was probably seven or eight by this time.

Years later, during the court hearing in 170 BCE (P. BM EA 10591), Tutu's wife Khratyankh would claim that Peteatum died before the contract made for Tufhapy was signed by the required sixteen witnesses. But somehow during the trial or the preceding hearings the contract apparently turned up in Tufhapy's papers, including the names of sixteen witnesses on the back of the papyrus, because we hear nothing of it later on. The protocol also tells us that Khratyankh filed three *shars*, or public protests, on behalf of her son Petewepwawet. It seems that her husband Tutu was keeping a low profile in this conflict.

Three public protests were required to maintain her claim—or deny someone else's—and pave the way for a court case. It so happens that P. Mattha (around 250 BCE) contains a lengthy passage about the proper way to file a public protest (P. Mattha col. II *l.* 12–25):

Here is the way to file a public protest that will be done regarding a house that is not pure (free from claims) for the man to whom it has been sold.

Regnal year so-and-so, month so-and-so. Mr. So-and-so filed a public protest against Mr. So-and-so, saying: "He has caused a contract to be made for Mr. So-and-so son of Mr. So-and-so regarding his house, which is in the town of So-and-so." And he will then describe its adjacent plots: south, north, east, and west. "This house, whose neighbors are described above, he (also) made a contract for me as a security. He owes me such-and-such money in year so-and-so, month so-and-so. Now he makes a contract regarding this house above, Mr.

So-and-so, even though he has nothing to do with the house mentioned above until he repays me in full my money about which he made a contract for me."

These public protests had to be filed in three consecutive years (P. Mattha col. II *l.* 17–18). This was probably done to keep people from making spurious claims against each other. So in theory this whole procedure could actually be wrapped up in three hundred and sixty-five days, plus two days, and still meet the requirements of the court:

> This is my public protest for each year. He will continue for three years filing an annual public protest regarding the property, three public protests being made about it (the property) according to what is written above. (. . .) This public protest may be made regarding anything that is being sold to prevent it from becoming pure (free from claims) for the person to whom it has been sold.

This public protest was made in the presence of the legal opponent and some witnesses (P. Mattha col. II *l.* 19–22):

> If a man files a public protest to the face he will do this in front of the witnesses who will write it for him, the man against whom a public file is made being present. (. . .) Every word that the man says will be recorded in the public protest, saying: "Mr. So-and-so son of Mr. So-and-so being present, he spoke such-and-such words," and if he does not speak they will write in the public protest: "Although Mr. So-and-so son of Mr. So-and-so is present, he remains silent and does not speak at all."

One can imagine that if Tufhapy was still a boy when these public protests were filed by his aunt Khratyankh, this procedure not only served to maintain or reinforce her claim but also probably did much to intimidate him, intended or not. Meanwhile the eldest brother, her husband Tutu, would be free to manage the physically undivided family estate and reserve the best produce for himself. It is unclear where Tufhapy's mother Tawa comes in, if she played a role at all.

On 17 May 173 BCE, Tufhapy wrote a petition—that is, he probably went to a scribe who wrote it for him—to Theomnestes, the Greek *strategos* of the Thebaid, who effectively ruled the south of Egypt. Theomnestes ordered the subordinate *strategos* of Asyut, another Greek called Timarchos, to investigate the matter. The result was that Tutu was ordered to draw up a division contract for his younger half-brother Tufhapy on 3 June 173 BCE, allotting to him one-third of their father's inheritance. Khratyankh explicitly consented to this agreement. The original petition was not found with Tufhapy's papers, but fortunately the trial record P. BM EA 10591 contains a copy.

The text on the recto also records Khratyankh's claim that some relatives of Tufhapy's mother—who were apparently working for the *strategos*—had her husband Tutu thrown in jail in an attempt to improve his skills of cooperation. According to Khratyankh, her consent to this division contract between her husband Tutu and Tufhapy (in 173 BCE) had only been given because they had used force on her. In court, Tufhapy flatly denied this accusation, saying that both he and Tutu belonged to the elders of the bread bakers of the temple of Wepwawet—in other words, they belonged to the same (religious) association—and for this reason alone he could never have forced Tutu to write a division contract. Also, the *strategos* had investigated the matter and relegated it to the authorities of Asyut. Tutu then realized that people would find out he was selling his younger brother short, and that may be why his wife Khratyankh came to play such a prominent role in later events. Tutu had every reason to stay well in the background. As soon as the *strategos* Theomnestes was gone from the scene, Khratyankh entered a petition of her own against Tufhapy with the new *strategos* Noumenios—another Greek—saying she wanted to take Tufhapy to court in Asyut. Meanwhile, the brothers would have to find a way to manage the estate together. This they did, but only for the time being.

As the trial record shows, the brothers worked their land together in 173–172 BCE. The next year they leased the land to a Greek cavalryman called Agylos, Tutu receiving two-thirds of the rent and Tufhapy one-third (P. BM EA 10595). The next year Tufhapy felt himself strong enough to lease his part of the land to another Greek cavalryman (P. BM EA 10597).

Tutu immediately wrote two petitions about this incident, as is shown by the trial record (P. BM EA 10591), but we do not know what came of them. That same year two official land surveyors measured Tufhapy's field, probably not by coincidence. They found that about one-quarter of a hectare belonging to his share of the inheritance had been withheld from him. So Tufhapy lost no time and filed another petition against

Tutu (P. BM EA 10598). It was probably then that the authorities decided enough was enough. With all parties having filed petitions against each other, it was clear that something needed to be done. The case would be placed before an Egyptian court of law on 22 June 170 BCE. Since all the documents pertaining to it were written in demotic, indigeneous law applied, not Ptolemaic Greek law. The judges were three priests of Wepwawet, seconded by a Greek called Andromachos. He acted as the *eisagogeus* ('who leads (people) in') and was probably the official representative of the Ptolemaic authorities, meaning that he kept tabs on things.

In the weeks before the trial, the statements, pleas, and accusations by both Khratyankh and Tufhapy had been collected, and these were now read aloud in front of the judges, Tufhapy, and Khratyankh. It may be worthwhile to note that once during the whole procedure when Khratyankh had been summoned by the authorities she did not appear, sending the message, "I am menstruating," which apparently was a valid excuse (see "The Days on Which Tsenhor Did Not Work" below). In any case, the *eisagogeus* started the trial by handing over the petition by Khratyankh from 173 BCE.

The main question was simple. Did Peteatum, the father of Tutu and Tufhapy, have the right to make a marital property agreement for his second wife Tawa, Tufhapy's mother, in 181 BCE, even though he had made one for his first wife Tsenese as well? In Khratyankh's view, her husband—Tufhapy's half-brother Tutu—had been robbed by the deal, even though he had consented to this second marital property agreement made by his father. Clearly Khratyankh had sought legal advice, because she cited a law from regnal year 21 of an unknown king:

If a man lives with a woman and he writes for her a contract of maintenance and they have a son and he divorces her and lives with another woman and he writes for her a contract of maintenance and then they have a son and the man mentioned above dies, it is to the children of the first wife, for whom he wrote a contract of maintenance first, that his property is given.

The record goes on to describe the events that had taken place in the previous years, and notes that both Khratyankh—at times represented by her lawyer (did she need a legal guardian in court?)—and Tufhapy stood by their statements. The judges then probably grilled both of them for the last time, and Tufhapy was asked to bring the marital property agreement made by Peteatum for his mother in 181 BCE, as well as the contract of division made for him on the same day. These were copied in the trial records. The judges would have been quick to note that Tufhapy's brother Tutu—Khratyankh's husband—had agreed to both deals. His signature is there. One takes it that at some point they retired to their office to go over the case. Maybe they even looked up what this law of regnal year 21 really said. They must have, because they referred to it in their final decision. Unfortunately for Khratyankh, they based their verdict on another section from the same law of regnal year 21:

> If a man writes a contract of maintenance for a woman and he gives some of his property to another man without the woman or her eldest son having assented to the contract involved, it is against the man to whom the property was given that the woman or her eldest son will (have to) bring suit. <The property> is not (legally) cleared for him. He is not put in possession thereof.

But Tutu *had* assented to the marital property agreement made by his father for his second wife, Tufhapy's mother. And then there was the other contract showing that Tufhapy was entitled to one-third of Peteatum's inheritance (referred to in the trial record and in P. BM EA 10599), with Tutu receiving two-thirds. The judges ordered Tutu and Khratyankh to hand Tufhapy's one-third share over to him. Khratyankh had to write a contract for Tufhapy stating that she would refrain from any claims going forward. We may assume that she actually did this, even though no contract to this effect was found with Tufhapy's papers. But the conflict did not end there.

The last document in the archive of Tufhapy is another petition written in 169 BCE (P. BM 10600), showing that Tutu had not learned anything from the trial that his wife had lost. One can only speculate about the role played by Khratyankh in this last incident, although it is clear that there was more than one side to a marital property agreement. For women it meant lifelong security. It also triggered greed:

> A petition for the village scribe of the west of the district of Asyut Mayhes from the lector-priest Tufhapy son of Peteatum:
> "I have suffered damage through the lector-priest Tutu son of Peteatum. There is a document he made for me in regnal year 8, first

month of the *shemu* season, day 2 of Pharaoh l.p.h. Ptolemy l.p.h., who lives forever, about some fields in the area of the southern highland of Asyut, his wife agreeing to said document from regnal year 8 until today. I was the one who worked said fields and paid their harvest tax to the granary of Pharaoh l.p.h.

"It happened in regnal year 12, fourth month of the *peret* season, day 11 that I went to said fields with my farmer to harvest them. Said man came to me and held me away from them. He did not let me harvest them and they are now left to the cows and the sheep, even though I am the one who worked them in the *peret* season.

"I beg you to cause that said man leaves my fields to me. If it happens that I (can) harvest them, I will pay their harvest tax to the granary of Pharaoh l.p.h. without lack or obstacle whatsoever. My petition is with you as a witness."

Written in regnal year 12, fourth month of the *peret* season, day 15.

The actual day date is a demotic reading problem. One would have expected Tufhapy to run straight to the scribal office after he was thrown off the land by Tutu.

Such was the power of the ancient Egyptian contract of maintenance. It could wreck entire families. But actually marriage and ancient Egyptian law produced even stranger results, as we can see from the famous Adoption Papyrus from the New Kingdom (1550–1070 BCE).

Why Not Simply Adopt Your Wife?

The Adoption Papyrus (P. Ashmolean Museum 1945.96) has fascinated everyone who has ever dealt with it, and in Egyptology this generally means that they feel they have to say something about it (including me). There is a reason for this. What happens in this papyrus, written in the reign of Ramesses XI (reigned 1107–1077 BCE), is totally unprecedented. The British Egyptologist Alan Gardiner, who acquired the papyrus—it came from the provincial town of Sepermeru in Middle Egypt—drily noted, "The language is barbarous, the composition execrable. Nonetheless the sense is clear and there is hardly a sentence that cannot be readily translated. The facts disclosed are amazing" (*Journal of Egyptian Archaeology* 26 (1941): 23).

Amazing, indeed. Because it shows that a husband who loved his barren wife could actually adopt her to make her his only heir and proceed—no doubt with the consent of his wife—to buy a slave girl to maintain the bloodline. This slave woman bore him three children, who were then set free by his official wife and adopted as her own children, along with her own younger brother who had married the eldest slave daughter.

Table 3. Family relations in the Adoption Papyrus

Stage 1: Nebnefer adopts his wife Naunefer (also known as Rennefer).

Stage 2: Nebnefer fathers three children with the slave woman Dinihutiry, two girls and one boy.

Stage 3: Naunefer adopts and frees the three slave children, and also adopts her own brother Pendiu (Padiu), who has married the eldest of the three.

The Adoption Papyrus starts with a statement by the official wife, Mrs. Naunefer—elsewhere in the papyrus called Rennefer—that she and her husband Nebnefer did not have any children so he adopted her as his daughter. This way, the inheritance would become hers and not be taken by Nebnefer's brothers and sisters. One of Nebnefer's sisters—a Mrs. Huirymu—was actually present when this deal was concluded, which probably means that she was his favorite sister and he had asked her to come by to represent the family.

Regnal year 1, third month of the *shemu* season under the Majesty of the King of Upper and Lower Egypt Ramesses Khaemwaset l.p.h. Meryamun, the God, Lord of Heliopolis l.p.h., given life forever and ever. This day (a) proclamation (was made) to this exalted deity, (viz.) Amun, who stands and appears, offering to Amun. "And Nebnefer, my husband, made a document for me, the singer of Seth Naunefer, making me for himself as a daughter. And he wrote for me all his property (?), because he had no son or daughter, except me. As for all profit that I acquired with her, I transfer it to Naunefer, my wife. And (if) my siblings stand up to claim from (?) her at my death on any given day in the future, and say: 'Give the share of my brother (text omitted).'"

In front of many, many witnesses:
The stablemaster Ruru
The stablemaster Kairsu

The stablemaster Beniry son of Duanefer
In front of the stablemaster Nebnefer son of Anerkaya
Before the Sherden Pakamen
Before the Sherden Satameniu (and) his wife Adjedaâ

See, I have handed (it) over to Rennefer, my wife, on this day in front of Huirymu, my sister.

Then, no doubt during the same session, the scribe started another legal contract, the first contract apparently serving as a preamble. The scene now shifts to regnal year 18 of Ramesses XI (1090 BCE). The text starts with the date and the parties involved, but the real question is whether Nebnefer was actually still alive by then. The impression given is that the first section of the second contract about the purchase of the slave girl and the three children partly comes from another contract of Nebnefer and Naunefer, and that it is actually the second preamble—the first establishing the right of Naunefer to dispose of her late husband's property, the second to establish that Nebnefer and Naunefer had bought the slave together—to what the Adoption Papyrus was all about: the adoption of the three slave children by Naunefer. From here on, the text sticks to "I" and "me" as the acting party, who can only have been the widow of Nebnefer, namely Naunefer. If she had died before him, the entire preamble would have been unnecessary because the property would still be with Nebnefer.

Also, the fact that "I" and "me" refer to the one who raised the three children to adulthood, receiving love and care from that person until the day of the contract, is something one would sooner associate with a woman talking than a man. The same can be seen in the statement by Mrs. Naunakhte in 1154 BCE, who was at the end of her life and, looking back, saw that some of her children had not been very good to her (see "When Old Age Sets In" below). A complicated case, indeed:

Regnal year 18, first month of the *akhet* season, day 10 under the Majesty of the King of Upper and Lower Egypt Menmaatra Setepenptah l.p.h., Son of Ra, Lord of Appearances, Ramesses Khaemwaset Meryamun, the God, Ruler of Heliopolis, given life forever and ever. On this day (it was) said by the stablemaster Nebnefer and his wife, the singer of Seth of Sepermeru Rennefer, namely: "We bought the female servant Dinihutiry and she has given birth to these three children, one male, two female, totaling three. And I took them and I fed them and let them reach maturity. I have come to this day with them, without them doing me any harm, (because) they did good things to me, whereas there is no son or daughter, but them."

The contract then moves on to the next issue, namely that one of the children by the slave girl Dinihutiry had evidently caught the eye—how much better do you want this story to get?—of Naunefer's younger brother, who is called both Pendiu and Padiu in the contract. Naunefer, now the *materfamilias*, set the girl free as a proper wedding gift.

And while she was at it, she also freed the two other children. They would live with the newlywed couple. To top things off, she adopted her younger brother Pendiu as her own son, stating that she also adopted the three slave children—who had just been freed—as her own. Apart from genuine love, the only reason for this seems to have been the family estate. But what is left unsaid is that this was actually a trade-off. The children and her younger brother would have to take care of Naunefer until she died. But they had already received the reward:

"The stablemaster Pendiu entered my house and he made Taamunniut, their eldest sister, as (his) wife, because he belongs to me, being my little brother. I received him for her and he is with her today. But see, I have made her a freewoman of the land of Pharaoh l.p.h., and if she gives birth to either a son or a daughter they will be free people of the land of Pharaoh l.p.h. in the very same manner, being with the stablemaster Pendiu, my little brother. The children shall be with their eldest sister in the house of Padiu, the stablemaster, my own little brother. Today I make him for me as a son, just like them."

She said: "As Amun endures, as the Ruler l.p.h. endures, I make these people that I put on record as free people of the land of Pharaoh l.p.h. and if (any) son, daughter, brother, or sister of their mother or their father raises an issue about them, except Pendiu, my own son, because they are not with him as slaves at all, they are with him as siblings and children, they being as free people of the land, a donkey will fornicate with him, a donkey will fornicate with his wife, whoever will say 'slave' about any one of them.

"If I have fields in the country or any property in the world, or if I have any assets, they will be divided among these four children,

Padiu being one of them. As for the things I have said, they are all entrusted to Padiu, this son of mine, who was good to me when I was a widow, because my husband had died."

Before many, many witnesses:
The stablemaster Setyemheb
The singer of Seth Tayuhery
The farmer Suawyamun
Before Taymutnefer
The singer of Anty Tanephthys.

Apart from the establishment of some of the most unheard-of family relations, there is still the question whether Nebnefer, the husband who presumably fathered the three siblings, had actually died when the contract about the manumission and subsequent adoption of the slave children was made in regnal year 18. He is, after all, listed as one of the declaring parties, making a statement about the purchase of the slave girl Dinihutiry, who would become the mother of—presumably—his children.

The American demotist Eugene Cruz-Uribe proposed that it was actually Nebnefer who made the next statement about the stablemaster Pendiu, who entered the house to marry the eldest of the slave children.[3] In other words, in that case Pendiu was Nebnefer's younger brother (and not his wife's), and he was then adopted by Nebnefer as his own son. Nebnefer had also declared that the bride, a slave girl (and presumably his own daughter), was no longer a slave, along with the couple's children. In Cruz-Uribe's interpretation, only then was an additional statement made by Nebnefer's wife, now called Rennefer instead of Naunefer, swearing that the two other slave children who were living with Pendiu were also no longer slaves, meanwhile calling the alleged brother of Nebnefer—Pendiu—her own son.

This new interpretation goes much further than the original publication by Gardiner, who believed that the first date referred to an earlier contract that was included in the real ('second') contract as a preamble that proved the rights of Mrs. Naunefer to draw up the 'second' contract (which in reality is the main contract), and that her husband Nebnefer had actually died before this 'second' contract was made.

In Gardiner's view, it was Naunefer who took on and raised the three slave children fathered by her husband as her own, marrying off the eldest slave girl to her—not her husband Nebnefer's—younger brother Padiu, then adopting him as her son and the slave children as her own children. This would also explain the inclusion of the contract that was written some seventeen years earlier, because this stated that her husband Nebnefer had adopted her as his daughter to secure her rights to his property. In other words, the childless couple used adoption as a very clever device to make sure their property would go to the people of their own choice. This meant the entire contract dated to regnal year 18 was Naunefer's doing, listing the earlier contract as proof of her rights.

One of the weak points in the theory that Nebnefer was still alive in year 18 is that it forced Cruz-Uribe to translate the text in verso *l.* 9–11 as follows: "As for these matters of which I have spoken in their entirety, they are passed on (handed over) to Padiu, this my son, that good might be done for me when I am a widow, when my husband is dead." There is a subtle difference with our rendering: "As for the things I have said, they are all entrusted to Padiu, this son of mine, who was good to me when I was a widow, because my husband had died."

If Nebnefer was deceased, this statement would make perfect sense, but what if he was still alive? In that case, just imagine what he must have felt when he listened to his wife Naunefer bluntly dividing the spoils.

Actually, the most devastating critique of the new hypothesis came from the Egyptian Egyptologist Schafik Allam, a leading expert in ancient Egyptian law and especially New Kingdom legal texts. He described Cruz-Uribe's translation as giving "rise to a whole series of unnecessary problems of a social and legal nature as well as to many a contradiction in the events narrated in the papyrus."[4] Indeed. But there is more.

It would be highly unusual in a contract to first introduce the two parties making a statement about the purchase of a slave woman, as is done here in the main contract from regnal year 18, after which the husband Nebnefer makes a statement about the marriage and subsequent adoption of his alleged younger brother Padiu, a.k.a. Pendiu, whose bride is one of the children of the slave woman bought by Nebnefer and his wife— and who was presumably impregnated by Nebnefer, because his wife was unable to have children—after which Nebnefer's own wife swears the official oath in which she anounces that all three slave children are to be set free and will henceforth be her children. On top of that, she also adopts Nebnefer's alleged younger brother as her own son. Yes, that complicated.

It would be far more logical to revert to the initial hypothesis proposed by Gardiner, meaning that—as one would expect—the person who makes the crucial declaration in a legal contract is the same as the one who swears the oath.

Finally, it is difficult to see why Nebnefer, who had adopted his own wife as his daughter to make sure that his property would go to her and *not* to his brothers and sisters—they are expressly forbidden to claim anything from his wife after his death—would adopt his alleged younger brother Padiu seventeen years later, creating all kinds of problems for his wife, whom he had adopted seventeen years earlier, in the process. If we stick to Gardiner's theory, things immediately clear up. This is a golden rule in hieratic and demotic papyrology: if your solution makes things more complicated, it is probably not the best solution. Nebnefer adopted his wife Naunefer and she in turn adopted her younger brother Padiu, who had married one of the slave girls presumably fathered by her husband Nebnefer. The freeing of the three slave children and their subsequent adoption meant that the property she had inherited from her husband would go to her adopted children and her younger brother Padiu, in return for a carefree old age.

Why then was Naunefer's deceased husband still listed as a declaring party at the beginning of the contract from year 18? The easiest solution is to assume that this is actually a summary of another contract showing that the couple had bought the slave who was to become the mother of Nebnefer's children. This would mean that the statement by Naunefer about freeing the slave children took place at a later date, or—and this somehow seems more likely—the contract itself was indeed made in year 18 and the statement about the purchase of the slave woman was slipped in between the dating and the main text spoken by Naunefer. This would not be entirely unexpected with the scribe of the Adoption Papyrus. Note, for instance, that in the summary of the contract made in year 1 of Ramesses XI (1107 BCE) the text jumps from the declaration by the wife Naunefer ("And he wrote for me all his property (?), because he had no son or daughter, except me") without any interruption to the declaration made by her husband in the original contract to that effect ("As for all profit that I acquired with her, I transfer it to Naunefer, my wife"). In other words, this scribe was prone to insert clauses from older contracts without any proper introduction.

It is time to return to Tsenhor. She had been fortunate. Although she was already in her thirties and a widow or a divorcee, she had found a new man, Psenese. And he was willing to settle the future of their children right from the start.

The Proud Father
29 February–29 March 517 BCE (P. BM EA 10120B)

Some time after Psenese and Tsenhor arranged their marital property through P. BM EA 10120A, the same scribe Teos son of Ip wrote P. BM EA 10120B on the same papyrus and to the left of the first contract. If we follow the order of events as proposed by Pieter Willem Pestman, this is what happened in March 517 BCE:

- Psenese has a marital property settlement made for his pregnant wife Tsenhor (P. BM EA 10120A).
- Tsenhor gives birth to their daughter Ruru.
- Psenese appoints his daughter Ruru as his rightful heir on the same papyrus that contains his marital property settlement with Tsenhor (P. BM EA 10120B).
- The scribe who wrote P. BM EA 10120A and 10120B is succeeded by his son Ip, who then writes P. Bibl. Nat. 216 and 217 in the same month.
- Tsenhor appoints her eldest son Peteamunhotep from her previous marriage as her rightful heir (P. Bibl. Nat. 216).
- Tsenhor appoints her baby daughter Ruru as her rightful heir (P. Bibl. Nat. 217).

If we understand correctly the content of P. BM EA 10120B, in which Psenese acknowledges the right of his newborn daughter Ruru to his inheritance, Psenese already had children and clearly expected to have some more. As far as we know, there are no other documented cases in demotic where someone marries a pregnant widow shortly before she is about to give birth and then, almost immediately after the baby is born, makes a second trip to the same scribe in the same notary office to acknowledge his child's rights to part of his inheritance. This was, after all, only a girl, in an era in which child mortality was rife. One is therefore tempted to look for a different explanation for why events unfolded as they did. Why would Psenese rush to the temple to have the rights of his baby daughter set down in a contract so shortly after she was born? Was it because Tsenhor was an exceptional woman used to seeing things go her way? The documents from her archive do show that she put the interests of her children before anything else. So here they were, Psenese, his daughter Ruru, Tsenhor, and perhaps also some of the other children from previous marriages:

Regnal year 5, third month of the *akhet* season under Pharaoh l.p.h. Darius l.p.h. The choachyte of the valley Psenese son of Heryrem, whose mother is Beniuutehtyes, has said to Ruru daughter of the choachyte of the valley Psenese son of Heryrem, whose mother is Tsenhor, his daughter:

"You are the sharing partner of my children who have been born and who will be born to me in everything that belongs to me and that I will acquire, namely houses, field, slaves, silver, copper, clothing, *it* grain, emmer, ox, donkey, or any other animal, any contract, and any other thing on earth. To you belongs one share of it in accordance with the number of my children who will be born, forever—as well as of my commissionings as a choachyte and *pastophoros* on the mountain (the Theban necropolis). To you belongs one share of it."

In the writing of the god's father of Montu Lord of Thebes, chief of priests of the temple of Montu Lord of Thebes in the fourth phyle and monthly priest in the second phyle Teos son of Ip.

The question is whether Tsenhor's own father Nesmin was already thinking about the future of his daughter—she would only be born a few years later—when he received eleven *aruras* of farm land as payment for his services as a choachyte in 556 BCE (P. Louvre E 10935). P. BM EA 10120B tells us this may well have been the case. Here a baby daughter—perhaps not coincidentally Nesmin's granddaughter—or a toddler between one and five years of age receives an equal share of her father's inheritance, including his tasks as a choachyte (and *pastophoros*) in the Theban necropolis and the income connected with this work. A *pastophoros* was originally a carrier of the holy shrine during religious processions (although some people think they were also the doorkeepers at the temple). From the demotic contracts written in Thebes in the Ptolemaic period we know that the people who were called shrine-bearers of Amunemope were actually choachytes. Now not only did Ruru—this little ancient Egyptian girl—receive an equal share according to the number of children Psenese would have, but the contract proving these rights was also written on the same sheet of papyrus that contained the marital property arrangement made for her mother. This was highly unusual, if not to say unique, so we must assume that Psenese and Tsenhor had a special reason to do this, something that has been speculated upon already above. And if it was not because of her half-brother Peteamunhotep who would not inherit from his stepfather

Psenese, the reason could have been that there were other children—something alluded to by Psenese in P. BM EA 10120B—and that Psenese had to prove beyond doubt that Ruru was born from his marriage to Tsenhor. But why? Did Psenese sense that Ruru needed special protection regarding her material future? To understand what could happen between children from first and second marriages, we only have to look at the notorious lawsuit between Tufhapy and his sister-in-law Khratyankh (see "A Woman with a Mind of Her Own" above). So maybe Tsenhor and Psenese decided to make absolutely sure that little Ruru would be all right.

How Many Visits to the Temple of Montu?

We can be sure that the contracts Ip son of Teos wrote on behalf of Tsenhor for her son and daughter (P. Bibl. Nat. 216 and 217) were written during a single session. The witnesses signed both texts on the back in the same order (see table 4). But the 'marriage contract' between Psenese and Tsenhor (P. BM EA 10120A) and the acknowledgment by Psenese of his baby daughter Ruru's rights to his inheritance (P. BM EA 10120B) were written by another scribe, Teos son of Ip, who was the father of the scribe Ip son of Teos. Also, there is something wrong with the order in which the witnesses signed the contracts written by Teos, suggesting the latter two texts were written on different days.

Table 4 lists the witnesses in the order in which they signed P. BM EA 10120A and P. BM EA 10120B, as well as P. Bibl. Nat. 216 and 217.

Teos son of Ip and his son Ip came from a Theban family of scribes all working as priests and professional scribes in the temple of Montu between 590 and 497 BCE. Montirtais son of Ip and Ip son of Montirtais are known from two abnormal hieratic marital property agreements from 590 BCE (P. Louvre E 7849) and 549 BCE (P. Louvre E 7846), respectively. In view of the handwriting in both texts—their handwriting is strikingly similar—it seems safe to say that Ip was trained in the office by his own father. Both texts were deposited in the archive of Djekhy & Son, whose archive directly precedes the Tsenhor papers.

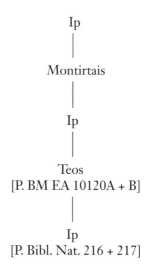

Ip
|
Montirtais
|
Ip
|
Teos
[P. BM EA 10120A + B]
|
Ip
[P. Bibl. Nat. 216 + 217]

Table 4. The witnesses to Tsenhor's contracts

P. BM EA 10120A	P. BM EA 10120B	P. Bibl. Nat. 216	P. Bibl. Nat. 217
Horwedja son of Bakrenef	Horwedja son of Bakrenef	Wennefer son of Wesirten	Wennefer son of Wesirten
Petenefer-hotep son of Ankhsematawy	Nanefer-ibra son of Naneferpsamtik	Petehorsema-tawy son of Petehorpakhrat	Petehorsema-tawy son of Petehorpakhrat
Nanefer-ibra son of Naneferpsamtik	Petenefer-hotep son of Ankhsematawy	Inaros son of Horsiese	Inaros son of Horsiese
Ankhhor son of Nesqayshuty	Horwedja son of Neshorpakhrat	Horwedja son of Neshor the overseer of the necropolis	Horwedja son of Neshor the overseer of the necropolis
Petesenty son of Neskhonsu	Ankhhor son of Nesqayshuty	Wennefer son of Horwedja	Wennefer son of Horwedja
Wennefer son of Petebastet	Wennefer son of Petebastet	Peteamun-nesutawy son of Iahmen	Peteamun-nesutawy son of Iahmen
Nesmin son of Petehorsema-tawy	Nesmin son of Petehorsema-tawy	Horwennefer son of Paqerer	Horwennefer son of Paqerer
Horwedja son of Neshorpakhrat	Nesdjehuty son of Nesby	Khonsuirtais son of Iturech	Khonsuirtais son of Iturech
Nesdjehuty son of Nesby			

During the reign of Amasis, abnormal hieratic was finally phased out in Thebes as a notary script and replaced by early demotic from Lower Egypt, the place of origin of the Saite kings. Under Psamtik I the Saites extended their hold over the whole of Egypt. This started a period that is sometimes referred to as the Saite Restoration, which included a thorough reorganization of the administration. The advantage of early demotic over Theban abnormal hieratic was that it came with a more or less standardized formulary that was far more abstract than the legal formulary used in Thebes until then. Gradually, some of the Theban scribes started to adopt this new demotic formulary, sometimes developing their own hybrid script that was no longer purely abnormal hieratic but also not early demotic.

The first scribe from the family who wrote early demotic is the same Teos son of Ip we met above. The first early demotic document written by him is P. Louvre E 7837 from 535 BCE, which also comes from the archive of Djekhy & Son. It was written for a cattle-keeper of the Domain of Montu called Petemontu, a well-known business partner of Iturech, the son in Djekhy & Son. One of the witnesses who signed P. Louvre E 7837 was the scribe's son Ip. So already in 535 BCE Teos son of Ip and his son Ip shared an office, where Ip was taught the tricks of the trade.

Teos son of Ip vanished from the stage after he wrote P. BM EA 10120A and P. BM EA 10120B for Psenese, Tsenhor, and their baby daughter Ruru in 517 BCE. His job was taken over by his son Ip. Ip was to become well acquainted with Tsenhor. Between 517 and 497 BCE he wrote no fewer than eight contracts for members of the family.[5]

So how many visits to the temple of Montu did Tsenhor and Psenese make in March 517 BCE? The first appears to be when they had P. BM EA 10120A written to arrange their marital property. Tsenhor was heavily pregnant, but—according to the dominant theory—the couple nonetheless went home carrying a contract on a papyrus that left enough room for another contract to be written directly beside it (which was unprecedented).

When Ruru was born the couple returned to the temple—again following the dominant theory—bringing the papyrus containing P. BM EA 10120A. On it, the same scribe wrote P. BM EA 10120B, in which Psenese acknowledges his daughter's rights to part of his inheritance. It is assumed that Ruru had only just been born (so why not wait until after Ruru was born and do it all at once? Or, why not stick to normal scribal practice and include the childrens' rights to the inheritance in the marital property arrangement itself?).

The third visit would have been by Tsenhor, Psenese, Peteamunhotep—Tsenhor's eldest son from a previous marriage—and the baby girl Ruru. The scribe Teos who wrote the first two documents was suddenly replaced by his son Ip (all according to the dominant theory), who wrote P. Bibl. Nat. 216 and 217 to settle the rights of Peteamunhotep and Ruru to Tsenhor's own inheritance.

So you're a woman of thirty-something in ancient Egypt—which was old—who is about to give birth and your husband drags you to the temple three times in a row in a single month to settle family matters? Somehow this does not make very much sense. Also, it is difficult to believe that Psenese and Tsenhor would rush to the temple the minute Ruru was born to have her rights laid down in writing. The ancient Egyptians were perfectly aware that many of their children would die well before their time (as would their mothers when giving birth). Why not wait until Ruru made it through her first year?

If the current theory seems to have its flaws, is there a better one? Actually, there may be. Suppose that Ruru had already reached the age of one or two in March 517 BCE. Tsenhor and Psenese had been together for some time, forming a family with Peteamunhotep—now about ten—and perhaps even some of Psenese's own children. The property rights of children, in other words their future, were a tricky issue. Children stood to inherit from both their father and their mother, but generally only if these were their own blood. Since Psenese and Tsenhor both had children from previous marriages, these would be their natural heirs, especially if they had a document to prove their rights. So something needed to be done to ensure the rights of Peteamunhotep and Ruru. It is easy to believe that the genius behind all this was probably Tsenhor, because these were her children. And while they were at it, why not marry as well?

In theory, therefore, Psenese and Tsenhor could easily have settled their family affairs on a single day in March 517 BCE. First, they had the marital property settlement P. BM EA 10120A drawn up by Teos, in his office in the temple of Montu. When this was done and the nine witnesses had signed the contract on the back, Psenese and the scribe Teos devised a second document—P. BM EA 10120B—to arrange Ruru's rights to his inheritance. While they were doing this, Tsenhor and her son Peteamunhotep walked over to the scribe's son, Ip son of Teos. Ip had been working as a professional scribe in his father's office since at least 535 BCE. After eighteen years he would be an accomplished professional scribe himself, so he was allowed to write the other contracts required by Psenese and Tsenhor (the woman was relegated to the secondary scribe, as it were).

They started with Peteamunhotep's rights to Tsenhor's inheritance (P. Bibl. Nat. 216) and, when Psenese and his daughter Ruru were done with the scribe Teos (son of Ip), they joined Tsenhor, Peteamunhotep, and the scribe Ip (son of Teos) to draw up a similar document to settle Ruru's rights to Tsenhor's inheritance (P. Bibl. Nat. 217). Both documents written by Ip were signed by the same witnesses, in the same order. The overseer of the necropolis Horwedja son of Neshorpakhrat—Neshor for short—countersigned all four documents.

This still leaves us with the witnesses in the contracts written by Teos son of Ip, P. BM EA 10120A and 10120B (see table 4). Much has been made of the fact that the witnesses did not sign these contracts in the same order, suggesting that the contracts were written with some time in between, namely the time that elapsed between the marital property arrangement P. BM EA 10120A and the arrangements made concerning Ruru's rights to her father's inheritance (P. BM EA 10120B).

There is also the question of why Psenese and Tsenhor had P. BM EA 10120A written on the right half of a papyrus and the remaining space reserved for P. BM EA 10120B. It would have been just as easy to have this contract written on a separate papyrus. The only reason for these two contracts being written on the same papyrus would have been to secure the rights of Ruru, their daughter. Egyptian women often entrusted their written marital property arrangements to third parties for safekeeping. Now, P. BM EA 10120A + B were acquired by the British Museum at the auction of the Anastasi collection in 1857 (see "The Collection of Bernardino Drovetti" below). Probably at the same auction, the Louvre bought P. Louvre E 3231A, proving Ruru's right to a piece of farm land that had been paid to her in return for her services as a choachyte. In other words, the papyri sold in 1857 were all proof of Ruru's rights, so the conclusion seems inescapable that they once formed part of her own archive or had been given by her to a trustee for safekeeping.

But how about these different lists of witnesses on the two papyri from the British Museum? If we look more closely, we see that apart from a Mr. Petesenty son of Neskhonsu, who signed the first contract as a witness, the witnesses to both contracts are the same, albeit listed in a different order. But there was probably no law saying that people had to sign contracts in the same order, so maybe Petesenty was sent on an errand after the scribe had written P. BM EA 10120A and hadn't returned by the time P. BM EA 10120B was finished. Or maybe the first contract was written and signed before lunch and the second after. All that remains to be proved then is whether there is a similar case in which two legal documents were undoubtedly written on a single day, with the witnesses signing both documents in a different order. In fact, there is the case of abnormal hieratic P. BM EA 10906 and 10907, at one time also known as P. Michaelides 2 and 1, respectively.

The Order of the Witness List

P. BM EA 10906 and 10907 deal with the transfer of a debt from one creditor to another. This case takes us back to Thebes, around 700 BCE. The texts were written by the same scribe. In P. BM EA 10907, the goatherd Paiuiuhor son of Nesamun states to his colleague Ityaâ son of Pawenesh that he owes him one deben and three kite of silver (slightly over 118 grams). This sum was paid by Ityaâ to yet another goatherd called Tjaynahebu son of Bay. The contract states that if Paiuiuhor tries to renege on this deal he will have to pay Ityaâ double the amount, or two deben and six kite of silver. P. BM EA 10906 is the receipt for the one deben and three kite paid by Ityaâ to Tjaynahebu, who states that he has received the silver from Ityaâ and that he no longer has a claim on Paiuiuhor, because Ityaâ has effectively become the new creditor. Why this deal was concluded is unknown, although one assumes that Paiuiuhor's actual creditor was a woman, who is simply referred to as "she" in P. BM EA 10907 *l.* 7. In that case we may be dealing with the financial wrap-up of a marriage gone wrong. The text runs:

> Regnal year 7, second month of the *peret* season. The goatherd Paiuiuhor son of Nesamun has said to the goatherd Ityaâ son of Pawenesh: "I have come to (the place) where you <are>," while they say (?): "As for the one deben and three kite of silver from the Treasury of Harsaphes to reimburse the goatherd Tjaynahebu son of Bay, which she has with me, I am with you under it. If <I> will leave you, because I prefer another man to you, I will give you the one deben and three kite of silver which are doubled, which are two deben and six kite. If <I> will find it (?) on a document in (?) your house, I will give them to you, it being . . . ." He said: "As Amun lives, as Pharaoh lives, I will not be able to withdraw the document."

After being signed by the scribe, the document was countersigned by one special witness called Hor son of Besmut on the recto of the papyrus, followed by eight witnesses on the verso. The scribe then wrote P. BM EA 10906, although this order of events is far from certain. It could also have been done the other way around, which in fact seems more probable.

> Regnal year 7, second month of the *peret* season. The goatherd Tjaynahebu son of Bay has said to the goatherd Ityaâ: "I have received from you the one deben and three kite of silver of the Treasury <of

Harsaphes>, which I have with Paiuiu<hor> son of Nesamun, the man from Gaza. I have received it from you today. For me there is no issue at all to discuss (any longer) with Paiuiuhor and his mother and all of his brothers, and there is also no (longer any) issue to discuss with you. You (?) will (now have to) discuss (the issue) with Paiuiuhor."

This time the name of the scribe on the recto, directly below the contract, is followed by the names of three witnesses. On the verso there are the names of five witnesses. Below this the scribe wrote, "Total: eight men who signed thus." The text on the verso ends with the signature of the special witness who signed directly below the name of the scribe on the recto of P. BM EA 10907 (see table 5).

Table 5. The witnesses in P. BM EA 10906 and 10907

P. BM EA 10907	Witness	Witness	P. BM EA 10906
Recto *l.* 15–16	Hor son of Besmut	Hormes son of Amunnakhte	Recto *l.* 16
Verso *l.* 1	Hormes son of Amunnakhte	Petewen son of Pakysis	Recto *l.* 17
Verso *l.* 2	Petewen son of Pakysis	Tipaâ son of Psengay	Recto *l.* 18
Verso *l.* 3	Payfibnakhte son of Pagoug	Pawerem son of Petous	Verso *l.* 1
Verso *l.* 4	Tipaâ son of Psengay	Payureba son of Pawerem	Verso *l.* 2
Verso *l.* 5	Pawerem son of Petous	Peteamun son of Ryry	Verso *l.* 3
Verso *l.* 6	Payureba son of Pawerem	Payfibnakhte son of Pagoug	Verso *l.* 4–5
Verso *l.* 7	Inaros son of Pakhar	Inaros son of Pakhar	Verso *l.* 6
Verso *l.* 8	Peteamun son of Ryry	Hor son of Besmut	Verso *l.* 8

The writing, the layout, and the arrangement itself suggest that the two papyri were written in a single session, although we do not know for certain which of the two documents was written first, the receipt for the money (P. BM EA 10906) or the IOU (P. BM EA 10907). What we do see is that there was apparently no golden rule that such documents had to be signed by the same witnesses *in the same order*. This is exactly what we had to prove for the case of P. BM EA 10120A and B, the documents that settled the marital property of Tsenhor and Psenese and the future rights of their daughter Ruru. So in the end it seems that Tsenhor and her husband may have had four documents drawn up on the same day in March 517 BCE after all (see "How Many Visits to the Temple of Montu?" above). The evidence is not against the theory.

A Very Fortunate Baby Daughter
29 February–29 March 517 BCE (P. Bibl. Nat. 216 and P. Bibl. Nat. 217)

Nobody knows when P. Bibliothèque Nationale 216 and 217 were acquired, or from whom, but the earliest work on these texts—which clearly belong together—was done by the famous German Egyptologist Heinrich Brugsch Bey, who published a facsimile of P. Bibl. Nat. 216 in his *Grammaire démotique* (Berlin: Dümmler, 1855). As is often the case in Egyptology the texts were republished independently in modern times by two scholars in 1979 and 1981, raising the interesting question of which of these authors actually had the publication rights, as well as illustrating that in the 1980s demotic studies still suffered from a severe backlog of reliable editions of the available demotic documentary material. The task ahead of us—keeping up with the material found every day and waiting in museum storerooms—is even more daunting.

As we saw above, the birth of their baby daughter Ruru prompted Tsenhor and Psenese to settle all their family matters together in March 517 BCE. Tsenhor wanted to provide for the future of both her children by putting on record that they would inherit equal shares from her. Taking into consideration that this decision was made by an Egyptian woman some 2,500 years ago, it was quite a revolutionary step. We may be reading more into it than was ever there, but even the dimensions of P. Bibl. Nat. 216 and 217—22.7 x 76.5 cm and 22.8 x 77.7 cm, respectively—show that ten-year-old Peteamunhotep and his baby sister Ruru were treated equally all the way. There would be no "my papyrus is bigger than yours" in the future. So could it be that Tsenhor—now thirty-three years old or so—had a number of miscarriages or saw some of her other children die before Ruru was born? One has to assume that she did.

Since P. Bibl. Nat 216 and 217 were most certainly written during a single session—the witnesses to the contracts signed in the same order on both—one takes it that on this day Psenese, Tsenhor, Peteamunhotep, and Ruru were all present in the office of the scribe Ip in the temple of Montu in Karnak. The inventory numbers suggest that these contracts were acquired by the Bibliothèque Nationale as a set, meaning that they were also found together. One would, however, have expected P. Bibl. Nat. 216 to have ended up in the archive of Peteamunhotep, and P. Bibl. Nat. 217 in the archive of his half-sister Ruru. This raises an interesting question regarding in whose archive these papyri were kept. Was it Tsenhor's? She would be the only person whose interests were to safeguard the rights of *both* Peteamunhotep and Ruru. In that case, does this mean that Peteamunhotep—of whom we learn nothing after Tsenhor appointed him as her heir in 517 BCE—died when he was very young? Otherwise P. Bibl. Nat. 216 should have ended up in his own archive, and it obviously did not.

It would have been very easy for Ip simply to copy P. Bibl. Nat. 216 and slip in the right names and feminine pronouns at the appropriate spots. But he was evidently not quite satisfied with the contract written for Peteamunhotep, which is suggested by the slight emendations that occur in P. Bibl. Nat. 217. Note that Ruru, who was a newborn baby or maybe a toddler, was already addressed as "the choachyte Mrs. Ruru." Apparently the ancient Egyptian legal mind considered Ruru to be a natural legal person even if she was too young to speak for herself.

Again we may be reading more into it than ever was there, but there is something about what happens when Tsenhor talks. Halfway through P. Bibl. Nat. 217—the record of a statement by Tsenhor—the scribe suddenly wrote "in the names of my mother and father," whereas the standard formula would always be "in the names of my father and mother," as seen elsewhere in P. Bibl. Nat. 216 and 217. Since ancient Egyptian contracts were a written record of a statement made in front of a professional scribe, one cannot help but wonder whether "in the names of my mother and father" is the verbatim record of what was actually said at that moment by Tsenhor, a woman who probably named both her daughter and son after her mother. It would make perfect sense, because on this day in March 517 BCE Tsenhor—holding little Ruru in her arms and thinking about her daughter's future—would also be thinking of her mum, and then having to make a statement. Of course, we have no way of knowing for sure.

Table 6. Parallel translation of the two promissory donations

P. Bibl. Nat. 216	P. Bibl. Nat. 217
Regnal year 5, third month of the *akhet* season under Pharaoh l.p.h. Darius l.p.h.	Regnal year 5, third month of the *akhet* season under Pharaoh l.p.h. Darius l.p.h.
The choachyte Mrs. Tsenhor daughter of the choachyte of the valley Nesmin, whose mother is Ruru, has said to the choachyte of the valley Peteamunhotep son of Inaros, whose mother is Tsenhor, her eldest son:	The choachyte Mrs. Tsenhor daughter of the choachyte of the valley Nesmin, whose mother is Ruru, has said to the choachyte Mrs. Ruru daughter of the choachyte of the valley Psenese, whose mother is Tsenhor, her daughter:
"To you belongs half of what I own in the field, the temple, and the city, namely houses, field, slaves, silver, copper, clothing, *it* grain, emmer, ox, donkey, tomb in the mountain, and anything else on earth.	"To you belongs half of what I own in the field, the temple, and the city, namely houses, field, slaves, silver, copper, clothing, *it* grain, emmer, ox, donkey, tomb in the mountain, and anything else on earth,
To you belongs half of everything on earth that belongs to the choachyte of the valley Nesmin son of Khausenwesir, my father, as well as half of everything on earth that belongs to Mrs. Ruru daughter of the choachyte of the valley Petemin, whose mother is Taydy, my mother.	as well as half of my share that comes to me in the name of the choachyte of the valley Nesmin son of Khausenwesir, my father, and (in the name of) Mrs. Ruru daughter of the choachyte of the valley Petemin, whose mother is Taydy, my mother.
To you belongs half of my share that comes to me in their name.	To you belongs half of my share that comes to me in the names of my mother and father mentioned above and in the names of their father and mother.
To you belongs half of what is rightfully mine, in my name and the names of my father and mother.	To you belongs (half of) what is rightfully mine, in their name.

To Ruru daughter of the choachyte of the vally Psenese, whose mother is Tsenhor, your younger sister, belongs the other half of the share that comes to me {in my name and} in the names of my father and mother mentioned above, again.

As for any child that I will bear in the future and who will live, his share will come from you two."

In the writing of Ip son of the god's father of Montu Lord of Thebes, chief of priests in the fourth phyle and monthly priest in the second phyle in the temple of Montu Lord of Thebes Teos son of Ip.

To the choachyte of the valley Peteamunhotep son of Inaros, whose mother is Tsenhor, your elder brother, belongs the other half.

As for any child that I will bear in the future and who will live, his share will come from you two."

In the writing of Ip son of the god's father of Montu Lord of Thebes, chief of priests in the fourth phyle and monthly priest in the second phyle in the temple of Montu Lord of Thebes Teos son of Ipy.

A 4,500-year-old Contract

One very profitable way of looking at ancient Egypt is simply to follow the money. Look at property relations. The ancient Egyptians were no different from us. They wanted their children to get a good start, just as we do today. What makes Tsenhor's papers so special is that they show that the leading women in the family—the Egyptian term was *nebet per*, or 'mistress of the house'—were treated equally to the men. Just like her three (half-)brothers, Tsenhor received an equal share of the inheritance of her father. Years later, her husband Psenese bequeathed half of his property to their daughter Ruru. Surprisingly, in Tsenhor's family there seems to have been no designated eldest son, with all the rights and duties that came with it, such as a larger share of the inheritance, although when it came to dividing the parental heritage it was her half-brother Nesamunhotep who took the lead.

Much of our knowledge of ancient Egyptian law comes from Late Period sources. This is simply a matter of statistics. If we go back in time, written sources that have survived—and especially papyri—become fewer. The chances of a papyrus from 2500 BCE surviving intact are lower than those of a papyrus from 500 BCE. But there are still important legal sources from very early Egyptian history, although they are not always written on papyrus. In fact, one of the most sensational legal texts from ancient Egypt comes from a *mastaba* tomb in Giza dating to around 2500 BCE. It was inscribed on one of the walls in the tomb chapel of a Mr. Wepemnefret—or Wep for short, as he is called in the actual contract—from the Fourth Dynasty. Wepemnefret was a prince, and one of the many sons of the legendary King Khufu (Kheops). This explains why he was allowed to build his tomb (G 1201) in the so-called western cemetery in Giza, near the pyramid of his father.

Although Mr. Wep is mainly known to the public from a beautifully painted limestone stela that is now kept in the Phoebe A. Hearst Museum of Anthropology in Berkeley (inv. nr. 6-19825), the will he had inscribed on one of the walls of his funerary chapel is probably more relevant for our understanding of ancient Egyptian society. Tomb G 1201 was excavated by the Egyptian archaeologist Selim Hassan (1887–1961). It was published as part of a series in his *Excavations at Gîza 1930–1931* (Cairo: Government Press, 1936), which is now online at the Giza Digital Library of the Museum of Fine Arts in Boston (see figs. 4–8).

At first glance the inscription, bordered in the left bottom corner by a 1.2-meter picture of the tomb owner and a much smaller one of his eldest son facing him, appears to be just another run-of-the-mill Old Kingdom tomb inscription. To the right of the inscription we see fifteen seated men, each inside a rectangular box that is preceded by separate boxes containing their names and titles (see fig. 8). The inscription of Wepemnefret is, in fact, one of the oldest legal contracts that has come down to us from ancient Egypt, showing that 4,500 years ago people already understood what was required to legally transfer property to another person and how to record this in writing as efficiently as possible. In view of the accomplished layout and content, we may safely extend this number to five thousand years ago. We must, however, keep in mind that the transaction recorded on behalf of Wepemnefret comes from the highest court circles and was probably not representative of the legal proceedings in everyday life. In 2500 BCE, as in later times, most contracts in Egypt would be concluded by mouth.

The will of Wep includes all the essential elements one would expect: a description of the declaring party, a description of the beneficiary, a date, a statement by the declaring party, a guarantee against future claims by third parties (family members), a statement about the health of the declaring party, a statement saying that the declaration by Wepemnefret was made in front of many witnesses, and a list of these witnesses. Directly above the figure of Wepemnefret are his name and titles, reading from top to bottom and from right to left (hieroglyphs always face the beginning of the line).

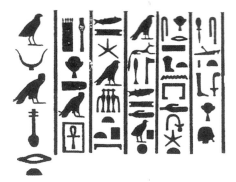

Figure 4. Name and titles of Wepemnefret [adapted from *Excavations at Gîza 1930–1931*]

(1) The unique friend, the most prominent of al-Kab, (2) the master of mysteries of the *duat* house, (3) the priest of Horus and Anubis, the domain manager of Buto, (4) the domain manager of the Star of Horus, prominent in the sky, (5) the chief of the palace, the head of . . . in the House of Life, (6) Wepemnefret.

The name and titles of his son Iby are listed directly above his own, in a much smaller picture, this time reading from left to right, and then from top to bottom and from left to right again.

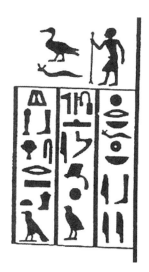

Figure 5. Name and titles of Iby son of Wepemnefret [adapted from *Excavations at Gîza 1930–1931*]

(1) His eldest son, (2) the lector-priest, the master of mysteries, (3) the scribe of the Divine Book, honorable (4) with his lord every day, Iby.

Figure 6. The will of Wepemnefret [adapted from *Excavations at Gîza 1930–1931*]

The actual contract was incised to the right of the depictions of Wepemnefret and Iby, the first four lines reading from left to right, followed by three columns that have to be read from top to bottom and then from left to right:

(1) The year of uniting the Two Lands, third month of the *peret* season, day 29, (2) the unique friend Wep, (3) he has said: "I have given to my eldest son, (4) the lector-priest Iby (5) the northern crypt and the northern offering chapel which is in my house of eternity in the necropolis, (6) so that he may be buried in it, *peret kheru* offerings being there for him, as an honored one. No brother, (7) wife, or children shall have a claim (?) on it except my son, the lector-priest Iby. I have given (it) to him."

The matter-of-factness of this very modern-looking property transfer—a will written 4,500 years ago—belies its real significance. By allotting a crypt and an offering chapel to his eldest son, Wepemnefret in fact provided him with a better chance at eternal life than most ancient Egyptians could ever hope to achieve. As one of a very few fortunate courtiers, Wepemnefret had been allowed to build his tomb in the direct vicinity of the great pyramid of Khufu (his dad), meaning that he was destined to serve King Khufu in the afterlife as well. As the representative of the gods on earth, Khufu would become an immortal soul, but even immortal souls would need courtiers to look after them. Just to make sure that there was no mistake about who was the new owner of the crypt and offering room in his own tomb, Wepemnefret included a clause to prevent any future claims by third parties, including his wife. This shows that even 4,500 years ago Egyptian women apparently had a big say in issues concerning the family estate, as they certainly would in Tsenhor's time. Otherwise Wep's wife would not have been listed among the potential future claimants.

To the right of the official contract, immediately before the picture of Wepemnefret, there is a small inscription stating that the contract was made in his presence and that he was healthy—or perhaps even *compos mentis*—when he made his statement. Ancient Egyptian law was based on oral statements made in court and in front of scribes and witnesses, which is not surprising in a country where perhaps 3 percent (or less) of the population could read and write (although Wepemnefret and his son probably could). This small inscription appears to be a later addition that could just as well have been included in the contract itself.

It is impossible to tell whether the image of Wepemnefret is pointing to the contract as a whole or to this specific text, which appears to have been added when the figure of Wepemnefret had already been drawn or even incised on the wall. This explains why the clause about his health runs from right to left whereas the rest of the text runs top to bottom. One can easily recognize the sign for *ankh*, 'to live,' and the group denoting his two feet (or rather legs, and, to add to the confusion, the order is in fact more complicated than that). There simply was no space for two longer lines instead of this layout, because otherwise the hieroglyphs would have been too close to Wepemnefret's face, meaning that he would have to spend his eternal life with hieroglyphs stuck to his face, which was not an attractive idea.

Figure 7. Addition to the actual will [adapted from *Excavations at Gîza 1930–1931*]

(1) Made in his own presence ('at his own side'), (2) while living on his two feet, (3) he has made the will ('the decree of words').

One would very much like to know more about the procedure that made his eldest son—who could be the biological eldest son but also a designated one—the new owner of a crypt and an offering chamber inside his father's tomb. Did Wepemnefret and Iby go to a scribe who recorded the contract on a piece of papyrus, after which they gave a copy of the contract to the artists decorating Wepemnefret's tomb to turn it into an everlasting monument in stone, or did the two men actually go to Wepemnefret's offering chapel inside the tomb to make the statement there? The latter hardly seems possible. The intricate layout of this unique inscription suggests it took the artists some time to assign each necessary piece of information its proper place, whereas the actual oral statement by Wepemnefret would have taken him less than a few minutes (and then only if he spoke very slowly), suggesting that this inscription was made using a copy of the contract on a papyrus (or an ostracon). If, on the other hand, the statement by Wepemnefret was indeed made inside the chapel, it may also have been problematic to accommodate all parties involved: Wepemnefret, Iby, some artists who could write, and no fewer than fifteen witnesses, who are all neatly listed to the right of the contract.

Figure 8. The fifteen witnesses to the contract [adapted from *Excavations at Gîza 1930–1931*]

The caption reads: "Given in the presence of many witnesses, and recorded in writing in his own presence."

One of the witnesses—second from the right in the bottom register—was a *ka* priest called Ptahhotep. Although the eldest son was supposed to perform the mortuary cult for his parents, and may have done so on specific dates that were important in the life of his father, just as in later times people would hire (lay) priests to do it for them, the work done by Mr. Ptahhotep in 2500 BCE was probably similar to the work done by Tsenhor two thousand years later. Could it be that Ptahhotep actually worked at tomb G 1201 in the western cemetery of Giza after Wepemnefret died?

The Law of Pharaoh

Tombs were a highly popular commodity in ancient Egypt, and more than once we see people ending up in court contesting the ownership of a tomb, as in the case of Mrs. Iryneferet. It started as a conflict about a young female slave (see "Women Owning Slaves" below), even though Iryneferet herself may have thought that she had a valid legal claim to the tomb involved. From the archive of Djekhy & Son—which directly precedes Tsenhor's papers—we have abnormal hieratic P. Louvre E 7848 from 558 BCE, in which the apparent owners of a tomb force their opponent to take an oath before the god stating that he (and his business partners) has no claim to their tomb. But these are all isolated cases. No written law about the ownership of tombs has come down to us. There is only one passage that resembles a law on the sale of tombs, and that is from the legal manual P. Mattha col. IX *l.* 30–32 (around 250 BCE):

> There are places made of natural stone or bricks in which to bury people. If nobody is buried there, the owner is at liberty to sell them to someone else. If people are buried there, the owner does not have the right to sell them.

It is an intriguing little text—with seemingly vast implications—that so far has sparked little comment from demotists or Egyptologists. But P. Mattha was dubbed a legal manual rather than a legal code by none other than Pestman, who was not a man to say things lightly. One should therefore be careful about denoting the above passage from P. Mattha as an actual law.

The demotic documents dealing with tombs clearly show that the rights to these tombs and their occupants could be transferred from one person to another, for instance as part of an inheritance. In the demotic P. Leiden I 379 from Memphis, in which the female choachyte Tetimuthes receives her share of the inheritance of her father, her eldest brother lists all the tombs and mummies from which she will derive her part of the family income (see "Mummies as a Source of Income" above). At the same time he states that she will not be allowed to lease out any rights to a mummy or tomb in the list if there is any connection with a Mrs. Nehoeris. She belonged to a different branch of the family that held the rights to these specific tombs before (P. Brussels 3). So apparently the rights had—perhaps through inheritance—gone over to the Leiden branch of the family, although from P. Leiden I 379 we may take it that there were still people from the Brussels branch disputing this. Now if Tetimuthes does not have the right to lease out the sensitive Brussels part of her tombs and mummies, this probably means that she could lease out the rest without a problem. And if she could lease them out to someone else, she could probably also sell them. Which is not to say that she owned the physical tombs.

Conflicts about tombs happened every day in every necropolis in Egypt, and we can safely assume that Tsenhor and her family had their share of conflicts about the ownership of a tomb. Tombs and mummies were business and business was money. And money creates greed.

Tsenhor and her children had a stake in various tombs in the Theban necropolis, but this does not necessarily mean that they owned them: (1) one-quarter of the tomb of the other Mrs. Tsenhor, acquired by Tsenhor's father Nesmin in 556 BCE, which Tsenhor probably shared with her three (half-)brothers (P. Louvre E 10935); (2) the tomb of Mrs. Tadyipwer, acquired by Tsenhor's daughter Ruru in 497 BCE (P. Louvre E 3231A); and (3) one-quarter of the tomb of the policeman Nespaser, which Tsenhor received from her eldest brother Nesamunhotep in 491 BCE (P. Turin 2127). Apart from these tombs, the children would also inherit the tombs—or the right to service the mummies inside the tombs—collected by their father Psenese. In P. Vienna KM 3853 (530–526 BCE), in which Psenese receives his inheritance, the list of items that will go to him consists of "field, houses, slaves, bread of the temple, bread of Osiris (income of a choachyte), tomb in the necropolis, and any other thing on earth," meaning that Psenese brought some tombs into the marriage as well.

In the documentary sources there is only one concrete reference to tomb ownership in connection with the law. It was written in hieratic in the New Kingdom (1550–1070 BCE), and its most likely provenance is—almost inevitably—the village of Deir al-Medina. This is where the men—and their families—lived who cut out the rock tombs in the Valley of Kings, decorating them with ritual scenes and inscriptions. They were privileged men who received good wages. They were also pampered by the Egyptian authorities because they knew state secrets, for instance where exactly the pharaohs had been buried and how you could get there unseen. The monthly salary of an ordinary workman was about four hundred liters of grain, more than enough to sustain a family. Apart from this, they received other rations, like beer, bread, cakes, fish, wood, and so forth. These people knew what they were worth.

But we have to return to our papyrus. It is 31 x 21 cm and has writing on both sides. According to the French Egyptologist Auguste Mariette it was found somewhere in the debris of Assasif, which is a rather vague provenance. Although it was assigned an official inventory number (P. Cairo CG 58092), most Egyptologists refer to it as P. Bulaq 10, and the name has stuck. The definitive edition of the text was published by Pestman and Janssen in 1968.

The text, probably from the reign of Ramesses VI (reigned for some years around 1140 BCE), appears to be the record of an official appeal to the oracle of the village by an anonymous Deir al-Medina workman, who was probably the grandson of the deceased people mentioned in the text. According to him, his father had taken care of the proper burial of his parents and perhaps also of their mortuary cult, whereas his brothers and sisters had sat and done nothing. But now suddenly they—the uncles and aunts of the speaker—had issued a claim to the property of their mother. Could it be that they had waited until their brother had died, only to strike when 'our' anonymous workman (we think it was Hay son of Hy) stood to inherit from him? Our workman directly addresses the 'Good Lord,' which means that he was standing in front of the oracle. This was most probably a statue of Amunhotep I, the founder and patron god of Deir al-Medina.

The speech to the oracle was most probably made during a court session, although it remains unclear where the direct speech begins: right at the beginning—one has to assume that the dry list at the beginning actually comes from a verbal statement—or at the point where our workman speaks to the oracle ("Now see, . . . ").

The list of objects he (the speaker's father) provided for Mrs. Tagemy, his mother (the speaker's grandmother): one place to bury, after he gave her coffin to N.N., makes forty deben. Again, what he provided for her: one coffin for her burial, whereas he had also provided the place of burial for Huynefer, his father. "Now see, the children of Mrs. Tagemy dispute this today, to claim her property. Yet they are not the ones who buried their father, and they did not bury <her>. It is her property that they claim today, even if they did not bury with (?) my father, like he buried his father and mother. Let the property be given to the one who buries, says the law of Pharaoh. My Good Lord! Look, I am with the officials, so cause that the right things will be done. See, the property of Taynehsy was given to Sawadjy when she was buried, because he provided her with his coffin. He was given her share in front of the officials, because it was Pharaoh Amunhotep (the oracle) who gave it to him in court."

So, not surprisingly, a Deir al-Medina court case could involve a decision by the divine oracle. There were many ways in which an oracle communicated with the people seeking justice. From Deir al-Medina we have a large collection of simple questions on ostraca, such as, "Did Amunnakhte steal my donkey?" and we assume that these ostraca were placed before the oracle, which would, especially if it was carried around in a procession, indicate by its movements—moving back meaning "no" and moving forward meaning "yes"—what the divine verdict was. Alternatively, people could lay an ostracon on each side of a road, one positive and one negative, and, when the procession passed, the oracle would swerve in the direction of the correct answer. Since the carrying of the divine oracle involved people from Deir al-Medina itself, this procedure was naturally prone to manipulation. But it was also a handy tool to give formal expression to what everybody in the village already thought or knew (this is speculation, not fact).

In P. Bulaq 10 the anonymous speaker seeks the assistance of the divine oracle, and just to make sure the oracle understands what is at stake, he cites a law about the ownership of tombs established by an earlier (or maybe the present) pharaoh, as well as an earlier, similar case.

By some magical quirk of fate the case of workman Sawadjy providing a coffin for Mrs. Taynehsy referred to in P. Bulaq 10 is quoted as the jurisprudence in deciding a similar case. In O. Petrie 16 from the Twentieth Dynasty—now O. UC (University College, London) 39617—one may assume that once again the divine oracle is addressed:

List of what the workman Nebsemen, my father, made for Mrs. Iner: one decorated wooden coffin, for her share which is the lower storehouse. "Now see, her daughter Wah has come to take a share in the storehouse, together with the workman [Huy]nefer. May My Lord cause that her share will be given to me."

Intriguingly, the speaker more or less tells the oracle exactly what it will have to say, and thus we discover that his opponents are probably his very own brothers and sisters and that Mrs. Iner was their mother. This is what the oracle will have to say: "You, the children of Nebsemen, share it, because he is the one who has buried her."

As so often with ancient Egyptian sources, much remains unsaid. This is in part because we lack the context that would have been obvious to the people living in Deir al-Medina. But it seems clear that we are right in the bloody aftermath of the division of the inheritance of the mother of the family. Apparently she had given her right to part of a storehouse to the workman Nebsemen in return for a decorated wooden coffin (or a complete burial?), and this right had in turn been promised by him to the anonymous claimant here in O. Petrie 16. He, in turn, was now being challenged by Mrs. Wah, who had taken a share in the same storehouse that partly belonged to her deceased mother. It is nowhere said, but the whole story suggests that Wah had contributed nothing to the burial of her mother. This is all the more likely in view of the jurisprudence adduced by the claimant. Again it is not clear where the direct speech should begin:

List of the things that the workman Sawadjy made to bury Mrs. Taynehsy, his mother, whereas his brothers and sisters did nothing to assist him: one wooden coffin, decorated and oiled, makes thirty-three deben (and) one small hollowed-out wooden coffin, makes twenty deben.

"May My Lord cause that they will share it with me because of these (things), because he took care of her when she died."

Once again, it was Sawadjy who needed to come to the rescue to help divide an inheritance. Not so Tsenhor. The very timely arrangements about their inheritance made by her and Psenese suggest that Tsenhor and her husband were well aware of the implications of an improper will.

4

Slave:
Tsenhor, 517 BCE

Two Owners within a Month
25 November–24 December 517 BCE (P. Turin 2122)

In the winter of 517 BCE a man called Amasis son of Psamtik sold Psenpaqed, a young boy, to a *pastophoros* of the temple of Amun in Karnak, a Mr.
Tjauheser son of Neskhonsu and Neskhonsu. Both parties to the contract
are only passersby in the Tsenhor papers. Tjauheser was to resell Psenpaqed
to Tsenhor one month later. Already in Tsenhor's days the ties between the
pastophoroi and the Theban choachytes were much closer than people think.
In P. BM EA 10120B (517 BCE) that Psenese made for Ruru, he explicitly mentions his "commissionings as a choachyte and *pastophoros* on the
mountain (the Theban necropolis)." In the Ptolemaic period the Theban
choachytes liked to call themselves *pastophoroi* in the written contracts. So
our buyer Mr. Tjauheser may very well have been a simple choachyte, too.

The names of the father and mother of the boy—Djehutymose and
Khedebirbin ('The evil eye is killed')—suggest that he was Egyptian. The
problem is that the word for 'boy' is *kher*, which may also mean 'Syrian,'
although in this case the sitting child determinative—the sign at the end
of a word denoting the word category—suggests the former. The seller
explicitly states that no brother, sister, father, or mother of his or any earlier
owner will be able to go back on this deal, meaning that the young slave
was his to sell. And if someone stakes a claim, the seller will have to pay an
excessively high fine, namely five deben, or about 450 grams of silver. This
would buy five cows. Such a steep fine is also seen in some early demotic
sales of cows—for instance, P. Michigan 3523 and 3525A and B (502 BCE)—
and there it is clearly more than just the cost of damages and replacement.

The fines mentioned in the other Tsenhor papers vary between half a deben and one deben (for example, in P. Louvre AF 9761 and P. Vienna KM 3853, respectively), suggesting that some risk was involved in this sale, so that the buyer of the slave boy Psenpaqed demanded additional security. Eight witnesses signed on the back of the papyrus.

> Regnal year 5, fourth month of the *shemu* season under Pharaoh l.p.h. Darius l.p.h. Amasis son of Psamtik, whose mother is Ituru, has said to the *pastophoros* of the temple of Amun Tjauheser son of Neskhonsu, whose mother is Neskhonsu:
>
> "You have satisfied my heart with the silver for the male child Psenpaqed son of Djehutymose, whose mother is Khedebirbin, my slave that I have handed over to you. He belongs to you, it is your slave.
>
> "As to the one who will come to you on account of him in my name or in the name of any other person on earth, namely brother or sister, father or mother, master or mistress—including me—saying, 'That is not your slave,' I will cause him to be far from you. If I do not cause him to be far from you, I will give you five (deben) of cast silver from the Treasury of Ptah, being four deben and 9 2/3 1/6 1/10 1/30 1/60 1/60 kite, again making five (deben) of silver from the Treasury of Ptah, whereas your slave and his children will still belong to you, forever."
>
> In the writing of Petosiriswennefer son of Inaros.

Within a month this contract would end up in Tsenhor's archive, when she bought Psenpaqed from Tjauheser.

Women Owning Slaves

The fact that Tsenhor would buy a slave is not surprising. Both she and Psenese probably already owned slaves, if we correctly interpret some of the earlier documents found with her papers. When Psenese received his share of the parental inheritance from his brother, the choachyte Rery son of Heryrem (P. Vienna KM 3853), slaves were among the property listed: "field, houses, slaves, bread of the temple, bread of Osiris, tomb in the necropolis, and any other thing on earth."

The same was done by Tsenhor when she divided her property equally between her two children in March 517 BCE through P. Bibl. Nat. 216 and 217. Each would receive half of her "houses, field, slaves, silver, copper, clothing, *it* grain, emmer, ox, donkey, tomb in the mountain, and anything else on earth." If the categories listed in the above examples were not general categories but specific to Tsenhor's household, both she and her husband already owned household slaves. This is not to say that owning slaves was common. In the Ptolemaic period, for instance, Egyptian households as a rule did not own slaves, whereas Greek households did.[1]

Being a slave was difficult in ancient Egypt, but the practice of slavery went unquestioned in society and was an embedded part of the social system. The evidence is sparse but suggests that the life of a slave in ancient Egypt might have been less harsh than, for example, that of a slave in a comparable situation in eighteenth- or nineteenth-century America. Note, for instance, that the slave boy bought by Tsenhor in January 516 BCE is allowed to make his own statement about the purchase (P. Bibl. Nat. 223). Then we have the famous Adoption Papyrus in which a childless couple buys a slave girl to maintain the bloodline. The children that were born were set free after they had been raised by the childless wife (see "Why Not Simply Adopt Your Wife?" above).

There were all kinds of categories of slaves, and the fate of state criminals, for instance, would be worse. The Petrie Museum of Egyptian Archaeology in London has an interesting collection of branding irons, and in most cases it is easy to see that they were used to brand cattle. In some cases these irons even seem to have been used for hair branding only, not scar branding. But in the case of inventory number UC 36437 the curators were not so sure. It is a bronze branding iron showing a cartouche with a human figure and the beginning of the name of Amasis I (better known as Ahmose I), one of the founders of the New Kingdom (1550–1070 BCE). This branding iron was probably used to brand slaves, not cattle.

Although the evidence is not conclusive, it appears slaves were used throughout ancient Egyptian history. Ancient Egyptians referred to them as *hem* and *bak*, and the controversy surrounding the exact meaning of these two words—and their mutual interrelation—rages as we speak. The obvious candidates for slavery would be criminals (and their families) and captive foreigners, although Late Period contracts suggest that people could also sell themselves into slavery to repay a debt (P. Rylands 5) or hand over one of their children as security for a loan (P. BM EA 10113). Some believe that these contracts in which people sell themselves as a slave were only temporary contracts of servitude. In that case one would expect the scribe to have included the precise duration of the period of servitude, which was never done.

A well-known category of foreign slaves in the Middle Kingdom (2040–1640 BCE) consisted of the so-called Aâmu ('Asiatics'). Interestingly, after many centuries this designation became the generic term for 'herdsman' in the demotic language. In the Middle Kingdom the Aâmu were still 'Asiatics' and some households or estates would house large numbers of them. P. Brooklyn 35.1446 from the Middle Kingdom is a relatively unknown documentary hieratic source telling us about these household slaves and their apparent owner, a Mrs. Senebtisy.

The papyrus was published by the American Egyptologist William Christopher Hayes as *A Papyrus of the Late Middle Kingdom in the Brooklyn Museum* (New York: Brooklyn Museum, 1955). It was bought in Egypt between 1881 and 1896 by the Amercian collector Charles Edwin Wilbour and presented to the Brooklyn Museum by his daughter in 1947. The papyrus measures a maximum of 29.7 x 182 cm but is badly damaged. In fact, it was reconstructed from more than six hundred small fragments between 1950 and 1952. The front contains eighty lines in several columns in Middle Kingdom hieratic, with some texts having been inserted in between, and on the back there are the names of ninety-five servants (or slaves). The texts were written by a number of scribes between regnal year 10 of Amenemhat III (around 1833 BCE) and regnal year 6 of Sobekhotep III (around 1745 BCE).

According to the text on the back of the papyrus, the slaves were both Egyptian and 'Asiatic,' the latter also receiving Egyptian names, which was more practical. The men were employed as domestic servants, brewers, cooks, and fieldworkers, whereas the women mostly worked in the production of linen. One of the women was a hairdresser and another a gardener. At first sight it seemed this papyrus was used over a period of many years for all kinds of notes and records, including a criminal register, an administrative letter, two royal decrees, a list of slaves recording changes in their owners, and a donation made by a husband for his wife. But then Hayes started thinking about the connection between the texts, finding that "the ultimate purpose of the greater part of the papyrus was apparently to establish the right of a woman named Senebtisy to the ownership of ninety-five household slaves," or the slaves mentioned on the back of the papyrus.

But how had she managed to obtain such a large number of slaves? That is where some of the interspersed texts on the back of the papyrus came in. Text C appears to be a claim that the slaves belonged to

Senebtisy as the result of a donation made in regnal year 2 of King Sobek-hotep III. Text B is a copy of the actual donation made by her husband, and text A finally explains how the slaves ended up in their household in the first place. In regnal year 1 of Sobekhotep, Senebtisy's husband had sent a petition to the government to this effect.

After this, Hayes had much less trouble explaining the interspersed texts on the front of the papyrus. The text labeled Insertion B dealt with the misconduct of the previous owner of the household slaves, and Insertion C was a citation from a royal decree from regnal year 6 of an unknown king stating that the slaves had to be transferred to a new owner or manager, which was presumably Senebtisy's husband. The only explanation for the inclusion of the criminal register on this papyrus is—unless one assumes that this was an early case of recycling—that it related to (some of) the forefathers of the household slaves, explaining why they were in the state they were in at present (but this would have been a cumbersome procedure). Which brings us to the question of ownership. Apparently the slaves had been transferred by royal decree to Senebtisy's husband to do with as he pleased. He donated them to his wife Senebtisy.

That is one version of the story. There are other voices saying that the whole thing really must come from some judicial institution. Its provenance would actually be one of the Thirteenth Dynasty tombs in the Theban necropolis. And instead of excerpts dealing with the slaves for Senebtisy's private use, this could be a document dealing with fugitives (avoiding the tasks assigned to them by the government, which was common practice in Egypt), slaves, and punishment. Well, maybe. According to the new theory, even the name of the former owner, Pay, the man whose slaves had been wrangled from him by Senebtisy's husband, was read the wrong way. The name Pay does not occur in the Middle Kingdom. It is even possible that Mrs. Senebtisy was actually the wife of the vizier Resseneb, which would explain why he had such quick access to the royal court (the papyrus contains some excerpts of royal decrees addressed to Resseneb's father Ankhu). Somewhere down the line there is also the case of Senebtisy's husband being sued by his daughter, because he wanted to give all those slaves to his wife and not to her. To summarize: the further we go back in time in ancient Egyptian history, the more Egyptologists seem to be groping in the dark. If there were ever one reason to stick to understandable sources from the New Kingdom (1550–1070 BCE) and later, it would probably be P. Brooklyn 35.1446.

If the legal status of women equaled that of their husbands, this means that judges held them accountable for their own offenses and, indeed, we have trial records showing that this was the case. In the thirteenth century BCE a Mrs. Iryneferet was summoned to court because people had accused her of buying two slaves with money that did not belong to her. The trial record is now kept in the Egyptian Museum in Cairo under the inventory number JdE (*Journal d'Entrée*) 65739. The text was—as so often and fortunately for us—published by Alan Gardiner. The handwriting is absolutely beautiful, carefully written New Kingdom hieratic. The scribe who wrote this trial record was in an excellent mood.

The beginning of the papyrus is lost, so we do not know the identities of the judges. Also lost is the opening statement by the accusing party, a soldier by the name of Nakhy. He produced six witnesses to support his accusation: a chief of police, a mayor of Thebes, and the elder brother of Iryneferet's husband Samut. These were people of importance. The witnesses also included three women, namely the wife of a deceased chief of police, a citizen without any further designation, and the elder sister of one of the women, called Bakmut, who allegedly was swindled out of her money by Iryneferet. But we do have the opening statement made by the accused party on this day:

> "[I am the wife of the superintendent of the district Samut] and it happened that I came to sit in his house (married him), and I worked on the [. . .] and I took care of my own clothing. Now, in regnal year 15, so seven years after entering the house of the superintendent of the district Samut, the merchant Raya came to me with the Syrian slave girl Gemenyherimentet ('I found (her) in the west'), she still being a [young] girl [and he] said to me: 'Buy (lit. 'bring') this young girl and give me her price,' so he said to me. I received the young girl and I gave him the price for her."

The fact that Iryneferet states that she "took care of her own clothing" may be a relevant detail. It reminds one of the food and clothing mentioned in the demotic marital property arrangements, suggesting she included this in her statement to show that although she was a married woman, she had money of her own. Iryneferet then gives a precise description of the items that made up the purchase sum for the slave girl, consisting of some garments, including their value, and several bronze items, mostly vessels. This time Iryneferet gives not only the value of these items but also the names of the people from whom she bought or borrowed them.

For some reason Gardiner, whose scientific commentary was not very extensive, which is very unlike him, did address the way Iryneferet presumably got the money to buy the slave girl. According to him, slave traders simply went from door to door, and when one came to Iryneferet's house he immediately realized he had found a buying customer.

But right at that point, things were going to take time. First Iryneferet and the dealer would have had to agree on a price for the girl, and then she would have had to scour the house looking for things that she could use to barter. The New Kingdom (1550–1070 BCE) was not a money economy, but people knew very well about the relative value of things. Apparently the tour of the house produced some precious garments (haggling with the dealer about their value would take another hour or so), but Iryneferet still needed more money. So she simply went around to some neighbors' house, where she either bought (but with what?) or borrowed some valuable items. If she had not compensated the neighbors in some way or was evading any talk about payback, this could well be one of the reasons why she was in court in the first place.

But let us assume that all the things Iryneferet gave to the slave trader were hers in the first place because she bought them long ago. In that case all she would have to do is go through the house, take the commodities out, and give them to the dealer. What is striking in the list of items used to pay is that the vessel she bought (or borrowed) from the priest Huy Panehsy weighing sixteen deben (about a kilogram and a half) cost only one and a half kite of silver, whereas one of the shawls she had used to buy the girl was apparently of such exceptional quality that it cost five kite of silver.

What must have really stung Iryneferet was that this same Huy Panehsy, her own brother-in-law, whose name ('Huy the Nubian') could be an allusion to his dark complexion, was among the witnesses produced by her opponent, the soldier Nakhy. After listing the total amount paid for the slave girl Gemenyherimentet—four deben and one kite of silver—Iryneferet states, "I gave them to the merchant Raya and there was no property of Bakmut among them. He gave me this young girl and I named her Gemenyherimentet."

The court proceeds by making Iryneferet take an oath stating that no property of Bakmut was used by her to buy the slave girl. If there was and she was found out, she would have received a hundred strokes of the stick and the girl would have been taken away from her.

The court then addresses the soldier Nakhy, but only at this point does it become clear that something more was afoot than just the one case of the Syrian slave girl (we must not forget, however, that the opening statement by the accuser is lost):

Said by the *qenbet* of hearers ('court of judges,' although 'hearing committee' would probably also be an apt translation) to the soldier Nakhy: "Produce for us the witnesses you say know about the silver of the citizen Bakmut that was given to buy the slave Gemenyherimentet, as well as the witnesses regarding this tomb of which you say, 'Look, the citizen Bakmut made it,' and then the citizen Iryneferet gave it to the merchant Nakht, and he gave her the slave Telptah."

From what appeared to be a simple case of two women bickering over money, a new pattern emerges. According to Nakhy, Iryneferet also took away a tomb built by Mrs. Bakmut—who one assumes must have been his wife, or in any case a relative—to buy a male slave. The phrasing, however, is, as so often, frustratingly brief and concise. It is difficult to imagine that Iryneferet could have just taken away someone else's tomb and then given it to a dealer as payment for a slave. Surely he would have demanded some proof of ownership from her.

This often happens in ancient Egyptian documents. They generate many questions. In this case one would very much like to know more about the family relations involved. Was Iryneferet in some way related to Bakmut, the woman who according to Nakhy was the formal owner of the tomb? And why would Iryneferet pay for a single slave with an entire tomb, particularly someone else's tomb? In ancient Egypt tombs were not just tombs, they were magical machines designed to provide immortality. They represented value.

At this point in the papyrus, the scribe made a list of the witnesses produced by Nakhy, three men and three women (listed above). Their titles or designations show that they belonged to the local ruling elite. Iryneferet was clearly in trouble.

Unfortunately, the papyrus breaks off after just a few lines, showing that the witnesses were questioned by the court, starting with Iryneferet's brother-in-law Huy Panehsy. Shortly before that, the court had imposed an oath on them. They presumably took this oath together:

"We will speak in truth, we will not speak falsehood. If we do speak falsehood, the slaves will be taken from us."

An interesting oath by all means. Did the witnesses by any chance have an interest in the slaves purchased by Iryneferet? It would seem so. Were the slaves still with Iryneferet or had they been impounded by the authorities awaiting the outcome of this trial? Or did the court simply mean that the witnesses of the prosecution would each have to pay a fine to the value of the two slaves if they made a false statement? This is where the ancient Egyptian sources fall silent and speculation begins.

Another papyrus from the New Kingdom (1550–1070 BCE), P. Gurob II 1, shows that people could indeed hire slaves for a specific period of time. In year 33 of Amunhotep III (around 1360 BCE) the herdsman Mesi and a Mrs. Pihy—accompanied by her son Miny—came to an agreement about the lease of two of Pihy's female slaves. The slave Kheryt was to work for seventeen days and Henut for four days. The payment was done in advance, consisting of several precious garments, a bull, eight goats, and one other item. The total amount was thirty-seven 'rings,' which Gardiner thought to be equivalent to slightly over three deben. But there is something very strange about this contract. To start with, it was made by an official scribe of accounts called Wennefer, a *wab* priest, and the whole procedure took place in the presence of a council consisting of five other priests and three witnesses from the nearby town. All this for a mere twenty-one days of work by two female slaves? Then there is the oath spoken by Pihy and (presumably) her son Miny: "Then they said: 'As the ruler endures (twice): if the days are hot they shall be made day by day. I have received their price in full.'"

In other words, the slave women were not allowed to work on days that were too hot. What we have here is preposterous compensation for relatively little work done by two slave women, a council consisting of priests, official witnesses, and a proviso under oath that the slaves cannot work on hot days (there were no collective labor agreements in ancient Egypt that we know of). This suggests that the slave women (or girls) were either capable of high-quality labor that was very hard to come by or, maybe worse, that they could have been hired to perform services of a sexual nature. The papyrus does not tell us.

Slavery would never be voluntary, but in some cases we get the impression that sometimes the ancient Egyptians did become slaves of their own free will, or rather were forced by circumstances. There is, for instance, the famous case of the Macedonian born in Egypt, Ptolemy, who lived in the second century BCE. When he was thirty years old he decided he no longer wanted to be a part of this world, so he settled in the Serapeum in Memphis as a recluse. Such a person was called a *katochos*, and it appears likely that this title had its counterpart in demotic, when people decided they would serve the god as a *bak*, or 'slave,' 'servant,' suggesting that the ancient Egyptian word for slave actually covered a much wider range of meanings than in English. The Greek papyrologists are not in agreement on whether this means that such a person was 'held fast (could not leave)' or 'held' in the sense that he or she was in some way possessed. The condition for becoming a *katochos* was that you no longer could leave the temple. Ptolemy had the habit of writing letters and petitions—to the king if need be—and keeping his drafts. They show that, although he was a recluse, he knew very well what happened on the outside. At one point he took in Egyptian twin girls called Thaues and Taous who had been kicked out of the house by their mother after their father died. Ptolemy has left us with forty-two letters dealing with these twins alone, showing that at times he dreamt about them and then tried to explain what this really meant. A good description of Ptolemy's adventures is found in a delightful book called *Reflections of Osiris: Lives from Ancient Egypt* (New York: Oxford University Press, 2002) by the British demotist John Ray.

Women could also decide to become a *bak* of the god. On 21 March 137 BCE, the scribe Pasis son of Marres, an official from the temple of the crocodile god Sobek of Tebtynis in the Fayoum, recorded a statement by a woman who was plagued by evil ghosts. She said that she wanted to become a *bak*—a slave—of Sobek and that she was willing to pay for this for a period of no fewer than ninety-nine years. How she was planning to do this the contract does not say. She would of course be dead long before the termination of her contract. Apparently the woman Tapanebtynis was in dire straits when she decided she wanted to become a recluse, and in this case the self-dedication as a *bak* almost looks like a health insurance contract.[2]

> Regnal year 33, second month of the *peret* season, day 23 under Pharaohs Ptolemy VIII and Cleopatra II (. . .) and Pharaoh Cleopatra III, his wife.
>
> Has said Mrs. Tapanebtynis, the slave, daughter of Sobekmen, her mother being Isiswery, before my master, Sobek Lord of Tebtynis, the Great God:

"I will be your slave, together with my children and the children of my children. I will not be able to act as a free person in your temple, forever and ever.

"You will protect me, save me, guard me, and keep me whole. You will protect me against any ghost on earth, against any water spirit, any sleepwalking man, any man having a divine illness, any drowned man, and deathbird, any . . . , any man from the river, any man from the riverside, any demon, any red person, any evil genius, any breath.

"I will give you 1¼ kite, half of which is . . . , makes 1¼ kite again in bronze, (counting) twenty-four obols for two kite as the salary for (your) work, each month from regnal year 33, second month of the *peret* season onward, to complete ninety-nine years, makes 1,204½ months, makes ninety-nine years again. I will give it to your priests each month without being able to hold back money for a (specific) month for one of the other months.

"You and your representatives are in control regarding anything that will be discussed with me in the name of every word above. I will do them at your request, compulsorily and without delay."

The contract does not state that Tapanebtynis would not have to pay if Sobek did not fulfill his end of the bargain, namely protecting her from sleepwalkers and epileptics, and more or less any evil spirit she could think of.

It is actually very difficult to label people as slaves when the ancient Egyptian terms used are *hem* and *bak*. There may have been subtle nuances in the language that we miss. But if we simply apply the principle that someone who is or can be sold by another man means that he (or she) is a slave, we are probably not far off. And sell the Egyptians did. For instance, the practice of selling people caught in battle or during raids as slaves continued in the Late Period. These people are often referred to as "from Gaza" or "from the north," the counterparts of the Aâmu or 'Asiatics' owned by Mrs. Senebtisy in the Middle Kingdom (2040–1640 BCE).

The Rijksmuseum van Oudheden in Leiden keeps a beautiful, tiny abnormal hieratic sales contract (F 1942/5.15) about such a man from the north, who was presumably captured during the reign of King Pye (reigned 746–716 BCE), who is also known as Piankhy. He was the second king of the Kushite or Twenty-fifth Dynasty, and his authority was constantly being tested by the Twenty-fourth or Libyan Dynasty in the north. Somewhere between 730 and 725 BCE the Libyans under Tefnakht managed to overthrow large parts of northern Egypt, even reaching as far as Hermopolis in Middle Egypt. This forced Pye to retaliate, which he did—and very successfully—from around 725 BCE onward.

Eventually Tefnakht had to retreat all the way into a tiny enclave in the Delta, from which he sent a message to Pye saying that he surrendered and recognized Pye as the pharaoh of Egypt. The whole episode is described in minute detail in the famous Piankhy Stela that is now kept in the Egyptian Museum in Cairo (St. Cairo JdE 48862).

The Leiden papyrus—dated to 30 March 726 BCE—appears to corroborate the success of the campaign mounted by Pye against the north, although it slightly predates the accepted date on which it started, so maybe our man from the north was captured during an earlier reconnaissance mission or raiding party. The label attached to the papyrus states that it is "A Small Papyrus taken from a Mummy by Belzoni," who was a famous circus strongman to whom we owe some irreplaceable Egyptian antiquities kept in museums today. Giovanni Battista Belzoni (1778–1823)—the Great Belzoni—is undoubtedly the most colorful personality among the nineteenth-century antiquities hunters. In the wake of Napoleon's attack on Italy, he emigrated to the Netherlands, working as a barber there between 1800 and 1803. He then emigrated to England, where he worked as a strongman at fairs and in the circus (he was more than two meters tall). He was also an inventor. This eventually brought him to Egypt, where he presented some hydraulic machine to the pasha himself, but the latter was not impressed enough to buy it. So there Belzoni was in Egypt, penniless and without any prospects. Fortunately he then met the famous art collector Henry Salt, who hired him to scout the country for antiquities. There was heavy competition here between France and England, and Bernardino Drovetti made life miserable for Belzoni from the French side. Completely undaunted, however, in 1816 Belzoni managed to procure and ship a colossal statue of Ramesses II (reigned 1290–1224 BCE) from the Ramesseum to the British Museum, where it still stands today. His other feats include the literal excavation of the Ramesside temple of Abu Simbel and the discovery of KV 17, the tomb of Sety I (reigned 1306–1290 BCE) in the Valley of the Kings, although he thought that he had found the tomb of Psamtik. This tomb is still known today as Belzoni's Tomb. In 1818 he even managed to find the—according to Herodotus nonexistent—way into the pyramid of Khafra (Khefren) and the Red Sea port of Berenike. He also, of course, found the abnormal hieratic papyrus P. Leiden F 1942/5.15, which still holds a label saying that he found it on a mummy in Thebes. Belzoni allegedly died of dysentery in an obscure African town, although some say he was murdered. Very appropriately, however, he died while on an expedition to find Timbuktu, at that time still a mysterious name.

So what does the papyrus say?

Regnal year 21, second month of the *akhet* season, day 8 under Pharaoh Pye, son of Isis (and) beloved of Amun.

Has said Payfditmen son of Paypenu to the choachyte Itshery son of Nesamun: "I have received from you the three deben and one kite of silver from the Treasury of Harsaphes as the silver for Paneferiu, the man from the northern area. I have given him to you in exchange for it today."

He said: "As Amun lives, as the king lives, may he be healthy. I do not have a son, daughter, brother, sister, or any person in the world who will be able to claim him. As to anyone who does claim him, his statement shall not be heard in any Hall of Documents, tomorrow and ever after."

The witness scribe Inaros son of Horsiese son of Basa.

The contract was signed by several witnesses. Since it still follows the abnormal hieratic tradition, they all copied a summary of the contract instead of just writing their names (which became the demotic practice). But we have to get back to Tsenhor and her slave Psenpaqed.

A Profitable Start to the New Year
30 December 517 BCE–29 January 516 BCE (P. Bibl. Nat. 223)

Regnal year 26 of Darius I had only just begun when Tjauheser son of Neskhonsu and Tsenhor visited the office of the scribe Ip son of Teos. They were accompanied by a number of witnesses[3] and the slave boy Psenpaqed. We may be sure that, shortly before, her husband Psenese and her son—his stepson—Peteamunhotep had attended the annual reception of the Association of Theban Choachytes to inaugurate the new year, as we know from their official records (P. Louvre E 7840). This is unless, of course, Peteamunhotep had already died some time before, as some believe. We may at least be sure that Tsenhor had not been invited to the meeting. She may have been a choachyte, but she was also a woman. There were other woman choachytes in Thebes. There was Mrs. Ruru daughter of Namenekhese, who owned some property in the Theban necropolis (P. Turin 2123) next to a building owned by Tsenhor and her husband. There was also Tsenhor's own daughter Ruru (P. Louvre E 3231A), and there must have been more. So maybe the women had their own party. In any case, today Tsenhor had other things on her mind, namely buying the slave boy Psenpaqed.

It is assumed that by now Ip's father Teos had left the office in the temple of Montu, finally making room for Ip. However, when Ip signed P. Bibl. Nat. 223 he referred to himself as "Ip son of the god's father of Montu Lord of Thebes and chief of priests in the fourth phyle Teos," mentioning his father's titles, so apparently the shadow of Teos still hung over the office. Ip had already written a few contracts for Tsenhor and was to write more. In these documents we actually see him experiment with his own signature, finally deciding on a catchy title: god's father of Montu Lord of Thebes Ip son of Teos.

We do not know who initiated this sale, but we can safely assume that it was Tsenhor who came up with the name of a reliable scribe. As part of the deal Tsenhor also received the contract of sale made one month earlier between Tjauheser and Amasis son of Psamtik. This was a straightforward sale, except for the inclusion of an oral statement by the slave boy Psenpaqed himself. Why he was sold is unknown.

> Regnal year 6, first month of the *akhet* season under Pharaoh l.p.h. Darius l.p.h. The *pastophoros* of the temple of Amun Tjauheser son of Neskhonsu, whose mother is Neskhonsu, has said to the choachyte Mrs. Tsenhor daughter of the choachyte of the valley Nesmin, whose mother is Ruru:
>
> "You have satisfied my heart with the silver for which the male child Psenpaqed son of Djehutymose, whose mother is Khedebirbin, will act as a slave for you, my slave that I have acquired for silver from Amasis son of Psamtik, whose mother is Ituru, for which he has made me a contract in regnal year 5, fourth month of the *shemu* season under Pharaoh l.p.h. Darius l.p.h.

Table 7. The scribe Ip playing with his signature

Source	Year	Signature by Ip
P. Louvre E 7837	535	Ipy son of Teos (witness to a contract written by his father)
P. Bibl. Nat. 216	517	Ip son of the god's father of Montu Lord of Thebes, chief of priests in the fourth phyle and monthly priest in the second phyle in the temple of Montu Lord of Thebes Teos son of Ip
P. Bibl. Nat. 217	517	Ip son of the god's father of Montu Lord of Thebes, chief of priests in the fourth phyle and monthly priest in the second phyle in the temple of Montu Lord of Thebes Teos son of Ip
P. Bibl. Nat. 223	517/ 516	Ip son of the god's father of Montu Lord of Thebes, chief of priests in the fourth phyle . . . Teos
P. Turin 2123	512	Ip son of the god's father of Montu Lord of Thebes Teos
P. Louvre E 7128	510	God's father of Montu Lord of Thebes, chief of priests in the fourth phyle Ip son of Teos son of Ip
P. Turin 2124	507	God's father of Montu Lord of Thebes Ip son of Teos
P. Louvre E 9293	498	God's father of Montu Lord of Thebes Ip son of Teos
P. Turin 2126	498	God's father of Montu Lord of Thebes Ip son of Teos
P. Louvre E 3231A	497	God's father of Montu Lord of Thebes Ip son of Teos

"I have given to you this slave. He belongs to you together with his children and everything that they own and will acquire. They cannot act as free men toward you. I have no issue whatsoever regarding them on this earth. No man on earth can exercise authority over them—including me—except you, from today onward forever and ever.

"As to the one who will come to you on account of them, in my name or in the name of any other person on earth, I will cause him to be far (from you). I will ensure that he will be clear of any title or claim on earth."

And the male child Psenpaqed son of Djehutymose, whose mother is Khedebirbin, stood up and said: "Record and do all that has been said above (about the sale). My heart is satisfied with it. I am your slave, together with my children and all that belongs to us and what we will still acquire. They will never be free before you forever and ever."

. In the writing of Ip son of the god's father of Montu Lord of Thebes and chief of priests in the fourth phyle . . . Teos.

The fact that the scribe recorded that Psenpaqed stood up in order to make his statement is a small but important detail, as is the fact that Psenpaqed—a slave boy—was allowed to speak for himself. What makes his statement so real, however, is that Ip may have written it all down the way Psenpaqed said it, because he first addressed the scribe ("Record and do all that has been said above") and then turned toward Tsenhor to continue his statement: "I am your slave, together with my children and all that belongs to us and what we will still acquire. They will never be free before you forever and ever."

This statement by a slave about to be sold is unique in the early demotic evidence from Thebes, and why it was included here is a mystery. The actual practice of including statements by other stakeholders to a contract did still exist in Late Period Thebes. It is, for instance, also found in early demotic P. BM EA 10117 (542 BCE), after which the practice seems to vanish from the Theban sources, although it was continued in other parts of Egypt.

In Memphite demotic from the Ptolemaic period, which in some respects is more uncial than Theban demotic, such a statement occurs much more often. In P. Leiden I 379, in which the choachyte Mrs. Tetimuthes receives a quarter of her father's inheritance from her eldest brother Petosiris, the two other parties involved make their own statement about this division. Her other brother Pagyr receives one-third and states that he is satisfied with the division as is, meaning that Tetimuthes probably did the same on the division contract that Petosiris made for Pagyr. Their mother Djedherbastet says that she allows them to divide her husband's inheritance—this would probably remain undivided and be managed by the eldest brother or by the three of them—as long as her eldest son will take care of her in accordance with the contract of maintenance her late husband had made for her.

Some of the mistakes in the contract made for Tsenhor by the scribe Ip, however, are telling. Taken at face value, the translation above appears to be a hallmark of female emancipation that some modern societies have yet to attain. But ancient Egyptian grammar requires separate masculine and feminine forms for 'you, your' and in no fewer than four cases Ip mistakenly wrote 'you, your' using the masculine form. He did correct most of these mistakes to the feminine form, but one wonders what happened here. There are two possible scenarios: either, as a woman, Tsenhor needed a legal guardian—which is something we rather associate with the Greek contracts from the Hellenistic period in Egypt—or Ip was simply not used to women showing up in his office ordering contracts and the legal formulary he had in his head (and fingers) would be the standard formulary for two male contracting parties. So even if in this case one of the parties was Tsenhor—a woman he knew very well from other contracts—his hand would inadvertently revert to the masculine form of 'you, your,' more or less the same way we need a week, if not more, to get the year right in letterheads in January. But, as we said, it could well be that Tsenhor needed a legal guardian. The most obvious candidate would in that case have been her husband Psenese, and this would explain the mistakes made by Ip on this day.

To You Belongs Their Fate

Women could do with their property what they liked, but the above sale of the slave Psenpaqed at least suggests that Tsenhor needed a male guardian to buy him in the first place. One also wonders why she bought the slave. Did this make her the sole owner? If he was to be a household slave or had to carry the water needed for their libation services in the necropolis, why did she and not Psenese buy the slave? In other words, which capital was used to buy Psenpaqed: Tsenhor's, Psenese's, or the conjugal capital?

In ancient Egyptian marriages there were three different kinds of property, namely the husband's property, the wife's property, and the conjugal property. This explains, for instance, why the lady Naunakhte (see "When Old Age Sets In" below), when she divided her inheritance, could disinherit some of her children from the one-third of the joint property that was hers to dispose of but not from the two-thirds that belonged to her husband. From a purely practical point of view, it would be difficult for Tsenhor to say that she was the buyer and that she would be the only one who could use Psenpaqed when he was just a slave. Even her children could boss him around, so we must assume that in Late Period Egypt there was always a clear understanding of who owned what in the house—which of course immediately changed once a couple decided to divorce—but underneath the surface there were subtle property mechanisms in play that are only rarely mentioned in the contracts. But sometimes they are.

In the Ptolemaic demotic P. BM EA 10394 (226 BCE) the Greek Melas and his Egyptian wife Tsenbastet make arrangements about their present and future property. Most of the clauses are as one would expect, and Melas acknowledges in writing the property that Tsenbastet has brought into the house, which included a piece of clothing of 1.6 deben, four times as expensive as her silver necklace. Then follows a cryptic statement from Melas about Tsenbastet's property that he has received: "When you are inside, you are inside with them. When you are outside, you are outside with them. To you belongs their *shy*, to me belongs their *sekhef*."

Half of this clause makes sense. The *shy* is 'fate' or 'ultimate destiny' and *sekhef* has the connotation of 'release,' which presumably means that Melas can sell the property if he so desires. In the case of a divorce he will have to pay their value to his wife. But the first part is a mystery (at least to me). No physical act can be meant here, because the property that Tsenbastet brought into the house included two beds and she would hardly want to take these with her whenever she went out. In other words, entering into a marriage meant that all sorts of subtle property mechanisms came into play (as they still do). If the wife received a marital property arrangement from her husband saying that he would maintain her during the marriage, his entire property became the security for this. And indeed there are contracts in which a husband sells his house or borrows some money—putting up the house as security—where we see his wife consenting to the agreement. But apparently at the same time the husband could use the capital brought by his wife into the marriage more or less the way he saw fit, unless the clause about the woman being inside and outside the house with her property meant that it would always be available in the house and could only be used by the husband as security for a loan, or something similar. But this is conjecture. Also, what the contracts never tell us about, but we know would have been there, is simple human emotion. Anyone living in a close-knit family can tell you that there is a whole world beyond mere contractual arrangements, dictated by emotion. One day you are going to get the house; the next day your parents decide it will be your no-good sister. This would have been the same in Tsenhor's household. And that is probably why she and Psenese let their children—boy or girl—each inherit an equal share of the family property. But only one of them could have the slave Psenpaqed.

5

Bricks: Tsenhor, Psenese, and Nesamunhotep, 512–506 BCE

The Tomb of Osorkon
28 January–26 February 512 BCE (P. Turin 2123)

For almost a century P. Turin 2123 was only known from a number of obsolete publications by Eugène Revillout written between 1895 and 1912, the last appearing shortly before his death. The first modern publication was by Pieter Willem Pestman in his scientific edition of the Tsenhor papers in 1994.

This easy-to-follow contract sheds revealing light on the kind of person Tsenhor may have been. She and Psenese were married for about five years and apparently she—now nearing forty, if our reconstruction is correct—had become a full business partner in some of the construction activities of her husband. Peteamunhotep, her eldest son from her previous marriage to Inaros, was now fifteen or sixteen, old enough to enter the family business (or, as some Egyptologists believe, he was no longer alive). Tsenhor's baby daughter Ruru was anywhere between five and maybe ten years old, often still clinging to her mother's skirts demanding attention or playing in the yard with the children of the other choachytes. One assumes that Psenese and Tsenhor lived on the east bank of the Nile, somewhere near the great temple of Amun in Karnak, maybe even in the neighborhood known as the House of the Cow (see fig. 9).[1] Their business as funerary service providers took place on the other side of the river in the Theban necropolis. Maybe this is also where the choachytes lived, as we know their Ptolemaic descendants did.

In any case, here Psenese had acquired a house or building plot. The term used is *per*, which literally translated means 'house,' so he had either bought a plot on which he intended to build something or he had bought a derelict house that he wanted to rebuild in some way. But in demotic a house was almost invariably called *awy*, so simply translating *per* as 'house' in demotic is actually a big problem.

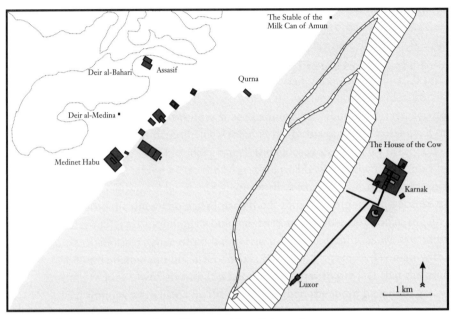

Figure 9. Thebes and surroundings [Courtesy Hans Schoens]

In New Kingdom Deir al-Medina there were structures then still called *at*—the forerunner of demotic *awy*—and *per*. Some of the greatest names in Egyptology came to grips with this apparent inconsistency, with sometimes stunning results. The German Egyptologist Wolfgang Helck, who more or less singlehandedly laid the foundation for social and economic research in Egyptology, thought that the *per* was the official residence connected with a position and the *at* was a private home built by people themselves. Others had even worse ideas. At this point the Dutch Egyptologist Rob Demarée—who probably knows more about Deir al-Medina than anyone else in the world today—decided to settle the issue once and for all. His conclusion, and with hindsight it seems difficult to see how anyone could have come to a different one, was that *per* was only used to denote the house(hold) inside the walled village itself, whereas the *at* was invariably situated outside the village and is most probably to be identified with the huts built by workmen near the tombs.[2] The dimensions of such an *at* could easily be 4 x 4.5 m. Here the workmen from Deir al-Medina relaxed—and slept—when they were working in the tombs, as returning to the village at the end of the day was not an option. It is both an intriguing and a vexing problem, because the New Kingdom *at* seems to be the predecessor of demotic *awy*, whereas *per* for house or household went into disuse. In the case of Tsenhor and her husband Psenese, it is therefore really impossible to decide what the scribe was thinking when he wrote that they were sharing a *per* together in the necropolis on the west bank of Thebes.

Whatever the truth, their plot—which will also be referred to as a house in the pages below for the sake of convenience—was located in a place called the Tomb of Pharaoh l.p.h. Osorkon l.p.h., which is also known from an abnormal hieratic papyrus from the archive of Djekhy & Son, P. Louvre E 7858 (609 BCE). The text of P. Turin 2123—and it may be worth noting that this contract does not tell us that Psenese and Tsenhor were in reality husband and wife—runs:

Regnal year 10, second month of the *akhet* season under Pharaoh l.p.h. Darius l.p.h. The choachyte of the valley Psenese son of Heryrem, whose mother is Beniuutehtyes, has said to the choachyte Mrs. Tsenhor daughter of the choachyte of the valley Nesmin, whose mother is Ituru:

"I have given to you half of this house in (or building site on) which I intend to build with you, which is in the west of Thebes in the Tomb of Pharaoh l.p.h. Osorkon l.p.h. Its south is the Processional Way of Amun, its north the house of the choachyte Mrs. Ruru daughter of Namenekhese, which is vacant, its west is the house of the choachyte Petehorresne son of Nesamunhotep, and its east the good house of Inaros son of Amunirdis. I have given to you half of this house (or building site) mentioned above. It is yours, while the other half is mine."

So according to the description of the neighbors in P. Turin 2123, the situation of their house in the Theban necropolis is shown in figure 10.

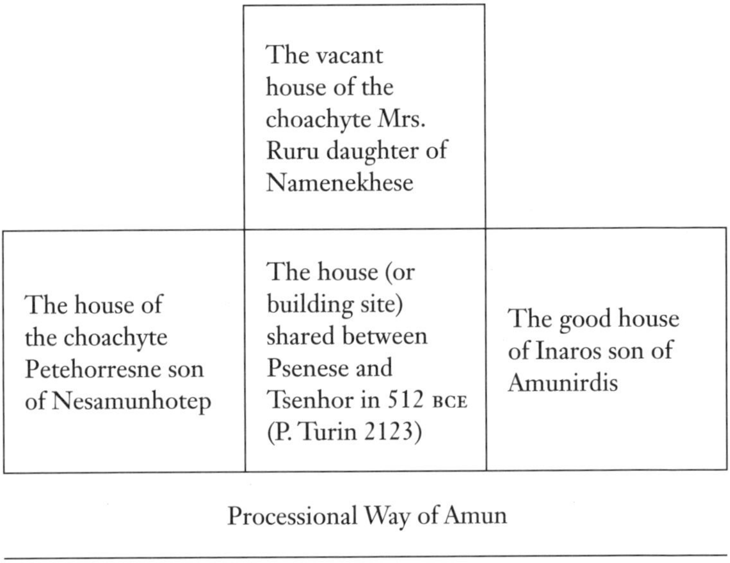

<table>
<tr><td></td><td>The vacant house of the choachyte Mrs. Ruru daughter of Namenekhese</td><td></td></tr>
<tr><td>The house of the choachyte Petehorresne son of Nesamunhotep</td><td>The house (or building site) shared between Psenese and Tsenhor in 512 BCE (P. Turin 2123)</td><td>The good house of Inaros son of Amunirdis</td></tr>
</table>

Processional Way of Amun

Figure 10. The neighbors of the house owned by Psenese and Tsenhor

As we will see below, the southern neighbor of the house divided between Psenese and Tsenhor was actually another property owned by the overseer of the necropolis Tjayutayudeny ('They have taken their share') son of Peteamunip. To the scribe, however, the Processional Way of Amun was the more obvious landmark. This area was clearly owned by a number of Theban choachytes' families. Two of the neighbors were choachytes and the southern neighbor—who was to sell the plot that separated the property owned by Psenese and Tsenhor from the Processional Way of Amun some two years later (in P. Louvre E 7128)—was an overseer of the necropolis. These overseers collected the mummy transfer taxes and settled the numerous business quarrels between the Theban choachytes, among other things. In the archive of Djekhy & Son we often see them act as professional scribes. They were so closely linked to the choachytes that they also attended the New Year's reception of the Association of Theban Choachytes (P. Louvre E 7840). The eastern neighbor was an embalmer's workshop.

The 'marriage contract' that Psenese made for Tsenhor in 517 BCE—P. BM EA 10120A—clearly states that in the case of a divorce Tsenhor would receive back the three deben (about 270 grams) of silver she had given him, as well as one-third of the capital they acquired during their marriage. But here we see Tsenhor receiving half of a house apparently owned by her husband. P. Turin 2123 is a donation, with only one proviso, namely that as the new co-owner Tsenhor share in the construction costs.

"You are accountable for half of the costs that we will make for it in view of construction work and the other half is mine. I have nothing on earth to say as far as the half of this house mentioned above is concerned, including half of any enclosure found there, the other half being mine.

"No man on earth—including me—will be able to exercise authority over it except you, forever and ever. As for the person who will come to you on account of it in my name or in the name of any person on earth, I will cause him to be far from you. I will ensure that it will be clear of any title or claim on earth. To you belongs half of its contracts wherever they will be."

In the writing of Ip son of the god's father of Montu Lord of Thebes Teos.

The contract ends with the usual demotic clauses stating that no third party has a claim on the property. It was signed by the scribe Ip below the text and by eight witnesses on the back of the papyrus. The first witness to sign also mentioned the name of his grandfather Nesmin, which happens only rarely. Perhaps the Nesmin he referred to was in fact Tsenhor's own father, in which case this witness was a member of the family who may have acted as Tsenhor's legal guardian.

Apart from P. Turin 2123, no previous title deeds to the property were handed over to Tsenhor—or, as in the case of P. Louvre E 10935 above, only as a symbolic gesture—but instead Psenese explicitly stated, "To you belong half of its contracts wherever they will be." In this case this would have been the house where the couple lived.

We do not know exactly where this new property was located, but we do know that it was close to one of the major roads in the necropolis, the Processional Way of Amun. In demotic contracts the public street is sometimes referred to as *pa myt Peraâ*, 'the road of Pharaoh,' using the masculine article *pa*. If the scribe wrote *ta myt* with the feminine article *ta*, he meant a much grander avenue, as is also reflected in Greek translations of *ta myt*, calling it either a dromos or *hè plateia hodos*, 'the large road.' The same Processional Way of Amun, running from east to west, is mentioned in P. Louvre E 7128, which was made for Tsenhor's husband

Psenese in 510 BCE. P. Turin 2125, in which Tsenhor inherits part of a building owned by her father, also mentions a Processional Way of Amun, this time running from south to north.

The Good House

One of the neighboring structures of the new property owned by Psenese and Tsenhor was an embalmer's workshop called a *per nefer*, or 'good house,' although some Egyptologists believe that in this case *nefer* does not mean 'good' but 'rejuvenation' or something similar. Above, it was shown that the translation 'house' for *per* in the Late Period is problematic. Such are the issues Egyptologists deal with.

One can imagine this to be the place where, according to several papyri describing the embalming ritual, like P. Bulaq 3 and P. Louvre 5.158, the master of secrets, the lector-priest, and the official called *khetemu-netjer*, who does not occur in Theban demotic contracts, joined the embalmer to help prepare the deceased for the afterlife, which of course involved a lot of magic and incantations.

The *per nefer* was a very ancient concept. One of the oldest references—and the reader is reminded that most of this material comes from a solid essay by the inspiring Danish Egyptologist Paul John Frandsen—is a stela found by Flinders Petrie in Dendara in the archaeological season of 1897–98. It was dated to between the death of Pepy II and the Eighth Dynasty (so between around 2246 and 2134 BCE). A *per nefer* also occurs in Spell 45 of the so-called Coffin Texts from the Middle Kingdom (2040–1640 BCE), where it almost works as a pun, underlined by the dry note—"i.e., killed them"—added by the British Egyptologist Raymond Faulkner, who translated the Coffin Texts: "Your father Geb has helped you (the deceased who is now Osiris). He has put your enemies who rebelled against you in the embalmer's workshop *(per nefer)*."

In the old days embalming took place at a location called the *wabet*, 'the pure (place).' Theban Tomb (TT) 110 from the Eighteenth Dynasty contains two stelae referring to this purification rite: "A perfect burial comes in peace, your seventy days having been completed in your *wabet*."

Statue Cairo JdE 86125 is a Twenty-first Dynasty Osiris statue that was made for a man called Ankhefenamun and his daughter. It was bought in July 1944 from a Cairo antiquities dealer. In two inscriptions it says: "He was placed in the *wabet* under the hands of Anubis (. . .) and he completed seventy-two (the other text has seventy) days in the *per nefer*."

At some point in time the term *wabet* became interchangeable with *per nefer*, as in stela Leiden AP 57 from the Saite period: "He was taken into the *per nefer* and spent forty-two days under the arms of Anubis."

Seventy-two, seventy, and forty-two days (would that be the cheaper option described by Herodotus?). Apparently some variation did exist, just as there were more variant words for this location, which may have come from local dialects. In P. Rylands 9, a papyrus that was written during the lifetime of Tsenhor, the scribe used a word spelled *syh*, prompting Günter Vittmann to remark that in this case *syh* probably has the same meaning as *wabet* and *per nefer*. Then there was also the *ibu* tent serving the same purpose: "The great harbor master Petiese spent seventy days in an embalming tent *(syh)* and he was buried in his tomb in Perwesiririr."

Since the property of Psenese and Tsenhor was in the Theban necropolis area, a place where mummies were processed would of course be a neighbor to expect. But there are all kinds of theories as to what the *per nefer* actually looked like. Was it really a tent erected near the entrance of a tomb or even inside the tomb, as some Egyptologists say? In that case, why would the scribe of P. Turin 2123 list it as a neighbor of Psenese's and Tsenhor's new property? Actually, we do have a picture of a *per nefer*. It comes from Theban Tomb C.4 from the time of Amunhotep III (1391–1353 BCE), which was visited and recorded more than once by early travelers. It is a small stone chapel with a door opening and the typical cavetto corniche crowning the roof. This makes perfect sense in a necropolis. And if we are to believe the Articles of Association and Rules of Procedure of the Theban choachytes from the Ptolemaic period (P. Berlin 3115), the funeral of a member would also involve two days of drinking at the *per nefer*.

The embalming workshop of Inaros and the house owned by Psenese and Tsenhor were located on the west bank of the Nile in the Tomb of Pharaoh l.p.h. Osorkon l.p.h. The name Osorkon takes us back to the dark ages of the Twenty-second to the Twenty-fourth Dynasties, a period of Libyan rule that lasted from around 945 BCE to 715 or 712 BCE. The Twenty-second Libyan Dynasty resided in Tanis, ruling Lower Egypt in the north. Middle and Upper Egypt were dominated by a line of priest-kings that would eventually become the Twenty-third Dynasty, likewise of Libyan origin. Some Egyptologists, however, believe that the Twenty-third Dynasty actually came from Lower Egypt and that this line of would-be kings from 'our' Twenty-third Dynasty in Upper Egypt was never included as a real dynasty in the famous classification of the royal houses of Egypt by the priest Manetho. The royal names used by both dynasties—Osorkon, Takelot, and Sheshonq—only add to the confusion. However, there was one Osorkon who was destined to become high priest of Amun in Thebes and eventually also the new pharaoh: Osorkon III, who ended a period of civil war in Thebes. But we have to start with his father Takelot II, who served as high priest of Amun in Thebes under the Tanite pharaoh Osorkon II. During the final years of this pharaoh's reign, which lasted from 872 to 837 BCE, Takelot proclaimed himself—or was proclaimed—the new king of Upper Egypt, ruling his part of the land as Takelot II (Takelot I again belonging to the line of Tanite kings). From his fortress in al-Hiba he continued to rule Thebes and surroundings under Pharaoh Sheshonq III, who succeeded Osorkon II in Tanis. Takelot's son Osorkon by his wife Karomama II—a daughter of Nimlot, Takelot's predecessor as high priest of Amun in Thebes—was destined to become the new high priest of Amun and pharaoh of Upper Egypt himself, and ultimately to change Egyptian history. But first he had to put down a number of revolts in Thebes, incited by an opponent known as Petebastet—often referred to as Pedubast or Pedubastis in the literature—and a would-be pharaoh called Sheshonq V. Or maybe that was IV (or VI).

Much of our information on this hazy period in Thebes comes from two inscriptions by a prince called Osorkon on the so-called Bubastite Gate in the forecourt of the temple of Amun in Karnak. These inscriptions are commonly referred to as *The Chronicle of Prince Osorkon*, following the scientific edition by Ricardo Caminos (Rome: Pontificium Institutum Biblicum, 1958). The first inscription tells of a successful military campaign by Osorkon—referring to himself as the "high priest of Amun, *generalissimo*, and leader Osorkon"—against the Theban insurgents in regnal year 11 of his father Takelot II (830 BCE). A large part of the first inscription, however, is taken up by a list of the lavish donations made by Osorkon to the Theban gods and their priesthoods.

The second inscription covers the regnal years 11–24 of Takelot II as well as years 22–29 of Sheshonq III, who succeeded Osorkon II in Tanis, ruling side by side with Takelot II in Upper Egypt. Since Osorkon also dated his inscription to the reign of Sheshonq III—who was the competing pharaoh from the north—we may assume that some form of courtesy was upheld between the ruling families. Osorkon was evidently not ready to proclaim himself pharaoh of Middle and Upper Egypt before he had stamped out the Theban rebellion once and for all.

In regnal year 11 of Takelot II, Osorkon, still based at the heavily fortified site of al-Hiba, took his army to Thebes, only to find that the inhabitants and the priests of the temple of Amun had opened the gates of the city and came out to offer flowers and prove their loyalty. They told Osorkon that he had saved them from a time "in which the laws had perished in the hands of those who rebelled against their lord, even though they were his own functionaries." This, of course, is once again the royal motif of a king restoring order, *ma'at*. To achieve this, the ringleaders of the Theban rebellion were led before Osorkon and after a summary trial they were burned alive to minimize their chances in the afterlife and as a warning to anyone wishing to rebel some more.

Osorkon also used this opportunity to issue an official decree that greatly benefited the divine domains of the Theban triad of Amun-Ra, Mut, and Khonsu, as well as the war god Montu and the goddess of justice Ma'at (as seen above, the inclusion of the latter two was no coincidence). However, it is probably correct to suggest that Osorkon's donations—including an eternal flame before the god, bird offerings, and tax exemptions for the priestly staff—may also have been designed to ensure the future loyalty of the Theban clergy.

The second inscription alludes to another revolt in regnal year 15 of Takelot II, sadly noting that "years went by in which one preyed upon his fellow unhindered." It seems Osorkon mounted another expedition, but unfortunately, or perhaps very conveniently, the inscription remains rather vague about the results. The only thing we learn is that once again the Theban priesthood—especially of Amun—was placated with donations, including a lotus-style silver altar of two hundred deben.

It may therefore have taken Osorkon years of struggle to get rid of the Theban insurgents. His reign as a true pharaoh only started around 777 (or 789) BCE, ending in 749 (or 761) BCE, meaning he may have been rather old when he came to the throne. Without further ado his son Takelot (III) was appointed as the new high priest of Amun in Thebes and his daughter Shepenupet became the divine adoratrice. In this way Osorkon III achieved a tight grip on the Theban priesthood. A few years before he died Takelot III became co-regent.

Some believe that King Osorkon lived to be ninety-three years old, a feat that has some parallels in ancient Egyptian history. Both Pepy II from the Old Kingdom (2575–2134 BCE) and Ramesses II from the New Kingdom (1550–1070 BCE) lived into their nineties. Age alone may therefore have made Osorkon something of a legendary figure in Thebes, as well as the fact that he had put an end to a period of civil war. This, then, would make him the most likely owner of the Tomb of Pharaoh l.p.h. Osorkon l.p.h., wherever this may be. Also, the other pharaohs called Osorkon are mostly associated with Lower Egypt, some being of very little significance. 'Our' Osorkon did build a new Osiris temple in the Karnak temple precinct and apparently was buried somewhere in the Theban necropolis, where his memory lingered on for centuries.

Expanding the Family Business
19 February 510 BCE (P. Louvre E 7128)

Elsewhere in the world great events were unfolding. The tyrant Hippias was chased out of Athens. In Italy the last Roman king, Lucius Tarquinius Superbus, gave way to the Roman Republic. He had come to power in 534 BCE, the same year in which Iturech, the second owner of the archive of Djekhy & Son, concluded a land lease with a beekeeper called Peteatum (P. Louvre E 7839). Shortly afterward Iturech was to vanish from the stage forever. And in 525 BCE the Persians had conquered Egypt.

But in Thebes in 510 BCE—far away from these events and under the strict but apparently just Persian rule of Darius I—business was good. Two years after Psenese and Tsenhor had decided to share a house of some sort in P. Turin 2123, they visited the office of the scribe Ip son of Teos once again. This time we even know the exact day on which this happened, 19 February 510 BCE. As a rule, early demotic contracts never mention the day date. The second witness on the back, however, was once again a grandson of a man called Nesmin (but not the same as in P. Turin 2123). Apparently he felt it would be wise to mention the date in a contract that concerned his aunt Tsenhor, who was a daughter of—perhaps—the same Nesmin.

Two years before, Psenese and Tsenhor had been planning to do some construction work on their shared new property in the necropolis. In the meantime the plot adjacent to theirs was put up for sale by the owner Tjayutayudeny son of Peteamunip, the overseer of the necropolis:

Regnal year 12, second month of the *akhet* season under Pharaoh l.p.h. Darius l.p.h. The overseer of the necropolis Tjayutayudeny son of Peteamunip, whose mother is Setairetbint, has said to the choachyte of the valley Psenese son of Heryrem, whose mother is Beniuutehtyes:

"You have satisfied my heart with the silver for this house (or building site) which is vacant in the Tomb of Pharaoh l.p.h. Osorkon in the west of Thebes, which is in ruins and measures five ground cubits, which makes five hundred square cubits, which makes five ground cubits again. Its south is the Processional Way of Amun, its north is the remainder of the house mentioned above, its west is the house of the choachyte of the valley Petehorresne son of Nesamunhotep, and its east is the good house of Inaros son of Iben. I have given to you this house mentioned above and you have satisfied my heart with the silver for it as well as the one-tenth for the representatives of Thebes to give it to the God's Offering of Amun."

After the opening statement, which is typical for an early demotic sale ("You have satisfied my heart with the silver for (item sold)"), Tjayuta-yudeny described the object sold. It was again called a *per*, so some kind of house or building site. It measured five ground cubits, which was five hundred square cubits. To avoid any tampering with the figures, the five ground cubits were broken into five hundred square cubits, making five ground cubits again. One square cubit being 0.275 square meters, the plot acquired by Psenese was 137.5 square meters, enough to build a house on but too small to grow crops.

"I have nothing to say whatsoever on account of it. No person on earth—including me—will be able to exercise authority over it except you, from today onward forever and ever. As to the person who will come to you on account of it in my name or in the name of any other person on earth, I will ensure that he will be far from you and that it is clear for you of any title or claim on earth. To you belong its contracts wherever they may be."

In the writing of the god's father of Montu Lord of Thebes and chief of priests of the temple of Montu in the fourth phyle Ip son of Teos son of Ip.

Psenese paid Tjayutayudeny not only the price—unlike in abnormal hieratic contracts, a price is never mentioned in early demotic sales—but also the 10 percent tax on sales payable to the representatives of Thebes to give it to the God's Offering of Amun, that is, the economic department of the Domain of Amun.

The 10 percent tax on sales of land and houses first occurs in abnormal hieratic sources from the seventh century BCE, such as P. Turin 2118 from regnal year 30 of Psamtik I (635 BCE). It was payable to a scribe of the Domain of Amun in Thebes, and sometimes also to people referred to as "the scribes and representatives in Thebes." In the Ptolemaic period many more taxes were invented to finance the state, including a poll tax, a tax on sheep, a dike tax, and many, many more, and the tax on sales now also included cattle and donations. All of a sudden, in the second century BCE, this tax appears to have been 5 percent, maybe the result of tax reform. In that case, why would the Ptolemaic kings—always looking for money to finance their court, economic projects, and wars—lower a tax that had already been set at 10 percent many centuries earlier? Then again, when Britain lowered the top rate from 60 to 40 percent in the 1980s, it actually increased tax revenues, because people became less inclined to find ways to avoid paying taxes.[3]

Although the tax on sales is not often mentioned in the Ptolemaic demotic contracts, people probably still had to pay it and then were given a separate receipt. Only later this receipt would be included in the (mandatory) Greek docket on demotic contracts.

If we now look at P. Louvre E 7128 again, we see that the tax was paid to the mysterious representatives of Thebes and that they would transfer the money to the God's Offering of Amun. One elegant way to make sense of this practice—for instance, why did people not simply pay directly to the scribes of Amun?—was proposed by the Dutch demotist Sven Vleeming, who investigated the tax. According to him, these representatives may have been representatives of the king, meaning that the revenues of this particular tax were probably divided between the royal and the divine domain, which would also help to explain the 5 and 10 percent figures.

Who Owns What?
The curious description of the northern neighbor to the plot sold in P. Louvre E 7128 raises a number of questions. We know—or at least we think we know—that the plot acquired here was adjacent to the plot divided between Psenese and Tsenhor in P. Turin 2123 some years before. Most of the neighbors mentioned in the two contracts are the same. In P. Turin 2123 the description says the southern neighbor was the Processional Way of Amun (see fig. 10).

However, the southern neighbor to Psenese's and Tsenhor's site listed in P. Turin 2123 was not the Processional Way of Amun after all. Apparently it was a property still owned by the overseer of the necropolis Tjayutayudeny.

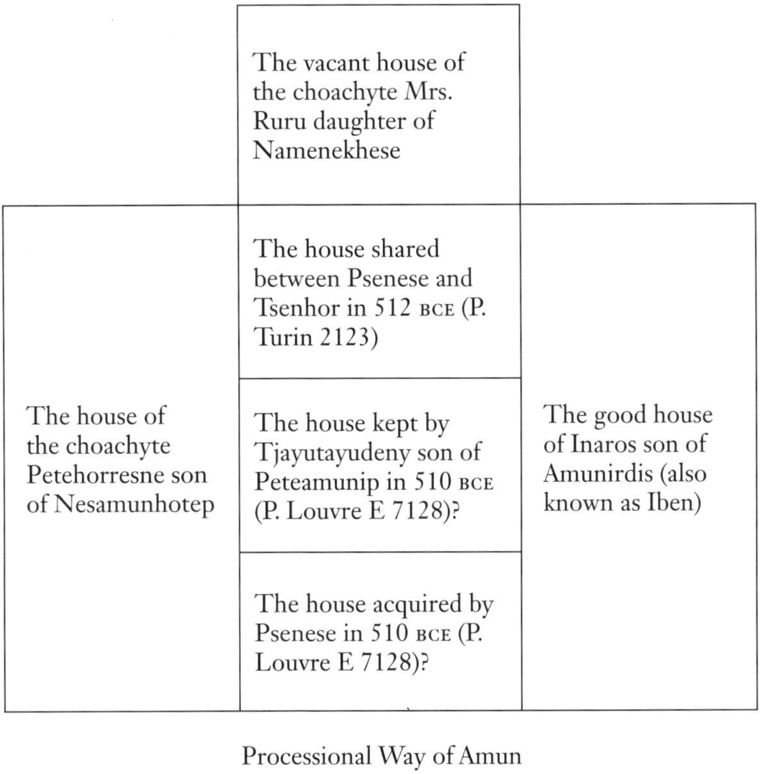

The vacant house of the choachyte Mrs. Ruru daughter of Namenekhese

The house of the choachyte Petehorresne son of Nesamunhotep

The house shared between Psenese and Tsenhor in 512 BCE (P. Turin 2123)

The house kept by Tjayutayudeny son of Peteamunip in 510 BCE (P. Louvre E 7128)?

The good house of Inaros son of Amunirdis (also known as Iben)

The house acquired by Psenese in 510 BCE (P. Louvre E 7128)?

Processional Way of Amun

Figure 11. Did Psenese and Tsenhor buy a split property?

Should one not expect the scribe Ip to have referred to the northern neighbor of the plot sold here in P. Louvre E 7128 as "your house, which is called the house of the choachyte Psenese son of Heryrem," or something similar? Instead, he described this northern neighbor as "the remainder of the house mentioned above," or what was left after the property was sold by Tjayutayudeny to Psenese. But that would create countless problems for Psenese and Tsenhor. What they hoped to achieve by buying the second property was of course direct access to the Processional Way of Amun, so it seems best to interpret Tjayutayudeny's statement "the remainder of the house mentioned above" as referring to the plot that had originally formed part of his property, which he had already sold to Psenese a few years before.

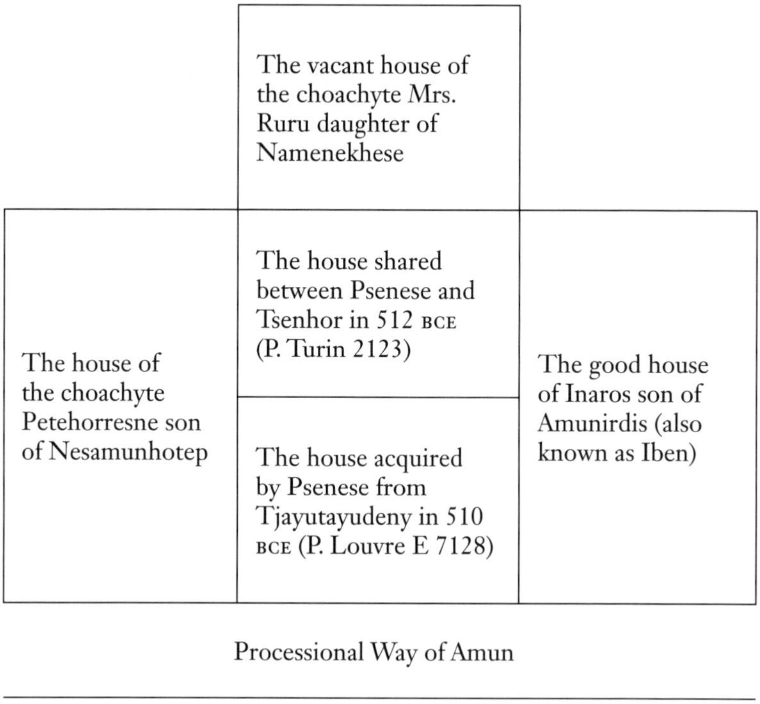

	The vacant house of the choachyte Mrs. Ruru daughter of Namenekhese	
The house of the choachyte Petehorresne son of Nesamunhotep	The house shared between Psenese and Tsenhor in 512 BCE (P. Turin 2123)	The good house of Inaros son of Amunirdis (also known as Iben)
	The house acquired by Psenese from Tjayutayudeny in 510 BCE (P. Louvre E 7128)	

Processional Way of Amun

Figure 12. The actual situation in 510 BCE

This would give Tsenhor and Psenese direct access to the Processional Way of Amun, without having to cross someone else's property, which could cause problems, and often did.

The Right of Way

Although P. Louvre E 7128 does not specifically mention it, the right of way was often a bone of contention in ancient Egypt. The Greek sources from Egypt generally contain a clause about the *eisodos* and *exodos*, 'entry to and exit from,' a plot or a house. These clauses are not as common in the demotic documents, although they are regularly found. Note, for instance, that when Tsenhor received a share of her father's house, she and her (half-)brother Nesamunhotep (and probably the other siblings, too) agreed to share the staircase (see "Dividing Dad's House" below). In the division of a house between Abigaia and Elizabeth (Coptic P. KRU 35), the two women involved made an agreement about the communal use of the door, the foyer, a water holder, and the staircase, although if at a later stage they decided to split up the house, each would be left with half a staircase. One assumes that the roof would also be shared, to sleep.

The most recent study of the right of way in legal documents was done by Schafik Allam.[4] In demotic P. Ashmolean Museum 14 and 15—a sale plus cession of property from 72 to 71 BCE—the seller is quite specific. The buyer gets the property,

> (. . .) (including) the path of exit [of the] house (and) its courtyard at its northern enclosure wall (. . .). And you will come in (and exit) through it together with your people and your goods so as to go to the house (. . .).

Since in demotic contracts concerning real estate the clause about the right of way is not a standard feature, this suggests that whenever it is there, it may have been included at the special request of the buyer, who had had a bad experience before. In the demotic P. BM EA 10071, for instance, the sale of part of a vineyard from the summer of 212 BCE, the seller—a Mrs. Horankh daughter of Hor and Tabastet—assures the buyer that "(the owner of the adjacent plot) will give you a path to the two plots in his share of the garden mentioned above (to) give water to your quarter of the garden mentioned above."

With a little imagination we can almost hear the buyer say in the scribe's office, "Yeah, right, and how do you propose I'm going to get to my plot once I've bought it?"

Once again P. Mattha (around 250 BCE), in this case col. VIII *l.* 1*ff.*, is able to enlighten us further, describing all sorts of bad things that could happen when people were building new houses. People could actually stop the building of a new house if the builder had stealthily extended the property by building on a public road. The builder would then be visited by the judicial authorities. Although the passage is severely damaged, it suggests that the judges would inspect the house and probably order the builder to pull down any part of it that had been built on the road. A man could also stop the building of a new house if the builder wanted to use his outer wall as his own. In that case the complainant would insist that there remain a space between his house and the new house of at least the length of a brick. And if we are to believe P. Mattha, it sometimes also happened that the builder of a new house simply appropriated a path belonging to the house that was already there (col. VIII *l.* 5–7 and 15–16). Some people are like that.

Dividing Dad's House
27 May–25 June 506 BCE (P. Turin 2125)

It was a hot day, probably between thirty-five and forty degrees Celsius. Tsenhor and her (half-)brother Nesamunhotep presented themselves in the office of the scribe Horsiese son of Psamtik. They had agreed to divide part of the inheritance of their father Nesmin, a building located on the west bank of the Nile, somewhere in the necropolis area.

From P. Louvre E 10935 we know that Nesmin was already active as a choachyte in 556 BCE, when he acquired a mortuary foundation field of eleven *aruras*—slightly over two and a half hectares—dedicated to an unknown Mrs. Tsenhor. If Nesmin was twenty years old when he closed this deal—sixteen being the likely age at which choachytes were expected to join the Association of Theban Choachytes—and if this division of the inheritance between Tsenhor and Nesamunhotep took place shortly after his death, this would mean Nesmin had reached the age of seventy, which was a rare occurrence in ancient Egypt. But the strange thing is that Nesmin is never mentioned in the official records of the Theban choachytes (P. Louvre E 7840). These were written between 542 and 538 BCE, which suggests that he did not attend the annual New Year's reception or the anniversary of the patron saint of the choachytes, Amunhotep son of Hapu, for at least four years in a row.

Apart from Nesamunhotep and Tsenhor, two other (half-)brothers were involved in the division of Nesmin's inheritance, which we may glean from a clause at the end of the contract : "(. . .) whereas the storehouse which is in the storehouse that I have given to you belongs to the four of us again." These (half-)brothers went by the names Inaros and Burekhef, but the name of their mother remains unknown. The division of the house of Nesmin therefore included at least two other contracts made by Nesamunhotep for Inaros and Burekhef, similar to the one made for Tsenhor:

Regnal year 16, second month of the *peret* season under Pharaoh l.p.h. Darius l.p.h. The choachyte of the valley Nesamunhotep son of Petemin, whose mother is Tays, has said to Mrs. Tsenhor daughter of Nesmin, whose mother is Ruru:

"I have given to you a large space of the house of Nesmin, our father. Its north is the house of Pakep, its south the house of Iturech son of Namenekhese, its east is the Processional Way of Amun, and its west is the . . . . Its staircase is shared between us, as is the large space that belongs to both of us. I have given to you the storehouse in the court, whereas the storehouse which is in the storehouse that I have given to you belongs to the four of us again."

In the writing of Horsiese son of Psamtik.

The house of Nesmin that was partly inherited by Tsenhor was adjacent to the Processional Way of Amun, so that once again this may have been a building in the Theban necropolis on the west bank of the Nile. We know, for instance, that the choachytes from the Ptolemaic period lived in and around Djeme on the west bank. But unlike the Processional Way of Amun mentioned in P. Turin 2123 and P. Louvre E 7128, this avenue ran from north to south, parallel to the Nile, perhaps—as has been suggested—leading to Medinet Habu. Once again the word used to denote Nesmin's property is *per*, a word that has a wide range of meanings, including 'house' (although in demotic one would expect *awy*), 'building site,' and '(divine) domain.' Some of the neighboring structures—from P. Louvre E 7840 we know that the southern neighbor Iturech son of Namenekhese was a choachyte as well—were also houses. Medinet Habu was an important burial site that contained private tombs and the tombs of a number of singers of the interior of Amun (see "Four Hundred and One Little Workers" below).

What if this house was located on the east bank of the Nile and really was a house to live in? What if this Processional Way of Amun was actually the large avenue that ran all the way from Karnak to Luxor, and the house was the house where Tsenhor was born?

Did Nesmin Make a Will?
We assume that Tsenhor's father Nesmin made a will in which he divided his possessions among his four children. If there was a will, it would have been kept by Tsenhor's eldest brother Nesamunhotep after their father died.

Although the division of Nesmin's house among his children does not mention the precise share received by Tsenhor—only referring to a large space and an additional storehouse, apart from the shared spaces—from P. Turin 2127 we know that Nesamunhotep gave her one-quarter of the revenues from the funerary services provided for a policeman and his family in 491 BCE in return for her work. Also, the fact that part of the house would be shared among the four siblings suggests that Tsenhor had in fact received one-quarter of the house as well, and that a will had been made by Nesmin listing the shares that were to be allotted to each of his surviving children.

It is not certain, however, that Nesmin had only recently died. It often happened that the parental estate would be managed by the eldest son for some time, with the revenues shared among the siblings. In fact, according to the famous demotic legal manual P. Mattha (around 250 BCE), if the father had neglected to make a will, the eldest son could do pretty much as he pleased, taking by far the largest share. He would then draw up a list of all the siblings who would share in the remainder of the inheritance, including the ones who had already died. This was important, because the shares of deceased siblings would fall to him. As is the case today, the division of an inheritance often led to friction in the family, as we saw in the case of Tufhapy and his sister-in-law Khratyankh (see "A Woman with a Mind of Her Own" above). If we combine this with the fact that the more dead siblings were listed by the eldest brother, the more he would get, we have all the necessary ingredients for a family feud (one other procedure to divide the inheritance, the casting of lots, would probably also often lead to sour faces).

The case below is from P. Mattha col. IX *l.* 5*ff*, neatly illustrating that conflict over an inheritance happened regularly, which is probably why it was included in the legal manual:

> If the younger brother files a complaint, saying: "The children of which our eldest brother says they are of our father: they are not the children of our father." As to the children of which the younger brother has said, "They are not of our father," one will oblige the eldest brother to swear an oath about them, saying, "The children of whom I said that they were of our father, they are (the children) of our father. I have not lied about them." One will then oblige him to say their names and at the same time (the name of) their mother. Template of the oath that one will make him swear, saying: "So-and-so son of So-and-so whose

mother is Mrs. So-and-so: they are the children of my father. They have died before their father died." As for the one about whom he has not sworn an oath, one cannot give him a share, but as to the one about whom he has sworn an oath, one will have to give him a share.

So even if the eldest son made a list that much favored him, and if a younger brother (or all of the siblings) filed a complaint against him, if he was prepared to take a false temple oath he could obtain the shares of any nonexistent brothers and sisters. This would essentially be a battle between fear of the gods and greed, one of the powerful human traits still shaping the face of this world today. Unfortunately P. Mattha is often not specific enough, although col. IX *l.* 9*ff* seems to suggest that even in this case there was still something the other siblings could do. One assumes that the case below also refers to an intestate division of the inheritance:

If a man dies and [his possessions are (already) in the hands of his] eldest [son], and if it so happens that the latter has a younger brother and that he files a complaint, saying, "Let them give us a share of the possessions of our father," one will divide [. . .] in accordance with the number of children, giving an additional share to the eldest son to complete two shares.

The fact that Tsenhor may have received one-quarter of her father's house—she would in fact herself divide her inheritance equally between her son and daughter in 517 BCE, stating that they would have to share with any future brothers or sisters—suggests that Nesmin made a will and that she shared equally with her three brothers. But is this proof that women always had the same rights as men in ancient Egypt? Probably not. It so happens that P. Mattha col. IX *l.* 14ff. informs us what would happen if a man died without a will, and, even worse, without a son:

If a man dies without having a male child, but having female children, one will have to divide his possessions into shares [in accordance with the number of his] female children, [and one will give a share to each of the] female children of his, except the additional share of a child. [One will] give it to his eldest daughter [. . .] to complete two shares. If the eldest daughter says, "My father had other children, but they have died. Let me be given their shares," one cannot give to her the shares of her brothers who died.

Some animals would always be more equal than others. So even if ancient Egyptian women were equal to men in a legal sense, in specific cases—such as an intestate inheritance—the sons of the family were slightly more equal.

If we now return to Tsenhor, who apparently received one-quarter of her father's inheritance, as did each of her three siblings, we are left with two questions. Did she not receive a dowry when she married for the first time? The dowry has been given as one possible reason why women often received less when the parental inheritance was divided. And does this mean that their father Nesmin did not allot an additional share to her eldest brother Nesamunhotep? In that case Tsenhor was indeed a very fortunate woman. It would also go a long way toward explaining why she divided her own inheritance equally between her son and daughter. As did her husband. No exceptions.

Inheriting a House in Coptic Djeme

Ideally, the study of ancient Egyptian legal documents should not be confined to demotic, although sadly this is exactly what mostly happens in Egyptology, partly because the discipline is split into different areas—Middle Egyptian, Late Egyptian, demotic, Coptic, archaeology, religion, and so forth—or specializations, and partly because it is dangerous to assume that things did not change over the course of thousands of years. One could of course argue that in order to understand the demotic legal texts better, one should have some idea of what happens in the hieratic and Coptic contracts. But in reality this is only seldom the case. Fortunately, once again Terry Wilfong's *Women of Jeme* (2002) comes to the rescue, in a chapter on the division of a house between two Coptic women living in Djeme in the eighth century AD. As will be seen later on, some of the specific clauses included in the contract would have been instantly understandable to Tsenhor, and fortunately also to us.

The women involved are Abigaia daughter of Samuel and Elizabeth daughter of Epiphanios. Abigaia's mother Tshenoute was Elizabeth's sister. When Tshenoute's and Elizabeth's father Epiphanios died, Elizabeth took their mother Maria into her home, where she lived with her second husband Abraham and their children Isak and Kyra. Elizabeth also had a son from her first marriage, Georgios, who often needed financial support.

Perhaps in AD 719 Maria died and left a house (see fig. 13). The division document, essentially similar to the document that Tsenhor received from Nesamunhotep, is P. KRU 35, a papyrus of 144 x 18 cm containing

115 lines of Coptic following a Kufic Arabic and Greek summary of the contract. That is indeed one of the differences between demotic and Coptic contracts: the latter are generally of sleep-inducing length. In fact, this contract forms part of an archive. It was written on 6 October AD 719, and starts with all sorts of pious invocations that most Coptologists (and we) will gladly skip.

Since most people have probably never laid eyes on a Coptic division of an inheritance, it may be a good thing to study it in some detail (so once again we will borrow heavily from Terry Wilfong's book on the women of Coptic Djeme):

On this day, the eighth day of Phaophi of the third indiction year (an administrative period), before the most honored and exalted Biktor son of the late Thomas and Ananias son of the late Abraham, the *lashanes* (financial managers) of the Kastron Djeme in the district of the city of Armant (Hermonthis), greetings.

I, Abigaia daughter of Samuel, deacon and monk of the mountain of Djeme, my mother being the late Tshenoute, with my husband Daniel, agreeing in everything, (we ourselves being also) people from the Kastron Djeme in the district of the city of Armant.

We write for Elizabeth daughter of the late Epiphanios, her mother being the late Maria, being people of the Kastron Djeme in the same district. We make this arrangement with each other and we will provide the ones who will sign below with trustworthy and reliable witnesses for them. These who will act as witnesses to this arrangement (do so) at our own request. Greetings.

At this point the first tangible thing about the division of the house still has to be said. Most Theban demotic scribes would have been finished by now, so in this respect the Arab rule of Egypt did not do much to alleviate the burden placed on its citizens by bureaucracy. But many of the clauses sound quite familiar, even if demotic—including its legal tradition—had been out of use for hundreds of years by now. So if the demotic clauses are actually the forerunners of the Coptic clauses we see here, this can only have happened through Greek, which filled the gap of a few hundred years between the written demotic and Coptic contracts.[5] Still, when it comes to the actual division of the three-story house this contract could have been written in Thebes or Memphis a thousand years earlier.

Although the contract makes mention of Abigaia's husband agreeing to this division, it is essentially a contract between two women only:

> Since at this time we agreed unanimously among ourselves to divide the house of our deceased one among ourselves in this manner, so that the portion of each will be evident, and we indicated them for you, namely Elizabeth, the sister of my late mother. You have received the room beneath the stairs and the room whose door opens north onto the stairs, and you control the whole veranda, whose door opens north onto the stairs, and the entire grain storage area, which is above the veranda, up to the top. As for the one who wants to build it, it is his to the limit, and he can bring up his staircase up to his portion. The outer door, the foyer, the water holder, and the stairway are common areas between us, unless building is carried out on the house. If building is done, then each one will bring his staircase to his portion, in such a way that we are each satisfied with the two portions.

Interestingly, the first room mentioned that Elizabeth will receive is also the most intimate one in the Egyptian woman's life, the space under the stairs, where the women would sit out their period of menstruation (see "The Days on Which Tsenhor Did Not Work" below). In total, the two women received approximately seventy square meters. In Wilfong's hypothetical reconstruction of the house we see that it would be more or less split into two equal parts—including the shared roof where they could sleep—and there is even a provision about making a separate entrance in the part of the house owned by Elizabeth.

There follows a description of the neighbors of the property that is also common in demotic contracts, as is the guarantee that the new owner is entitled to his or her part of the property. At this point in demotic sales we often also see a guarantee clause against third parties who may claim (part of) the property, for instance if a house had already been promised to them as security for a loan. In that case the seller would have to pay a fine. And indeed it is also there in P. KRU 35. The women promise not to file suit against each other, which extends to their children, heirs, or legal representatives, or else they will have to pay four ounces of gold or twenty-four four-and-a-half-gram *solidi* of pure gold. Ridiculous fines such as this, probably two or three times the value of the house, are very common in such Coptic documents. After a pious oath the whole arrangement closes with a statement that the contract will be in duplicate—one for each party—and that the sale has been publicly announced, carrying the risk that an old creditor might turn up on Abigaia's or Elizabeth's doorstep. The contract was signed by a number of witnesses. In some ways Egyptian culture remained unchanged for thousands of years indeed.

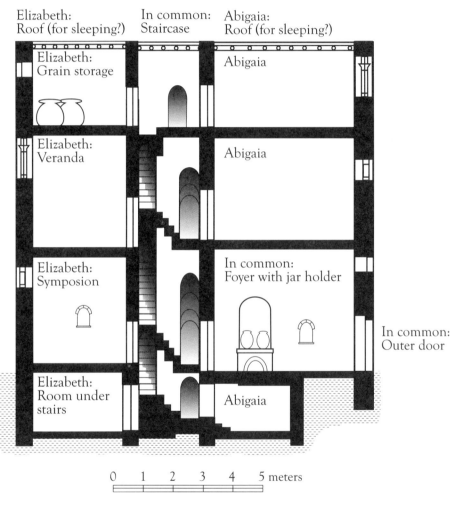

Figure 13. The house of Abigaia and Elizabeth in Coptic Djeme [from Terry Wilfong, *Women of Jeme: Lives in a Coptic Town in Late Antique Egypt* (Ann Arbor, MI: University of Michigan Press, 2002), 52]

6

Cattle: Burekhef and Ituru, 507–487 BCE

Was There a Rent-a-Cow in Thebes?
26 July–24 August 507 BCE (P. Turin 2124)

P. Turin 2124 was made out by the cattle-keeper of the Domain of Montu Pawahamun son of Petemontu for Burekhef, the (half-)brother of Tsenhor. In this contract—a receipt—Pawahamun states that he is satisfied with the compensation for a cow that Burekhef leased the previous year, presumably to work some fields.

Pawahamun's father, the cattle-keeper of the Domain of Montu Petemontu, is well known from the archive of Djekhy & Son, where he is seen leasing land from one of the owners of the archive (P. Louvre E 7836) as well as from a priest called Wedjahor (P. Louvre E 7833 and 7837). All the papyri dealing with Petemontu were found with the archive of Djekhy & Son, meaning that Petemontu and Iturech—the son and second owner of the archive—had a close (business) relationship. The explanation for this may in part be that, as a cattle-keeper of Montu Petemontu could easily lay his hands on the livestock needed to work the extended fields of Djekhy & Son. In other words, he had access to the boss's John Deere tractor on the weekends, and Iturech owned more than ten hectares of land located somewhere to the north of Qurna on the west bank of the Nile, which would have been a few miles from Thebes, where he lived.

As so often in ancient Egyptian sources, we do not know who actually owned these cows. Did Petemontu use cows that belonged to the Domain of Montu for some moonlighting on the side? Or did he have his own regular Rent-a-Cow that in due time was inherited by his son Pawahamun, the declaring party in P. Turin 2124?

P. Turin 2124 came to the Museo Egizio in Turin in 1823 as part of a lot that had been kept together since antiquity, as the consecutive inventory numbers P. Turin 2122–2128 suggest. They can all be tied in with Tsenhor and her relatives. The only logical conclusion is that this lot from Turin was most certainly once an integral part of Tsenhor's archive.

Table 8. The Turin papyri from Tsenhor's archive

P. Turin	Beneficiary
2122	Tsenhor
2123	Tsenhor
2124	Brother of Tsenhor
2125	Tsenhor
2126	Daughter of Tsenhor (Ruru)
2127	Tsenhor
2128	Son of Tsenhor (Ituru)

P. Turin 2122 seems the odd one out, because this contract was made for a Mr. Tjauheser, who was no relative of Tsenhor. It is the title deed to a young slave made in 517 BCE. Almost immediately after he bought the slave, Tjauheser sold him to Tsenhor (P. Bibl. Nat. 223), who also received the title deed P. Turin 2122 as the new owner. If the Turin lot 2122–2128 was indeed part of Tsenhor's own archive, how did P. Turin 2124 end up there? This contract was made for Tsenhor's brother Burekhef, who had apparently leased a cow to plow a field. But which field, and why didn't Burekhef deposit it in his own archive? We know that Tsenhor and her three brothers divided part of the inheritance of their father Nesmin in 506 BCE (P. Turin 2125).

Some Egyptologists believe that Tsenhor also inherited the eleven *aruras* acquired by Nesmin in 556 BCE (P. Louvre E 10935). If these had been donated to her directly by her father—because she was given the exclusive right to look after the needs of her namesake, the deceased Mrs. Tsenhor, who died in or shortly before 556 BCE—this could only have happened with the explicit consent of her brothers. Since the eldest son Nesamunhotep could exercise major rights over the inheritance (see "Did Nesmin Make a Will?" above), it is difficult to see how Tsenhor's brothers would have consented to letting her have eleven *aruras* of high-quality farmland without any compensation, so their father Nesmin would have had some difficulty compensating her three brothers for the loss of these *aruras*.

A typical and perfect ancient Egyptian solution would have been to leave the property intact, as in the case of the house that Tsenhor and her brother Nesamunhotep divided only in 506 BCE—a deal that also involved their (half-)brothers Inaros and Burekhef (P. Turin 2125). It is also probably not a coincidence that Tsenhor's eldest brother allotted a quarter of the income from some mummies to Tsenhor in 491 BCE (P. Turin 2127). It was often better to co-own a property and to share the revenues. This would be where P. Turin 2124 fits in. Could it be that Burekhef leased the cow from Pawahamun to work the eleven *aruras* that were actually only co-owned by Tsenhor together with her three brothers? It is at least a convenient explanation.

Regnal year 15, fourth month of the *peret* season under Pharaoh l.p.h. Darius l.p.h. The cattle-keeper of the Domain of Montu Lord of Thebes Pawahamun son of Petemontu, whose mother is Nesirkay, has said to the choachyte of the valley Burekhef son of Nesmin:

"You have satisfied my heart with the compensation for my red female plowing ox, which is called by the name of Ta . . . that I gave you to plow with from regnal year 14 to regnal year 15. My heart is satisfied with its compensation.

"I have nothing on earth to say against you on account of it. As for the person who will come to you on account of it in my name or in the name of any other person on earth, I will cause him to be far from you. If I do not cause him to be far from you, I will give you one (deben) of cast silver from the Treasury of Ptah because of it."

In the writing of the god's father of Montu Lord of Thebes Ip son of Teos.

Pawahamun states before Burekhef, "You have satisfied my heart with the compensation for my red female plowing ox." This is a free variant of the opening statement of an early demotic sale, "You have satisfied my heart with the silver for (item sold)." Although many of the clauses in this contract remind one of a sale, the use of 'compensation' instead of 'silver' suggests that this is actually a receipt for Burekhef after he paid for the lease of the cow. Since it was paid sometime in July or August, the obvious conclusion is that Pawahamun was paid in kind with a share of the harvest of the eleven (and most likely more) *aruras* owned by Tsenhor and her brothers.

Even if cattle daily eat up to 4 percent of their own body weight, depending on the quality of feed, starting a Rent-a-Cow business could be lucrative, as the example of P. Louvre E 7833 and 7837 (535 BCE) from the archive of Djekhy & Son shows. These leases feature a lessor-priest called Wedjahor and Pawahamun's father Petemontu. Both texts are land leases dealing with a number of fields. Since Petemontu was a cattle-keeper of Montu, one assumes that he would have been the one to supply the plowing animals, but in both contracts it was actually Wedjahor who managed to slip in his own cows to increase his profit. In P. Louvre E 7833 Wedjahor received one-third of the harvest as the landlord and an additional half because he provided the seed corn and two cows belonging to his brother. As the landlord in P. Louvre E 7837 he managed to wangle one-third of the harvest and an additional 11.1 percent for one cow supplied by him (the lessees brought in five cows). Wedjahor obviously liked to play hardball.

The Collection of Bernardino Drovetti

The Tsenhor papers from Turin (P. Turin 2122–2128) all come from the Drovetti collection. After joining the Piedmontese Hussars—who would eventually be incorporated into the French army—Bernardino Michele Maria Drovetti (1776–1852) worked as a judge and minister of war in the province of Piedmont. He also served as Napoleon's consul-general in Alexandria, where he became an avid collector and antiquities dealer with a knack for overpricing and destroying artefacts to increase the value of the remaining pieces.

When in 1823 or 1824 he sold his collection, which was to become the backbone of the Museo Egizio in Turin, no fewer than 5,268 items—including 170 papyri—changed hands. Tsenhor's papers were a part of this. Other lots were sold to the Louvre (1827) and the Berlin Museum (1836). These later sales did not include any Tsenhor papyri. As we will see below, some of the other Tsenhor papyri were acquired by one of Drovetti's competitors, Giovanni Anastasi (1780–1860), to be sold in 1857 at an auction to the Louvre and the British Museum.

The nineteenth century was the era of the great collectors of Egyptian antiquities, such as Drovetti, Salt, Anastasi, and Belzoni. The European market was flooded with Egyptian antiquities in the years after Napoleon's expedition to Egypt (1798–1801), which included a team of scientists tasked with preparing a description of the land and its cultural treasures. The expedition was not a huge military success, despite a massive task

Table 9. Where do Tsenhor's papyri come from?

Inventory Number	Acquired	From
P. Bibl. Nat. 216	Unknown	Unknown
P. Bibl. Nat. 217	Unknown	Unknown
P. Bibl. Nat. 223	Unknown	Unknown
P. BM EA 10120A	1857	Anastasi collection
P. BM EA 10120B	1857	Anastasi collection
P. Louvre AF 9761	Unknown	Unknown
P. Louvre E 3231A	1857	Anastasi collection
P. Louvre E 3231B*	1857	Anastasi collection
P. Louvre E 3231C*	1857	Anastasi collection
P. Louvre E 7128	1881	Publisher Leroux
P. Louvre E 10935	1901	Public auction in Paris
P. Turin 2122	1823 or 1824	Drovetti collection
P. Turin 2123	1823 or 1824	Drovetti collection
P. Turin 2124	1823 or 1824	Drovetti collection
P. Turin 2125	1823 or 1824	Drovetti collection
P. Turin 2126	1823 or 1824	Drovetti collection
P. Turin 2127	1823 or 1824	Drovetti collection
P. Turin 2128	1823 or 1824	Drovetti collection
P. Vienna KM 3853	1821 (?)	Inscribed in the inventory book of the museum in 1824

* For P. Louvre E 3231B and C, see "The Missing Tsenhor Papyri" below.

force that included thirteen ships of the line, forty-two frigates, and 130 transport ships carrying thirty-four thousand troops, seven hundred horses, and a thousand field guns (about as many as the Dutch army had in 1940 to repel the German invasion). The British were evidently not deceived—at least not for very long—by the false rumor that Napoleon was planning to invade Ireland. In the end Horatio Nelson beat the French near the Egyptian coast, cutting off the French ground troops from their homeland (and essential logistics) and forcing Napoleon to flee to France in disgrace. If he had won the war, the famous Rosetta Stone—found in 1799 by French officer Pierre-François Bouchard—would now be in the Louvre instead of the British Museum.

The scientific part of the expedition, however, was a huge success. The *Description de l'Égypte* became the final product of approximately 160 scientists and two thousand artists. It was published in twenty-three volumes in 1809, for the first time revealing the full splendor of ancient Egypt to a mass audience. It caused a collective hype that would become known as 'Egyptomania,' which spread rapidly across Europe, influencing fashion and furniture and creating a healthy appetite for Egyptian antiquities with the European elite (and museums).

If we then try to group the Tsenhor papyri—seventeen if we follow the traditional classification and nineteen if we include P. Louvre E 3231B and C—we see that seven of them were sold by Drovetti in 1823 or 1824. These were given consecutive inventory numbers in the Museo Egizio, which means that within the large Drovetti collection they still formed a separate lot that could therefore only have been stashed away in antiquity by Tsenhor herself (or one of her children). Around this time P. Vienna KM 3853 was sold to the Kunsthistorisches Museum in Vienna, so even if this had been found with the Turin lot it was not sold to Drovetti by one of his many Egyptian agents but to someone else. It could of course be that P. Vienna KM 3853 was not found with the Turin papyri.

The second large sale was in 1857, when two Tsenhor papyri were sold to the British Museum (P. BM EA 10120A and B) and three to the Louvre (P. Louvre E 3231A through C). P. BM EA 10120B was written for Tsenhor's husband Psenese in March 517 BCE to establish the rights to the inheritance of his (and Tsenhor's) daughter Ruru, who must have been a small child at that time. In P. Louvre E 3231A (497 BCE) the same Ruru receives four *aruras* of land in return for her services as a choachyte. Both documents should have been kept together, either in Ruru's own archive or in the archive of her husband (or a trustee) or even as part of the greater Tsenhor archive. Does this mean that these five documents—including P. BM EA 10120A, the marital property settlement between Psenese and Tsenhor—were all kept together already in antiquity, presumably by Tsenhor and then by her daughter Ruru, or do we have to assume that through sheer luck Giovanni Anastasi acquired no fewer than five Tsenhor papyri from various dealers? Another distinct possibility (even though we cannot prove it) is that Anastasi acquired all of the remaining Tsenhor papyri that did not end up in Vienna and Turin, meaning that P. Bibl. Nat. 216, 217, and 223 (acquisition date and provenance unknown), P. Louvre E 7128 (from the private collection of Leroux in 1881), and P. Louvre AF 9761 (bought at a public auction in Paris in 1901) can all be traced back to the Paris Anastasi sale of 1857, first going to private collections and then ending up in the Bibliothèque Nationale and the Louvre. This appears to be a scenario worth investigating in the future. In that case, the Tsenhor papers would have been found as two lots, or three if we count the Vienna papyrus as a separate find, which is somehow difficult to believe in view of the dates of purchase. There are other documented cases in which a family archive was found hidden in a number of separate jugs. In any case there is some comfort to be found here: *Si non è vero, è ben trovato.*

A Cow Branded with the Milk Can
21 June–20 July 487 BCE (P. Turin 2128)

Some time after their daughter Ruru was born in or before 517 BCE, Tsenhor and her husband Psenese had a son who was named Ituru. Tsenhor's mother had been called Ituru and Ruru for short, so it appears that both children were named after Tsenhor's mother. This would be in line with the picture we have of a no-nonsense businesswoman used to making her own decisions. We know that Tsenhor had three (half-)brothers, and we also know that ancient Egyptians liked to name their children after their parents, so there were most likely already several cousins called Petemin or Nesmin in the family, after Tsenhor's father.

If we assume that Tsenhor did have her way, this would suggest that Psenese—an ancient Egyptian man living 2,500 years ago—was liberal enough to let her decide. Or maybe she was simply wearing the pants. It is an attractive thought, but we have no way of knowing and in all likelihood we are seeing things through a modern looking-glass that were never actually there.

In any case Ituru would have been born after 517 BCE, but this could easily also be 510 BCE if Tsenhor had any miscarriages or lost some children in the period in between. Also, nothing is heard of her son Peteamunhotep after he first appears in the Tsenhor papers in 517 BCE. Did he die, move to another city, or fall out with his parents? The fact that the contract that gave him the rights to half of Tsenhor's possessions (P. Bibl. Nat. 216) was found with its counterpart for his sister Ruru (P. Bibl. Nat. 217)—which may have been part of a larger find of Tsenhor papyri (see "The Collection of Bernardino Drovetti" above)—is slightly worrying. In order to prove his right to his mother's inheritance, Peteamunhotep should have kept this document in his own archive. Unless of course Tsenhor had insisted that she would keep the documents herself as long as she was alive (which is what most people do).

The problem with Tsenhor is that we know of only three of her children who lived beyond the crucial age of five. Ancient Egyptian women of course used contraceptives, like a pessary made from crocodile dung and tampons soaked in honey and date paste. Alternatively, Tsenhor could have taken a mixture of beer, celery, and oil that was heated and drunk for four days in a row. Most treatments probably also included magic spells. While some of these household solutions may have worked—the thought of having sex with a woman smelling of crocodile dung in a specific place may not have acted as a powerful aphrodisiac in the first place—ancient Egyptian women nonetheless generally had a lot of children. And many women and children died in childbirth.

If the contraceptives and the magic did not work, Tsenhor may have been pregnant at least ten times between her fourteenth and thirty-fifth years, which is probably a low figure. Even if the death of newborn children was a fact of life—just as Tsenhor's survival of another delivery each time would have been something of a miracle—it may be that at times something snapped in her head and her reproductive system. This is not at all far-fetched.

In my family archive—which starts in the nineteenth century, although we can trace the family name back to the sixteenth century, where the trail disappears—I keep a photo of a baby. Most people think this is my dad. He was born in 1927, even though his passport said 1928 (it is a long story). The baby has a very dark complexion. It is clearly a child of mixed Dutch–Indonesian blood (we come from the former Dutch East Indies, and many of my forefathers married or cohabitated with local women). This is my father's eldest sister Joyce. She was born and died in 1916. They say my Indonesian grandmother's grief was so great that she did not have another pregnancy for years on end. Her body simply refused to consider it. My father was only born eleven years after his sister's death. He became my grandmother's favorite child.

After 2,500 years, it is of course impossible to reconstruct what happened in Tsenhor's household (or her mind) after she gave birth to Ruru in 517 BCE or in some earlier year. But it would not be a big surprise if something similar happened here. Also, it is by no means certain that Ituru was born soon after Ruru.

In the end Ruru and Ituru would be the only living children Tsenhor and Psenese had (the son from her first marriage is believed to have died in the meantime). Very modern, of course, but a family of four was extremely small by Egyptian standards. Still, Ituru lived, and by the time P. Turin 2128 was written he would have been in his twenties or his early thirties. By this time Tsenhor was about sixty-three, well over the ancient Egyptian retirement age.

The contract between the unknown cattle-keeper Iturech son of Horemsaf ('Horus is his protection') and Ituru, who is referred to as "the choachyte of the necropolis of Djeme," is—as so often—straightforward. Ituru gave a cow to Iturech and received one in return. What is striking, however, is that the cow coming from Ituru's or his parents' stable was branded with a mark designating a Theban agricultural area that is well known from the archive of Djekhy & Son. It was a mark in the shape of a milk can. The Domain of Amun owned a piece of land on the west bank of the Nile, slightly to the north of Qurna. It was known as The Stable of the Milk Can of Amun. This area, which is also mentioned in P. Louvre E 3231A, was used to grow crops and graze the cattle of Amun, which were branded with the mark in the shape of a milk can. The question then becomes how Tsenhor or her son Ituru acquired this cow, which at some point was obviously owned by Amun. It seems unlikely that they stole it. The mere fact that the actual brand is mentioned in the contract suggests that it was Ituru's cow. Apparently the Domain of Amun sold off its surplus cows, the same way governments sell their surplus cars today (this is actually still called the domain sale in the Netherlands).

Regnal year 35, third month of the *peret* season under Pharaoh l.p.h. Darius l.p.h. The cattle-keeper Iturech son of Horemsaf, whose mother is Neshor, has said to the choachyte of the necropolis of Djeme Ituru son of Psenese, whose mother is Tsenhor:
"I have given to you this red cow branded with the three . . . on its hind leg in exchange for your female red cow branded with the milk can that you have given to me. It is yours, it is your cow.

"As for the person who will come to you on account of it, saying, 'This is not your cow,' I will cause him to be far from you. If I do not cause him to be far from you, I will give you one (deben) of cast silver from the Treasury of Ptah without citing any contract on earth against you."

In the writing of Wesirweris son of Nespameter.

If the cow had been stolen, one would assume that Tsenhor's son would at least have taken the trouble to change the brand. There is one papyrus from the New Kingdom (1550–1070 BCE)—believed by some to belong to the famous Harem Conspiracy Papyri—showing that the practice of rebranding cattle did exist. It is a fragmentary papyrus containing only three lines and a tiny fraction of a fourth that was found in Thebes in the coffin of a mummy. It is now kept in the Musée Auguste Grasset in Varzy, hence the name Papyrus de Varzy. Although the gist of the text is difficult to grasp, it seems the papyrus was written during a legal inquiry involving some cattle that had been stolen from a man and subsequently rebranded.

Cows branded with a mark of a divine domain were actually traded more often, and one supposes that in those cases this was also done in good faith. The demotic P. Loeb 41 was written in regnal year 2 of Psamtik IV (485 BCE), who was a short-lived native king in the period when Darius I was succeeded by Xerxes I, although some authors believe that the Psamtik mentioned could also be Psamtik I or even Psamtik III (this is what keeps Egyptologists busy). In the contract one party addresses the other, stating, "You are my business partner in half of this female red cow, which is branded with the obelisk and the milk can, which we have bought between us, the two men."

Since the name of the god Amun was sometimes written with the sign for an obelisk, this brand could very well be interpreted as a designation of The Stable of the Milk Can of Amun, especially because the rules of Egyptian writing require the god's name to be written first. This is called 'honorific transposition' and it happens all the time in ancient Egyptian. It is a very clever solution (not mine), although the unsurpassed *Wörterbuch der Aegyptischen Sprache* only lists writings of Amun with just an obelisk for the Ptolemaic period, when hieroglyphic writing became highly cryptic (very much on purpose) and the number of available hieroglyphs rose from a few hundred to thousands. During this period scribes started assigning different phonetic meanings to known hieroglyphs used on temple walls, but this was centuries after P. Loeb 41 was written.

So, if anyone living in Thebes was buying or selling a cow with the brand of an obelisk and a milk can on its hind part and was asked to describe the brand of the cow for a scribe to record, and if the obelisk really represented Amun, wouldn't he or she just have said "(the brand of) the Milk Can of Amun" instead of "the obelisk and the milk can"?

Actually there is another papyrus from the reign of Hakoris (reigned around 392–380 BCE), P. BM EA 10846.1–2, in which a calf is said to be branded with "the obelisk," but this time the word for obelisk is written in full, including a determinative, rendering a reading of the obelisk as Amun even more uncertain. So the discussion about this extremely small detail from ancient Egyptian agrarian history seems far from over. It could well be that the obelisk and the milk can represented the two domains this cow belonged to, the last being The Stable of the Milk Can of Amun.

P. Turin 2128 belongs to the Turin lot assembled in antiquity by Tsenhor, meaning that it comes from Tsenhor's archive proper. By now, Tsenhor was sixty-three years old, which was ancient. Was it about this time that Ruru and Ituru were taking over the family business? In the everyday life of physical hard work, they probably had done so twenty years earlier.

Four Hundred and One Little Workers

It is not difficult to pinpoint the exact location of the necropolis of Djeme, where Ituru worked: Medinet Habu—the name is believed by some to derive from the nearby temple of the famous sage Amunhotep son of Hapu—on the west bank of the Nile. This was still a sacred place in the Late Period. The divine adoratrices selected this spot for building their mortuary chapels to the south of the Eighteenth Dynasty small temple in front of the first pylon of the large temple built by Ramesses III (reigned 1194–1163 BCE). The mortuary cults for the divine adoratrices would have been commissioned to people of more elevated rank than Ituru, who was after all just a private choachyte.

For instance, the well-known divine adoratrice Amunirdis had her own choachyte, who had probably already been appointed to this position while she was alive (so did they discuss her weekly requirements when she would be dead?). An Osiris statue of this choachyte is kept in the Ny Carlsberg Glyptothek in Copenhagen under the inventory number

AEIN 72. His name was Hor, and he was the servant of the entrance of the palace of the divine adoratrice Amunirdis. It so happens that we know many of the functionaries who were attached to her palace. All of these men may have brought libations to their employers, even if the sources do not explicitly tell us (if people do not mention their daily tasks on their statues, we do not know). We know that many other people were involved in the mortuary cult of the divine adoratrice, often a priest or a monthly priest, and in one specific case even the first prophet—the economic director of the divine domain—attended to this cult. So it is difficult to imagine that Tsenhor's children would ever have been able to add a divine adoratrice to the family portfolio. But there were of course plenty of people who could afford to be buried in the near vicinity and hire a choachyte to carry out their mortuary cult.

Medinet Habu has been the subject of an ongoing campaign by the Oriental Institute of Chicago that started in 1924 and continues to this day. This has included going over some of the nineteenth-century excavations by the French Egyptologist Georges Daressy. Daressy noted that many of the tombs he found at Medinet Habu had been pillaged in antiquity, although he did find a number of cachettes containing hoards of bronze votive statues, some even measuring up to fifty centimeters. Popular cults attracted many pilgrims from all over Egypt who were seeking a favor from or fulfilling an obligation to a deity. In the course of time their votive offerings—often bronze statuettes—would start to crowd the places of worship, so once in a while they were all discarded together to make room for new items. The famous Karnak Cachette found by the French Egyptologist Georges Legrain in 1903 in the courtyard in front of the seventh pylon of the Karnak temple contained seven hundred stone and seventeen thousand bronze statues, statuettes, and other items. All of these were likely discarded by pious priests to make room for new pilgrims, for paying customers.

Within the temple precinct, the team from the Oriental Institute also found a number of nonroyal tombs from the Twenty-fifth and Twenty-sixth Dynasties. Whenever they were able to identify the owners, they turned out to be the (female) courtiers of the divine adoratrice. For example, Tomb 24—hidden below Room 7 of the large temple—belonged to a singer of the interior of Amun Ankhamunirdis from the Twenty-fifth Dynasty. Most tombs only contained small items like coffin and mummy parts, canopic jars, a pet monkey, jewelry, and *ushabti*s.

Apparently ancient tomb robbers were not particularly interested in these *ushabti*s, mostly stone or faience statuettes that would answer *(usheb)* if the tomb owner was summoned to do work in the afterlife. It is often overlooked, but the ancient Egyptians were a very practical people in their religious beliefs (as long as it worked), and in a sense the hiring of *ushabti*s to do all the work in the afterlife, alongside various kinds of rituals to turn the deceased into an Osiris, the services of a choachyte, and the mummification process, may be seen as an added insurance policy to ensure a happy time in the afterlife. For extra security, people who could afford it would take a Book of the Dead, and in later periods there were other funerary texts such as the Book of Traversing Eternity—which allowed the deceased to take part in all the important national religious festivals, of which there were many—and the Book of Breathing. Some of the nonroyal tombs published by Uvo Hölscher in *The Excavation of Medinet Habu, Volume 5: Post-Ramessid Remains* (Chicago: University of Chicago Press, 1954) as Tombs 3–31 contained hundreds of *ushabti*s. Many were uninscribed and of rather poor quality, which suggests that they were mass produced. Excavators found 373 *ushabti*s in Tomb 22, 240 in Tomb 23, 266 in Tomb 24, 195 unbaked ones in Tomb 26, and 429 in Tomb 29.

These numbers suggest that, at one time at least, some of these tombs may have contained 401 *ushabti*s, as happened more often in the Late Period. For some people a proper burial required 365 workers and thirty-six managers.

We know, for instance, that in 1903 the Italian Egyptologist Alessandro Barsanti—who was to become famous for his discovery of the tomb of Akhenaten near Amarna in 1891—found the intact tomb of the overseer of the royal ships Hekaemsaf (reign of Amasis II) in Saqqara, somewhere to the east of the Unas pyramid. It contained 401 *ushabti*s of very high quality that subsequently found their way into collections, including private collections, all over the world. To this day the whereabouts of only about seventy of Hekaemsaf's *ushabti*s are known. He was an important man, as is shown by his titles: prince, seal-bearer of the king of Lower Egypt, unique friend, controller of the palace, overseer of the storehouse of refreshments, and overseer of the double treasury of the residence, in addition to overseer of the royal ships.

In some cases the Late Period tombs from Saqqara yielded only four hundred *ushabti*s, like Tomb 23 of Horiraâ to the southeast of the Step

Pyramid of King Djoser. The same number was found in the tomb of Horkheby—located between the pyramids of Djoser and Unas—thirty-six of them being inscribed. The nearby tomb of a man called Padineith, a chief of scribes of the royal cattle and overseer of horses, likewise contained four hundred *ushabti*s. It would be a strange coincidence if just one *ushabti* were missing in all the above cases, so apparently for some tomb owners four hundred *ushabti*s would do just as well. However, in the tomb of the overseer Tjaynahebu, like that of Hekaemsaf overseer of the royal ships, south of the Unas pyramid, Alessandro Barsanti once again found 401 *ushabti*s of exceptional quality.

In fact, we even have a bill of sale for 401 *ushabti*s from a slightly earlier period, the eighth century BCE. It is now kept in the British Museum as P. BM EA 10800. Even though the writing in this text is believed by some to contain several abnormal hieratic signs, the scribe actually wrote isolated, rather crude signs and sign-groups with a thick brush. There are far fewer ligatures and abbreviations than one would expect in a proto–abnormal hieratic text. In many cases the hieroglyphic origin of signs and sign-groups can be distinguished with ease. P. BM EA 10800 is phrased as a legal document, although it was clearly designed for use in the afterlife. At one point, the man who manufactured the *ushabti*s speaks to them directly. The witnesses to this contract are the gods:

> Regnal year 14, second month of the *akhet* season, day 8. Has said Petekhonsu son of Nespenankh son of Hor, the chief manufacturer of amulets of the temple of Amun, to the priest beloved by the god, Nespernub son of Ihafy son of Iufenkhonsu:
>
> "May Amun, the Great One, endure. I have received from you the silver for these 365 *ushabti*s and their 36 managers, in total 401, my heart being satisfied. They are male servants and female servants. I have received from you the cast silver for them, the 401 *ushabti*s.
>
> "(So) hurry and work to replace the Osiris beloved by god, the priest Ihafy. Say 'We will do' at any hour he will ask you to do the daily service. I have received from him the silver for you."
>
> So he declared before . . . Ptah and Horus, the Great One of the Sacred Place. So he declared, speaking with his own mouth.
>
> The witness-scribe Pamy son of Ankhpakhrat son of Djedkhon-suiufankh . . . .

There has been some discussion about who is actually being paid in this document. Some Egyptologists believe that the *ushabti*s needed a guarantee that they had been paid in advance for their work (otherwise they might go on strike), and indeed the fashioner of amulets Petekhonsu urges them to go to work if they are summoned, because the money to do so is already in the bank. In that case one would have to assume that this document was placed with the *ushabti*s in Ihafy's tomb. If ever they did not feel like working, the manager could take it out to prove that Ihafy's son had already paid their wages. The fact that the witnesses to this contract are deities, including Ptah and Horus, renders this hypothesis all the more likely.

The gods are definitely involved in two writing boards belonging to a woman called Neskhonsu. Her tomb is mostly referred to as DB (Deir al-Bahari) 320, but it is also known as TT (Theban Tomb) 320. It was made for her husband, the high priest of Amun Pinodjem II (which is disputed by some Egyptologists), who lived during the Twenty-first Dynasty. The tomb became famous as the last hiding place of scores of royal mummies that were discovered in 1881. DB 320 was found by members of the famous al-Rasul family, who then started to sell the high-quality inventory piecemeal, thereby attracting the attention of the Egyptian authorities. Among the antiquities sold by the al-Rasuls were the McCullum Tablet (T. BM EA 16672), bought in Luxor in 1874, and the identical Rogers Tablet (T. Louvre E 6858), acquired in 1878. They were most probably placed in Neskhonsu's tomb with the *ushabti* boxes, informing us that none other than Amun-Ra King of Gods guaranteed that the *ushabti*s would work for Neskhonsu whenever she was summoned. That is why this text is also known as the Neskhonsu Decree. It was issued nineteen days before her funeral, some fifty days after she died. T. BM EA 16672 runs as follows:

Amun-Ra King of Gods, the Great God, the most ancient to come into being, has said: "I will commission these *ushabti*s that were made for Neskhonsu, the daughter of Tahendjehuty, to cause that they do all the work for Neskhonsu, the daughter of Tahendjehuty, namely the sort of work that *ushabti*s can do, being in the service of a person who died and has been taken to the necropolis, having become a god, without them leaving any remainder." It is what Amun has said: "I will cause that they will do the things for Neskhonsu, the daughter of Tahendjehuty."

Amun-Ra King of Gods, the Great God, the most ancient to come into being, has said: "I will commission these *ushabtis* that were made for Neskhonsu, the daughter of Tahendjehuty, to cause that they do all the work for which they were manufactured to exempt each magnificent spirit, to cause that they do it to exempt Neskhonsu. I will commission them to exempt her in every year, every month, every decade, and every day, including the five epagomenal days."

Copy of the writings that were put before Amunnestytawy of the Mansion of the Benben in regnal year 5, fourth month of the *shemu* season, day 2.

Amunnestytawy of the Mansion of the Benben, the Great God, has said on two pieces of writing *(text continues on verso)* that testify to all that has been given to the faience-makers to compensate for the *ushabtis* that were made for Neskhonsu, the daughter of Tahendjehuty in the form of any copper, clothing, *ak* bread, *shay* cakes, fish that were given to them as their compensation or will be paid to them: "The faience-makers have been paid for them with the silver to compensate for them, regarding everything that was done for the *ushabtis* to compensate them, to have them manufactured in order to replace a person at work, saying, 'I shall do all that should be done,' so that the *ushabtis* will do the things to replace Neskhonsu, the daughter of Tahendjehuty. They will be good to her and they will do good things for her."

In both contracts the scribe specifically states that payments have been made, using legal formulas from everyday contracts, but there is still a debate whether the faience-makers were paid or the *ushabtis* themselves. In a way the *ushabtis* had agreed to be sold into slavery in the afterlife. The actual reward they received would be that the faience-makers had brought them to life, even if it was just in the afterlife.

Some believe that this would include an 'opening of the mouth' ritual to imbue the *ushabtis* with life, and in that case one rather hopes that performing this ritual on a single *ushabti* would suffice for the entire lot. This brings us to another question. Late Period tombs often contain sets of very crude *ushabtis*, almost homemade. Would these work just as well in the afterlife as the ones that had been manufactured—and magically processed—in temple workshops?

Of course even in death there was inequality. Neskhonsu belonged to the upper elite, meaning that her funerary equipment was of the highest quality, as would be the mortuary services performed for her. Still, the upper elite also had its choachytes, popping up in the papyri every now and then. In abnormal hieratic P. Vienna 12002, for instance, we see a choachyte of the fourth prophet of Amun Nesptah, who is none other than the son of the famous Theban strongman Montuemhat. Above, we saw that the divine adoratrice Amunirdis had her own choachyte. But we cannot be sure that these people were really professional choachytes like Tsenhor. Maybe in the case of Amunirdis the word 'choachyte' simply denoted one of the extra tasks (or functions) performed by her courtier.

Still, even Tsenhor had at least one client who had been rich enough to pay with eleven *aruras* for the choachytes' services on behalf of a single woman (P. Louvre E 10935). But we do not have—as we do in the case of Djekhy & Son, who counted a member of the famous Besmut family among their clientele, whose coffin is now kept in the Cairo Museum under the inventory number CG 41011—a tangible piece of funerary equipment or a tomb of which we can say that it was once seen—or better still, touched—by Tsenhor. As we saw above, the well-known tomb of Pabasa may have had a special meaning for her (see "A Tomb in the Assasif").

Most people could not afford to pay eleven *aruras* to a choachyte and, if their children could or would not perform these services themselves, they were left to rely on the good will of strangers passing by, which was probably the reality for most.

As if to underline the wide gap between Egyptology and demotic studies, much of what we have learned so far about Tsenhor and her colleagues and the way they did business will never make it into the mainstream literature on the ancient Egyptian mortuary cult, where—as far as one can see—even the existence of the choachytes seems to remain a well-hidden secret known only to papyrologists and the odd colleague working with New Kingdom material. This may be just as well.

7

Love and Death: Tsenhor, Psenese, Ituru, and Ruru, 498–494 BCE

Psenese Becomes Ill
24 July–22 August 498 BCE (P. Turin 2126)

When their daughter Ruru was born in 517 BCE, or perhaps a few years before, Tsenhor's husband Psenese was quick to acknowledge her rights to his inheritance. This was done through P. BM EA 10120B, in which the scribe Teos—the father of the scribe Ip who wrote our P. Turin 2126—recorded Psenese's oral statement in writing:

> "You are the sharing-partner of my children who have been born and who will be born to me in everything that I own and will acquire (. . .). To you (Ruru) belongs one share of it (Psenese's inheritance) in accordance with the number of my children who will be born."

So apparently Ruru would have to share with the children from Psenese's previous marriage and those that he would have with Tsenhor. But here in P. Turin 2126 the scribe Ip wrote, "To you belongs half of everything that belongs to me and that I will acquire (. . .)." The other half would go to Ruru's younger brother Ituru. It was, of course, Psenese's prerogative to divide his inheritance as he saw fit, and the fact that he divided it equally between his two children by Tsenhor, one of whom was a girl, suggests that this was a happy household and that the children from his previous marriage—mentioned in P. BM EA 10120B from 517 BCE—for whatever reason no longer played a part in his life. Some even believe that the scribe of P. BM EA 10120B made a mistake here and that Psenese never had any children from a previous marriage. In that case, someone

173

should have noticed when the scribe read back what he had written in front of Psenese and the witnesses. Alternatively, this was simply a stock phrase used by the scribe to cover every eventuality.

It would also mean that Ruru would be Psenese's first-born and that he became a father only when he was probably well into his thirties. This sounds slightly more modern than sixth-century-BCE Thebes. The fact that Ruru received half is remarkable, because as a rule sons inherited more than their sisters. Whether she took on the designated role as the eldest son—with all the privileges and responsibilities involved—remains a moot point, especially because she had a younger brother. But from the looks of it, each received an equal share of their parents' inheritance.

According to the legal manual P. Mattha—dating to around 250 BCE but showing traces of a much older original—if a man died without having made a will the eldest son could dispose of the inheritance in any manner that he liked, meaning that he could select the shares he wanted. Only then were the other brothers and sisters allowed to choose (P. Mattha col. IX *l.* 1–2). One should note, however, that the cases about an intestate property division recorded in P. Mattha are listed side by side, meaning that apparently several procedures could be followed.

> As far as the remainder of the possessions is concerned, these should be divided according to the number of his (the deceased father's) children. The male children may then choose their shares according to their date of birth, and subsequently his female children may choose (their shares) according to their date of birth.

As noted above, the ancient Egyptians were—and this message mostly does not go down well with the many pyramidiots Egyptologists have to deal with—a highly practical people, so P. Mattha lists a number of similar cases, including the ultimate nightmare scenario, dying without a son (P. Mattha col. IX *l.* 14–17):

> If a man dies without having a male child, but having female children, his possessions should be divided into shares [according to the number of] female children [and one share will be given to each] of his female children except an additional children's share: this will be given to his eldest daughter to complete two shares. If the eldest daughter says, "My father had other children, but they

died. Cause that their shares are given to me," the shares of her brothers who died cannot be given to her.

Fortunately for Psenese, he did have a son, and one assumes that Ruru's brother was present on this day to receive his own contract similar to P. Turin 2126. It has been suggested that Psenese was already very ill when he had his will drawn up by Ip in 498 BCE, but how old was he? His wife Tsenhor was born around 550 BCE, so she was now fifty-two years old or so. Psenese is not mentioned in the only official records of the Association of Theban Choachytes we have, namely P. Louvre E 7840 from 542–538 BCE. If sixteen was the age at which you could become a member and if—this is just a hypothesis—Psenese became sixteen in 537 BCE, he would have been born around 553 BCE, which would have made him fifty-five in 498 BCE, when he dictated his will to Ip:

Regnal year 24, fourth month of the *peret* season under Pharaoh l.p.h. Darius l.p.h. The choachyte of the valley Psenese son of Heryrem, whose mother is Beniuutehtyes, has said to Mrs. Ruru daughter of the choachyte of the valley Psenese son of Heryrem, whose mother is Tsenhor, his daughter:

"To you belongs half of everything that belongs to me and that I will acquire in the field, the temple and the city, namely houses, field, slave, silver, copper, clothing, *it* grain, emmer, [ox], donkey, tomb in the necropolis, bread of Osiris, and any other thing on earth. (These) are yours and I have nothing to say on earth on account of them. I have given them to you as your share, whereas the other share belongs to the choachyte of the valley Ituru son of Psenese son of Heryrem, whose mother is Tsenhor, my son and your brother.

"As for the person who will come to you on account of them in my name or in the name of any other person on earth, I will cause that he will be far from you. To you belong their contracts wherever they may be. To you belongs my right derived from them."

In the writing of the god's father of Montu [Lord of Thebes] Ip son of Teos.

One takes it that Psenese made his last will because the end was near and there were only two children to inherit his possessions. Nineteen years earlier Psenese had already allotted a share to Ruru (P. BM EA

10120B), but this was done before it was entirely clear who would be there to divide the inheritance. By now they all knew that Psenese had only two children who would inherit from him. Ruru's younger brother Ituru had not yet been born when Psenese appointed Ruru as his heir the first time. He was now perhaps eighteen years old. Table 10 shows what Ruru would inherit from her father.

Table 10. Ruru's inheritance

Year	Share	Description of inheritance
517 BCE (P. BM EA 10120B)	One share according to the number of children that have been and will be born	Everything that belongs to Psenese and that he will acquire, viz., houses, field, slaves, silver, copper, clothing, *it* grain, emmer, ox, donkey, or any other animal, any contract, and any other thing on earth.
498 BCE (P. Turin 2126)	Half	Everything that belongs to Psenese and that he will acquire in the field, the temple, and the city, viz., houses, field, slave, silver, copper, clothing, *it* grain, emmer, meat, [ox], donkey, tomb in the necropolis, bread of Osiris, and any other thing on earth.

The Days on Which Tsenhor Did Not Work

Hiring Tsenhor came with a price and, while she was still of childbearing age, most probably with a special labor agreement, because she was, as will be seen below, probably not allowed to work as a choachyte when she had her period. As long as she was pregnant—and this may have been a semipermanent condition for many women in ancient Egypt—she could fulfill her obligations. During the week of her period, however, the work would probably be done by her husband or her children. Perhaps her husband had to do the cooking as well, because cooking during your period may have been taboo in ancient Egypt (the sources are not clear, but somehow a view of ancient Egyptian husbands cooking and doing the dishes seems utterly unlikely). Sources like P. Jumilhac XII *l*. 16–17 do suggest, however, that menstruation—called an "abomination" in the text—was rated among evil omens such as the howling of a dog, a dream, the grunting of a pig, and worse.

As we saw earlier and will also see below, according to the demotic sources women having their period could use a space under the stairs in the house (not the whole time, one assumes, but to wash or sit out difficult moments),[1] but the relevant sources are few and not necessarily representative of customs elsewhere in Egypt (and how did they do it—by locking their women in?). There may have been other solutions. In many cultures there was—and still is—a hut outside the village where women could go to sit out their monthly ordeal.

In Indonesia, Huaulu women retreat to a menstrual hut just outside the village, but they are still allowed to go into the jungle, as long as they do not cross any hunting trails or eat game. Washing—a deeply felt need when menstruating—is done in special places that are strictly off limits to their men. The pattern is more or less the same among the Dogon in Mali, where women are confined to a special hut. They are not allowed to go into the village or their family homes. Sex and cooking for their husbands are not allowed. Orthodox Jews really get the short end of the stick because women are not to have sex with their husbands during their period *and* a week after, and the husband is not allowed to share a bed with her, look at her clothes, or hear her sing.

In Pliny's *Natural History* menstruating women are described as being responsible for turning wine into vinegar, blunting razors, and causing mares to have miscarriages and fruit to fall from trees, and these are only some of the lesser evils ascribed to them. Even today Russian Orthodox women are believed to repel fish and game, and have a bad influence on the weather, too, when menstruating. In most cultures, therefore, menstruation had—and still has—a deep impact on daily life, and we may assume that this was in many ways not so different in ancient Egypt.

If we want to look at the impact of menstruation on daily life in ancient Egypt, we inevitably—once again—end up at Deir al-Medina. The village scribes have left us literally thousands of accounts, letters, trial records, and work journals. These work journals are especially interesting because they show that a woman having her period was a valid excuse for a workman to stay home from work.

The most famous work journal comes from regnal year 40 of Ramesses II (1290–1224 BCE). It lists the attendance and absence of the individual workmen from Deir al-Medina in the Valley of Kings during the entire year (O. BM EA 5634). It shows that apart from being stung by a scorpion or taking funerary offerings to their relatives—the verb used, *wah mu*, is actually the same as the professional title of Tsenhor—the workmen were also excused if their closest female relatives were having their periods. This is corroborated by a number of other work journals written in the Nineteenth and Twentieth Dynasties by the Deir al-Medina scribes—for example, O. Ashmolean Museum 167, O. Cairo CG 25782 and 25784, O. DeM 898 and 908, O. MMA 14.6.217, and O. Turin N. 57388—which suggests that the women in Deir al-Medina expected their husbands to be at home to do the housework when they were menstruating. O. Cairo CG 25784 is no longer counted among the evidence, because it was shown that the enigmatic sign-group that had been read as 'menstruating' could actually also be a way to write 'offering,' although this view could change any day. In Egyptology, one quickly becomes used to accepted interpretations changing back and forth for a hundred years or so without any direct result.

Until 1999, probably no one in Egyptology devoted too much attention to the practical problems of women having their period in Egypt. Except Jack Janssen, that is, who made a special study of O. BM EA 5634. On account of the infrequent absences of specific workmen in connection with their wives' alleged periods, he suggested that the term generally translated as 'menstruation'—for which see below—was actually a purification ceremony after childbirth, and with good reason, because the Egyptian word for menstruation also means 'purification.'

In 1999 Terry Wilfong published a damaged but very important little ostracon of only a few lines known as O. OIM 13512. In the course of his research he retraced Janssen's work, finding that in one specific case the Deir al-Medina workman Samut was absent from work twice in a period of three months, on day 25 of the first month of the *peret* season and on day 23 of the fourth month of the same season. Something of a coincidence and also very easily explained by the menstrual cycle.

Naturally, Janssen had noticed the Samut case as well. His explanation was that in the case of day 25 of the first month of the *peret* season, Samut's wife had had a purification ceremony after childbirth, and another three months later because of a miscarriage, which of course frequently happened. In fact, some of the demotic papyri made for the Memphite choachytes—like P. Leiden I 379, mentioned earlier—seem to suggest that they also serviced the miscarriages of their clients. Memphite choachytes' contracts—never those written in Thebes—sometimes refer to a category of dead people called *huhet* or *wehyt*, which is exactly matched by Sahidic Coptic *huhe*, 'untimely birth,' and the Bohairic Coptic variant *wehe*, which was translated as '*foetus abortif*' and '*Fehlgeburt*' by Eugène Revillout and Wilhelm Spiegelberg in 1881 and 1921, respectively. In the case of the wife of Samut, the natural menstrual cycle seems to explain it all.

What makes OIM 13512 so special is that it is the only known reference to a special hut where wives and daughters went when they were menstruating, which suggests that the cycles of the eight women on their way to this menstrual hut had apparently become synchronized. This is not surprising, because O. OIM 13512 probably comes from Deir al-Medina, where people lived on top of each other. The text seems simple and straightforward, although it is much battered:

> Regnal year 9, fourth month of the *akhet* season, day 13. The day on which these eight women went out [to/of the] place of women, they being in their period, reaching the rear of the house [. . .] the three walls.

If the official scribe of Deir al-Medina affairs devoted a note to it, this means something unusual happened. Unfortunately we do not know if the women were going to the menstrual hut and were held up at some mysterious three walls or had actually come out and had decided—a lot of emotion goes on between eight women sitting together in a menstrual hut while having their period, and in the stifling heat—that they had had enough and wanted to go back to the village *right now*, somehow circumventing the three walls, which are believed by some to be guard posts, and were finally stopped at the back of a house (which in Deir al-Medina probably meant they were still outside the walled village).

The assumption we have to make here is that—as in many cultures—physical contact between men and menstruating women was not considered a very good thing. In the case of the workmen of Deir al-Medina, one may argue that they were working on a magical machine that was to keep the king alive forever after death. In that case it would make sense to assume that the official scribe thought he had to make a note that the women had actually left their menstrual hut and come back to the village even while they were still having their periods, thus somehow magically connecting the 'abomination' of menstrual blood with the sacred task of preparing the king's grave (yes, I found it difficult to write this down, too). This ancient Egyptian source generates more questions than answers, as ancient Egyptian sources tend to do. So what did OIM 13512 say to Terry Wilfong?

> The basic sense of the text is clear. Eight women who were menstruating came out of the village on their way to or from a location called 'the place of women.' Something (lost in the lacuna) happened on the way after they had reached the rear of a house; the event appears to have had something to do with another place known literally as 'the three walls.'[2]

In other words, while we would like to see the women come out of the hut and head toward the village, it may actually have been the other way around. But in that case one would almost have to assume that the periods of these eight women all started on the same day. Can that be done? If there was a special hut for menstruating women, they would have to go there the moment their periods started.

There is one other text that mentions a woman—the daughter of a widow—reaching a wall near Deir al-Medina, who consequently had to be heard by the authorities (O. Cairo CG 25831), but the crucial parts are damaged and the context is unclear (this happens more often than not).

Women menstruating in Deir al-Medina are always described to be in a state of *hesmen*. The word *hesmen* can also mean 'natron' or 'purification.' But the ancient Egyptian medical treatises describe *hesmen* as a condition of women that may come or stay away, and they refer to the blood of a woman whose *hesmen* has come. A single example from the Edwin Smith Surgical Papyrus (verso col. 20 *l.* 13–15) should suffice to support the translation 'menstruation': "If you examine a woman with pain in her stomach and *hesmen* does not come to her (. . .) you will say about it, 'This is a case of an obstruction of the blood in her womb.'"

The debate over whether *hesmen* means menstruation or purification was effectively brought to an end by Paul John Frandsen in a ground-breaking article called "The Menstrual 'Taboo' in Ancient Egypt" (*Journal of Near Eastern Studies*, vol. 66, no. 2 (2007): 81–106), from which we have borrowed, once again, many examples cited here. Frandsen suggests that 'purification' was simply a euphemism for menstruation. In other words, it was a taboo word: "The woman rids herself of the blood and is thereby purified, that is, restored to her normal status."

However, we must get back to O. BM EA 5634. One of the interesting conclusions reached by Wilfong is that the synchronization of the menstrual cycle can be demonstrated in this ostracon, whereas according to O. Cairo CG 25782, between day 24 and 26 of the first month of the *shemu* season in regnal year 3 of Amenmesse no fewer than seven workmen did not show up for work on account of a female relative being in a state of *hesmen*. In fact, the menstrual synchrony of women living in close proximity such as dormitories, prisons, and bordellos—also known as the McClintock Effect or the Wellesley Effect—is still a hotly debated subject, or perhaps even no subject at all. In the 1990s Houston Clyde Wilson of the department of anthropology of the University of Missouri went through all the data from the fundamental studies underlying the McClintock Effect—including those that failed to find any evidence for menstrual synchrony—uncovering sufficient errors and inconsistencies to state that once these studies were corrected for such errors an objective researcher would have to conclude that there really was no evidence for menstrual synchrony. So are we back to square one? Then how do we explain the overwhelming anecdotal evidence for menstrual synchrony, going back to the ancient Greeks and coming into the present? There still is a strong perception among women that it occurs, independent of medical evidence.

Probably in June 506 BCE, Tsenhor and her eldest (half-)brother Nesamunhotep decided to divide the house that had belonged to their father Nesmin (P. Turin 2125). Although this division is not very specific—Tsenhor receives a large space and a storehouse in the court for her own use—we know that their other two (half-)brothers were also involved. Some parts of the house remained in co-ownership as shared property, like the staircase. In this case the mention of the staircase probably means just that: the siblings all had the right to use the staircase.

In other demotic contracts the space below the staircase is the place where women were expected to sit out their period, which is a change from the women of Deir al-Medina being sent out of the village to a menstrual hut. If menstruation was so taboo, then why keep a ritually unclean woman in the house? And why under the stairs?

The space below the staircase reserved for women menstruating was called the *khereret*, with variant spellings such as *kherkheret* and *khelylet*. The reason for not finding such a space in the cramped living space of Deir al-Medina may be just that, namely lack of space. People literally lived on top of each other in relatively small houses, ranging anywhere between 4 x 13 and 6 x 27 m (which on second thought is not exactly that small). But there would always be a staircase leading up to the roof with—one assumes—a space underneath. In fact, the suggestion has been made that the women of Deir al-Medina may have menstruated in some back room of the house after all, but this suggestion was never substantiated. By contrast, some demotic sales explicitly mention this menstrual space, including the activities taking place in it. In P. Louvre N 2424 from 267 BCE, half of a house is sold by a woman to a man. Both practical and sensible people. So some of these slight irritations that can so easily become large nuisances—and can also be so easily avoided—were carefully laid down in writing: "You (the buyer) will go out using the middle door of the house abovementioned (. . .) and your women will menstruate in the *kherkheret* according to (its) half."

This can only mean that the other half of this room under the stairs would remain in use with the female relatives of the co-owner of the house. A practical if perhaps somewhat inconvenient arrangement for the prudish. This passage is by no means a hapax, because it also occurs in other demotic contracts (for example, P. Louvre N 2443 from 249 BCE).

In fact, this special space still existed in Byzantine Egypt. In the sixth century—or to be more precise, in AD 530, 586, and 590—three contracts about the sale of a house were written (for example, P. London V 1722.20) at Aswan in the south of Egypt. The contracting parties were Christians, but they included a special place called the *khrere* or *tkhrere* (the 't' being the Coptic article) under the stairs or, in Greek, a *hypopession*. If we understand correctly the evidence collected by the French Egyptologist (and papyrologist) Frédéric Colin, according to one Greek papyrus even in Hellenistic Egypt there were collective or maybe even public spaces where women could have their periods. Strangely enough, the example cited by him appears to have been near a temple.

And finally, according to one reference by the British Egyptologist Stephen Glanville, in Upper Egypt (which is actually the south of the country) people still use the word *kharara* to denote the water closet or bathroom, so that the meaning of the word may have changed over time but not the notion that it is a place people associate with getting clean.

However, in the case of the division of their father's house between Tsenhor and her three (half-)brothers, the only thing we read is that the four co-owners were all permitted to use the stairs, nothing about what went on beneath them. If Tsenhor had such a room, it would be in her own house.

Closing the Account
25 March–23 April 494 BCE (P. Louvre AF 9761)

In the spring of 494 BCE Tsenhor and a Mr. Djedamuniufankh son of Payftjauawykhonsu appeared before the scribe Horwedja son of Neshorpakhrat. In this particular case, it is not certain whether they came to Horwedja's office, because there were only two witnesses present: Tsenhor's eldest (half-)brother Nesamunhotep, called Amunhotep in this contract, and Neshorbes, the son of the scribe. It would have been just as easy for Horwedja to call on Tsenhor at home in view of her advanced age.

Djedamuniufankh—a former business partner of Tsenhor's husband Psenese—apparently was an intimate acquaintance of the family. Four years earlier he had been one of the witnesses to P. Turin 2126, in which Psenese bequeathed half of his inheritance to his daughter Ruru. But his ties with the family went back further than that. P. Louvre AF 9761 is about a deal between Djedamuniufankh and Psenese that was concluded in 503 BCE, nine years earlier. We do not know what it was about, but it involved some obligation Djedamuniufankh had toward Psenese. Since Tsenhor finalized the deal in the new contract by stating that Djedamuniufankh had fulfilled his obligation and that she had no further claims on him, one assumes that Psenese had died and that Tsenhor was wrapping up her husband's business, and the paperwork it involved.

Tsenhor was supported by her brother, who signed the contract as a witness. This was, of course, no coincidence. Tsenhor was fifty-six years old and probably quite sad. From what we have seen in the documents she left us, Psenese had been a good husband. And being a widow in ancient Egypt was not the best possible prospect.

P. Louvre AF 9761, which was written on a reused slip of papyrus of 25.5 x 12.5 cm, does not belong with her papers but to the archive of Djedamuniufankh, unless of course this was a copy made for her.

Regnal year 28, fourth month of the *akhet* season under Pharaoh l.p.h. Darius l.p.h. Mrs. Tsenhor daughter of Nesmin, whose mother is Ruru, has said to Djedamuniufankh son of Payftjauawykhonsu:

"You have satisfied my heart with the obligations from the contract that you made for Psenese son of Heryrem, my husband, in regnal year 19, first month of the *shemu* season.

"I am far from you. As for the person who will come to you on account of it (the contract) in my name or in the name of any other person on earth, I will cause him to be far from you <and if I do not cause him to be far from you> I will give you five kite of silver from the Treasury of Ptah, without citing any contract against you."

In the writing of Horwedja son of Neshorpakhrat.

We will never know what deal was made between Psenese and Djedamuniufankh, but even the fine that Tsenhor would incur if people bothered him about it again is low, just half a deben. It is almost as if both parties wanted to get this over with as quickly as possible.

When Old Age Sets In

It is very difficult to say anything definite about aging women in Egypt in general. Just like today, the elite had a better chance of reaching old age than the average woman in the street. The office of the divine adoratrice—the highest priestess of the land—seems to have been a particularly healthy one. Shepenupet II held office from 710 to 650 BCE and Ankhnesneferibra from 595 to 525 BCE, when the office was abolished by the Persians. For one thing, ordinary ancient Egyptian women—if there was such a thing—appear far less often than elite women in the written sources, and mostly not in relevant strings of sources covering a period of six to seven decades, as in the case of Tsenhor's papers.

Also, maybe we have it all wrong and Tsenhor was not really born around 550 BCE but in 532 BCE, so that she was actually only fifteen years old in 517 BCE when she married Psenese—her second marriage already—and made a will for the children from her two marriages, meaning that when she died sometime after 490 BCE she was in reality only forty-two instead of the sixty-three I would so much like to ascribe to her (and did in this book).

A very handy definition of old age in ancient Egypt comes from one of the few real specialists in ancient Egyptian women, Deborah Sweeney of Tel Aviv University, in a delightful chapter entitled "Women Growing Older in Deir el-Medina": "As a rough guess, we might argue that people could be considered old when they had grandchildren, or . . . several adult children."[3]

Or could it be when they could no longer give birth? According to Sweeney, the transition to menopause may not have been easy to detect, although the external signs would have been there, such as osteoporosis, increased tooth loss, and wrinkled skin, and all that in an age where the average life expectancy may have been as low as thirty. There was an upside, probably. Even today in some parts of Egypt mourners at a funeral are preferably women way past their prime. This is to prevent an unborn child from being harmed the moment the mourners cross the border between life and death. It is complicated.

But there would always be exceptions. The lady Naunakhte may have reached the age of sixty-nine. One would expect her to have gradually started doing less and less in the house—probably without losing her status of *nebet per*, 'mistress of the house,' because her record shows that right until the end she remained very much in charge of her life—but there were many things even old women could do, such as textile work of any kind, trade, bringing libations to the dead while the men were working in the Valley of Kings (nice thought), looking after the grandchildren, acting as midwife, or more if they had creative children.

In Deir al-Medina there were also women called *rekhet*, 'wise woman' or, literally, '(female) knower,' and one supposes that here age and life experience really would have counted. The wise woman acted as a mediator between the villagers and the gods, telling them which god had caused which mishap (for a fee, of course). Wise women could also tell why people fell ill, which would often have a supernatural cause. But we cannot dismiss the possibility that some of these wise women were actually wise women, as we can still find in village communities all over the world today. The only question that remains, however, is just how many wise women a tiny village such as Deir al-Medina could accommodate.

Anyone trying to sort out the legal status of ancient Egyptian women will sooner or later have to go through the demotic evidence—assuming he or she can read it (the abnormal hieratic evidence is generally ignored or, at best, taken from translations)—to finally end up in the New Kingdom village of Deir al-Medina. There, we often see women briskly going about their business and, just like their men, appearing in the local legal court, the *qenbet*, to face charges. If, however, statistics say anything about the actual legal status of women in official life, the fact that they only seldom appear as active members of this court is telling us something.

Although the many thousands of written sources from Deir al-Medina have been published in all sorts of books and academic journals, there are two outstanding publications that give a full overview of the legal procedures and the position of women in the village during the New Kingdom (1550–1070 BCE). The first is *Jurisdiction in the Workmen's Community of Deir El-Medîna* (Leiden: Netherlands Institute for the Near East, 1990) by the American Egyptologist Andrea McDowell (who now works as a judge), and the second is *Women at Deir el-Medina: A Study of the Status and Roles of the Female Inhabitants in the Workmen's Community during the Ramesside Period* (Leiden: Netherlands Institute for the Near East, 2001) by the Finnish Egyptologist and archaeologist Jaana Toivari. These books are the first highly successful syntheses of the evidence that has come to us from Deir al-Medina on these two specific subjects.

One of the famous sources treated by both authors is the so-called Will of Naunakhte, which is actually a series of papyri connected with the inheritance of a woman who lived in Deir-al Medina in the Twentieth Dynasty. Two were acquired by Alan Gardiner sometime after 1928 and two others were found in situ during the excavations in Deir al-Medina by the IFAO in 1928, so presumably all four papyri were found together and then two were stolen and sold on the market. The excavation team also found a large number of fragments, which turned out to be letters and a literary text. The largest papyrus—43 x 192 cm in the handwriting of two different scribes— is now kept in Oxford under the inventory number P. Ashmolean Museum 1945.97. It was written in regnal year 3 of Ramesses V (c. 1145 BCE).

It records the oral statement by a Mrs. Naunakhte before the local court of Deir al-Medina. Apparently she was very old and did not have much longer to live. What she has to say in court sheds some light on the position of the ancient Egyptian *materfamilias* and her right to divide the family estate.

Qenhirkhopshef x *Naunakhte* x Khaemnun
|
    Maanynakhtef
    Qenhirkhopshef
    Amunnakhte
    Wasetnakhte
    Menatnakhte
    Neferhotep
    Henutshenu
    Khatanub

The names of the women are in italics.

In P. Ashmolean Museum 1945.97 Naunakhte states that several of her children by her second husband will not inherit from her because they did not look after her when she became old. Likewise they will not share in the division of the estate of her first husband, the prominent scribe Qenhirkhopshef, although they will inherit from the property of their own father Khaemnun, Naunakhte's second husband. It is believed that when Naunakhte married Qenhirkhopshef, the latter was about forty years older than she. Behind the statement by Naunakhte we sense the age-old family problem still encountered today: it is always the same brothers and sisters caring for their parents, while the others prefer to look the other way or are too busy leading their own lives. This brings up an intriguing question: what would have happened if Naunakhte had died before she went to court?

According to the official record, Naunakhte, described as a citizen, made her statement in regnal year 3, fourth month of the *akhet* season, day 5 of the reign of Ramesses V. This would be about October, c. 1145 BCE. The court where she did this comprised no fewer than fourteen men (no women), including the two managers of the workmen of Deir al-Medina, two scribes, two draftsmen, two district officers, and several workmen. Although it is nowhere explicitly stated, one assumes that her children were present as well, and probably even many of the village people who had a day off and were looking for some recreation. After these preliminaries, Naunakhte's statement reads as follows:

"As far as I am concerned, I am a free woman of the land of Pharaoh l.p.h. I have raised these eight servants of yours. I gave them a household outfit of all things that is usually made for the likes of them. But see, I have grown old. But see, they are not caring for me in turn. As for anyone among them who laid his hand on my hand (cared for me), I will give him my things. As to the one who has not given to me, I will not give him from my things."

Then there is a list of the children who will inherit from her and those who will not. What is striking is that her son Qenhirkhopshef—clearly named after her first husband—receives an extra portion. This may have been because, as we will see below, he would take care of his father after Naunakhte had died. One daughter, the citizen Menatnakhte, inherits some of Naunakhte's property, but slightly less than her siblings, so she probably also did less for her mother than the others:

List of the workmen and women to whom she has given: the workman Maanynakhtef, the workman Qenhirkhopshef. She said:

"I have given to him a bronze washbowl as a reward and as an additional share above the others also ten sacks of emmer corn."

(And) the workman Amunnakhte, the citizen Wasetnakhte, and the citizen Menatnakhte. As for the citizen Menatnakhte, she said about her:

"She will have a share in the division of all my things, except the *oipe* of emmer corn that my three male children and also the citizen Wasetnakhte have given me, and my *hin* of fat that they gave me in the same manner."

The inheritance divided by Naunakhte consists of various lots: a storeroom she inherited from her father, the property of her first husband Qenhirkhopshef, the property acquired by her and Qenhirkhopshef, and the property acquired by her and her second husband Khaemnun, of which one-third was hers to dispose of. Some of this would also go to the children who had been negligent toward her, but her own property and the property inherited from Qenhirkhopshef was hers to divide, and hers alone. From this they would get nothing.

This explains the next division listed by the scribe, who makes a crucial mistake, once forgetting to write 'not' where he should have:

List of her children of whom she had said:

"They will not enter into the division of my one-third, but they will enter into the division of the two-thirds of their father."

The workman Neferhotep, the citizen Menatnakhte, the citizen Henutshenu, and the citizen Khatanub.

"As far as these four children of mine are concerned, they will <not> enter into the division of all my things. And as for all the things of the scribe Qenhirkhopshef, my husband, and also his places and this storehouse of my father and likewise this *oipe* of emmer corn that I and my husband collected, they will not share in them."

Four children were excluded from the division of the property from Naunakhte's first marriage with Qenhirkhopshef, although she could not prevent them from sharing in the inheritance of their own father Khaemnun. So far the statement is not entirely clear about the share that her daughter Menatnakhte will or will not receive. Also, the fact that the scribe once forgot to write 'not' at a crucial spot in the statement—indicated by the pointed brackets—could have led to fierce legal battles afterward: "As far as these eight children of mine are concerned, they will enter into the division of the things of their father, each (receiving) a single share."

The atmosphere was probably very tense when this document was written, because we have to assume that all the stakeholders in the division of Naunakhte's inheritance were present at this court session. We do not know—although it seems likely—whether Naunakhte had discussed her plans with her husband and (some of) her children. If not, this would have been the hour of truth, and Naunakhte would have had to make a coherent oral statement with all these people staring at her, including the children who would be disinherited, so one would very much like to know how she felt when she made it. Was she sad because her life was drawing to a close? Was she elated because this was payback time? Or was it a mix of these and many more emotions?

Although the good guys won the day, this session most likely meant that family relations would remain sour for the next generation or so, as most of the people involved would still be living in—or rather confined to—the same small gated community of Deir al-Medina. But Naunakhte was far from finished. One of her sons was to receive some extra punishment, although curiously enough he is not mentioned by name. This was clearly the black sheep who needed support, time and again (and probably was too lazy to get a job).

> As for the kettle that I gave him to buy bread for himself, and likewise the chisel of seven deben and likewise the *irer* vase of seven deben, and likewise the adze of six deben, which makes forty deben, they will form his share. He will not enter into the division of any copper. It will be for his brothers and sisters.

The record was signed by the scribe Amunnakhte, the same who wrote the famous Turin Strike Papyrus—about the strikes in regnal year 29 of Ramesses III—and many other documents from Deir al-Medina. Then there is a little addendum to the official record that is dated one year later, in regnal year 4, third month of the *akhet* season, day 17. It says that on this day the workman Khaemnun—who can be none other than Naunakhte's second husband—and his children went to court again.

This time, the court consisted of the two managers of the crew, the scribe Horshery (the son of the scribe Amunnakhte), and two district officers, one of whom witnessed the official declaration by Naunakhte the year before. Khaemnun—who was not a very rich man—and his children had come to make a statement:

> As far as the writings are concerned which the citizen Naunakhte has made about her things, they are thus exactly, exactly. The workman Neferhotep will not share in them. He will take an oath with the Lord l.p.h., saying: "If I turn back on my word again, he shall receive a hundred blows and be deprived of his things."

From this we may surmise that—as was to be expected—Naunakhte's will had created quite some uproar in the family. Her son Neferhotep, for instance, clearly did not agree with the way things had gone, and the fact that the addendum states that Khaemnun and his children had gone to court again probably does not refer to the time they were there to hear Naunakhte's statement the year before, but rather to subsequent hearings about the validity of the division.

We do have two more papyri showing that some of the property owned by Naunakhte was physically divided among her children. These were found by the French excavation team in Deir al-Medina in 1928, and they are now known as P. DeM 23 and 25. Both are about 21 cm x 11 cm, but they are written in different hands. They record the division of some of the things belonging to '(y)our mother'—Naunakhte—and their content is nearly identical, mentioning the items received by Amunnakhte, Wasetnakhte, Maanynakhtef, Menatnakhte, Nebnakhte, and Qenhirkhopshef.

Nebnakhte is the odd one out. He is not listed among Naunakhte's children who are mentioned in her own statement, but he does appear in the last papyrus of the series as a witness to a statement made by Naunakhte's second husband Khaemnun.

The fourth papyrus from the series is not as straightforward as the rest. It actually predates the will of Naunakhte by a few weeks. Formerly owned by Alan Gardiner, the papyrus, which measures 21 x 43 cm, is now known as P. Ashmolean Museum 1945.95. The inventory number 1945.96 was assigned to the famous Adoption Papyrus (see "Why Not Simply Adopt Your Wife?" above), which was also owned by Gardiner.

According to its editor, Jaroslav Černý, the papyrus was in two hands, one neat and professional and the other rather sloppy. It is not certain whether we are dealing with another court session here, since the following transaction between Naunakhte's second husband Khaemnun and their son Qenhirkhopshef only involves ordinary workmen, asked to witness the transaction. Some of the people present were his brothers:

> Has said the workman Khaemnun before the workman Anynakhte, the workman Qedakhetef, the workman Hornefer, the workman Neferhotep, the workman Amunnakhte, the workman Maanynakhtef, and the workman Khonsu: "Look, I give this washbowl which is thirteen deben of copper. It is for Qenhirkhopshef. No son or daughter will discuss it. His statement shall not be heard. It is not in any (other) division."

Since the economy of Deir al-Medina revolved around bronze and copper weights that were used to express relative value, thereby allowing trade (coined money was a much later invention), this represented a serious amount of cash. Why Khaemnun gave it to his son Qenhirkhopshef is unknown, but it seems reasonable to assume that this washbowl is the same as the one mentioned by Naunakhte in her court statement a few weeks later.

Khaemnun explicitly states that the washbowl will not be part of any division, presumably of Naunakhte's inheritance. The statement made by Khaemnun was then formally put into writing again, meaning that it was recorded twice, the second time with an official date. It could also be that Khaemnun first stated his plan to donate the washbowl to Qenhirkhopshef in front of witnesses and that after this—and not necessarily on the same day—they went to court or an individual scribe to have it recorded in writing. Either way it is strange to see his statement recorded twice on the same papyrus.

Only then are we told why the washbowl was given. We know that Naunakhte was old and intended to make the statement in court about her inheritance a few weeks later. We also know that Khaemnun was not a rich man and that in ancient Egypt children were a man's (and woman's) pension:

> Delivering on this day in front of the workman Anynakhte, the workman Qedakhetef, the workman Nebnakhte, the workman Khonsu, the

workman Neferhotep, the workman Amunnakhte, and the workman Khaemnun himself, whereas the workman Qenhirkhopshef has said: "I will give to him 2¾ sacks (of grain)." And he took an oath with the Lord l.p.h., saying: "As Amun endures, as the Ruler endures l.p.h. If I take away the ration of my father my reward shall be taken away. I will give a pair of sandals to the workman Amunnakhte and he (I?) will give to him a chest, namely Maanynakhtef, on account of the writings that were made concerning the statement of their father."

Although the last part of this text is particularly obscure, it seems that Qenhirkhopshef had promised to take care of his father after the death of Naunakhte. In return he received the washbowl as a bonus on top of his share of the inheritance. Since two and three-quarters sacks were slightly more than two hundred liters of grain, one does wonder about the precise arrangement between father and son. Two and three-quarters sacks would be more than half of the normal monthly income of a workman, and it seems unlikely that Qenhirkhopshef would agree to give this to his father each month, unless perhaps there would be some future compensation, such as a larger part of the inheritance of his father. Two and three-quarters sacks per year would be even more unlikely, unless all eight children of Khaemnun and Naunakhte were to chip in, so that Khaemnun actually received eight times two and three-quarters sacks, or twenty-two sacks per year, which would be a reasonably good pension. As intricate and sometimes incomprehensible as this arrangement may seem, the general impression is that Naunakhte was in a position to divide her wealth as she pleased. Just like Tsenhor centuries later.

Who Gets Mum's Library?
Naunakhte's will was deposited in her own archive, and this archive may originally have contained at least forty literary and administrative papyri, including the famous Chester Beatty Papyri 1–19—which should not be confused with the famous Biblical papyri in Greek known by the same name—and P. DeM 1–17. The dockets and internal evidence show that the library covers a period of well over a hundred years, beginning in the reign of Ramesses II (reigned 1290–1224 BCE) and ending in the reign of Ramesses IX (reigned 1131–1112 BCE). This should not come as a big surprise, because when Naunakhte was very young she was married off to the scribe Qenhirkhopshef, the charismatic, overbearing, and

weighty character who was a village scribe for decades. Qenhirkhopshef was the first known owner of the archive, and when he died it passed to Naunakhte. It then went to their son, the scribe Amunnakhte—not *the* Amunnakhte—and after that to Amunnakhte's brother Maanynakhtef, who, like his brother, deposited his own papers in it.

8
Earth and Water: Tsenhor, Ruru, and Nesamunhotep, 497–491 BCE

Ruru Takes Over
21 September–20 October 497 BCE (P. Louvre E 3231A)

By now Tsenhor was well into her fifties and most probably a widow. Psenese had made his last will in 498 BCE (P. Turin 2126), and in 494 BCE Tsenhor wrapped up a deal started by her husband in 503 BCE (P. Louvre AF 9761), suggesting that he died in the meantime. Their daughter Ruru was now twenty years old, or slightly older, and she was working in the family business. Female choachytes concluded their own deals with clients, as Ruru did in P. Louvre E 3231A in the late summer of 497 BCE.

In this same year Darius I visited Egypt for the festive opening of a major building project, a canal that ran all the way from modern Zagazig in the eastern delta—a few miles from the ancient city of Bubastis—to Suez. This would include all kinds of festive ceremonies, very nervous Persian and Egyptian authorities, and a protocol that left nothing to chance. But that was far away from Thebes, so Tsenhor and Ruru may not have heard about this great event for some time.

In Thebes it was business as usual, and we may assume that Ruru was now doing Tsenhor's work as well. Tsenhor probably had taken Ruru on her trips through the Theban necropolis from an early age, perhaps pointing out the tomb of Pabasa and telling her why this was such an important tomb for the family. When they passed their graves, she probably taught Ruru to say a prayer for her siblings who died long before she was born, and for whoever else was left of Tsenhor's children and grandchildren. Tsenhor at this point may have been living with her daughter's or son's family, or they may have moved in with her.

In the New Kingdom (1550–1070 BCE) professional choachytes were attached to the cults of the elite, and the workmen of Deir al-Medina did this service themselves. Nothing is heard of women pouring water for their relatives, but they were of course not included in the official records. The men would often be absent, working in the Valley of Kings, and one has trouble imagining that a woman like Naunakhte—so much in charge of her own life, at least near the end—would not have been allowed to bring libations to her first husband Qenhirkhopshef.

Professional female choachytes are mentioned for the first time in the Twenty-fifth Dynasty, for example, in the abnormal hieratic P. Vienna 12003 (648 BCE) and P. Louvre E 7858, 7857C, and 7845, fragments 6–7, from 609 BCE (see "The Hidden Treasures of the Louvre" below). Unless we want to assume—on the basis of this slim evidence—that female choachytes were a southern Egyptian (abnormal hieratic) invention dating back to the Kushite period, the fact that there is no evidence of this for Dynasties Eighteen up to and including Twenty-four may simply be a case of statistics (again). No female choachyte is mentioned in P. Louvre E 7840, the official records of the Association of Theban Choachytes (542–538 BCE), but this probably only means that women were not allowed to become members of the club.

The Theban choachytes were not at the high end of the mortuary business and, for instance, the lamentations and glorifications to turn the deceased into an exalted spirit were in most cases probably performed by lector-priests rather than the choachytes themselves, although one is severely tempted to assume that—apart from the daily or weekly service for the mummies entrusted to them—women like Tsenhor could have been involved in some private ceremonies at the tombs of her clients as part of the so-called Khoiak mysteries in the fourth month of the *akhet* season.

P. Vienna KM 3865 is a hieratic ritual text from the first or second century AD from Thebes. It was to be recited by a priest assuming the role of Horus "with raised arm, sovereign in front of his Ipet, king of the gods, who shows himself in Waset (Thebes) at the beginning of each decade, to bring offerings to his forefathers," and especially Osiris-Wennefer. Directly after this, mention is made of Isis performing a *peret er kheru* for Osiris—the ancient ritual already known from the Old Kingdom (2575–2134 BCE)—and Nephthys who pours water for him, so here she does the work that was normally done by the choachytes.

Days 25 and 26 of the fourth month of the *akhet* season were of special significance. Allusions to what happened on those days and especially on the night of day 25 are even found on a relatively plain mummy board such as BM EA 35464. It measures 144 x 12 cm, and apart from a demotic inscription of thirty-nine lines it shows the *ba* spirit of a deceased woman called Tabastet, some magical amulets, and the jackal god Anubis with the deceased on a stretcher. The captions with the images are in rather clumsy hieroglyphs (with some hieratic signs), but the inscription itself—said to be the recitation by Isis and Nephthys—is in perfect demotic. After a pious wish by these goddesses that the soul of Tabastet will be received in the *duat*—the netherworld—before Osiris-Wennefer, the king of the entire land, Tabastet is said to be justified before Osiris:

> You will travel to This and sail to Abydos and they will pour water on your altar in the fourth month of the *akhet* season on day 25, in the morning of day 26, and at the remainder of the burial of the king l.p.h. of the entire land. (. . .) May you be provided with a perfect burial, and Isis, the Mistress of the West and Mistress of Burial, will salute you. (. . .) May they receive for you water of rejuvenation every day, Tabastet who was borne by Tasua.

Water of rejuvenation, indeed. It is tempting to assume that the actual work done at the tomb by the choachytes involved not just offerings and pouring water, but also some prayer like the above. However, we must return to Tsenhor's only daughter Ruru, who received a contract.

Once again the scribe is Ip son of Teos. He started his career as a witness in P. Louvre E 7837 (535 BCE) from the archive of Djekhy & Son. This was his thirty-eighth year in office, which is long even by today's standards. Ip knew Ruru as a baby. Now she was a businesswoman in her own right. Next to Ruru stood a high dignitary of the temple of Amun, Ankhefenkhonsu, who was a scribe of the Divine Book. They had come to arrange the payment for the funerary services to be performed by Ruru—probably including weekly libations—for a deceased woman called Tadyipwer, who may have been Ankhefenkhonsu's wife or mother. The payment consisted of four *arura*s of farm land, including some trees, that is, just over one hectare. This field formed the southern end of Ankhefenkhonsu's land, once again located in the well-known farming area of The Stable of the Milk Can of Amun.

The contract made for Ruru explicitly states that she is the new owner. Still, one has to assume that this would only last for as long as the funerary rites for Tadyipwer were performed by Ruru to Ankhefenkhonsu's satisfaction. He countersigned the contract in his own handwriting:

Regnal year 25, second month of the *shemu* season under [Pharaoh l.p.h.] Darius l.p.h. The god's father [and priest of Amun-Ra] King of Gods and scribe of Amun Ankhefenkhonsu son of Nespayutawy, the scribe of the Divine Book, has said to the choachyte Mrs. Ruru daughter of Psenese, whose mother is Tsenhor:

"I have given to you the four *arura*s of land [which] are located in my field [in the high land of The] Stable of the Milk Can of Amun, as the [(mortuary) foundation for] Mrs. Tadyipwer daughter of the god's father Hor, whose mother is Taweher. The neighbors of the four *arura*s of land mentioned above are: their south is the Field of the Hairdresser, their north are my lands, their west are the lands of [. . .] son of Sheshonq, and their east are the lands of Namenekhamun son of Peteratawy. To you belong the four *arura*s of land mentioned above as well as their trees.

"I have nothing on earth to say on account of them."

In the writing of the god's father of Montu Lord of Thebes Ip [son of] Teos.

In the writing of the god's father and priest of Amun-Ra [King] of Gods and scribe of Amun Ankhefenkhonsu son of Nespayutawy, the scribe of the Divine Book, in person.

Some Egyptologists believe that Ruru died soon after P. Louvre E 3231A was written, because this is the last time she is mentioned, whereas the last document in the Tsenhor papers dates to 487 BCE (P. Turin 2128), which is ten years later. However, one should keep in mind that although the title *Les papyrus démotiques de Tsenhor: Les archives privées d'une femme égyptienne du temps de Darius Ier* suggests that the Tsenhor papers published by Pestman form an archive, they are in fact what we call a dossier, an incomplete set of papers dealing with one or more people from antiquity that was composed in modern times. An archive is a collection of papers that we can *prove* were kept together in antiquity.

There is no way of knowing whether Ruru died or not. It could well be that Tsenhor's papers all went to Ruru's brother Ituru, including P. Louvre E 3231A, and that Ruru deposited her own contracts in her husband's archive after 497 BCE (we do not even know whether Ruru married). For her there was no real pressing need to keep the contract herself, because if she had worked the land each year after she acquired it from Ankhefenkhonsu in 497 BCE, nobody would contest her right to the property. Most people will only go and look for a contract the moment they need it to prove their rights (at least I do). Every so often early demotic contracts state that owners have a right to a property and their contracts, wherever they are. Besides, the Theban choachytes formed a small and tightly knit community where people knew all about each other. Also, maybe the land acquired by Ruru formed part of what in reality was a family enterprise consisting of Tsenhor (and her husband Psenese) and Tsenhor's three (half-)brothers that was now carried on by Ruru, her brother Ituru, and other relatives.

The Hidden Treasures of the Louvre

Female choachytes were not so special in ancient Egypt. They are already found in abnormal hieratic papyri from the Kushite period, albeit only occasionally. But the problem with abnormal hieratic sources is that only a few Egyptologists can read them, so publication is slow. This is actually very good news for those who can read them. Museum collections still keep abnormal hieratic gems that have not been read by anyone for the past 2,700 years or so. One of these is P. Louvre E 7858 (as well as 7857C and 7845, fragments 6–7). It was found with the archive of Djekhy & Son, predating it by about forty years.

The text was written on 21 May 609 BCE, during the reign of Nekau (Necho) II. It is the only legal contract on papyrus known from his reign. Apart from being in abnormal hieratic, it is also very damaged, which has rendered large parts of the text illegible. The contract, consisting of two columns—the main contract, a full witness copy, and a number of smaller witness signatures—is lost at the beginning. At least six and a half centimeters of text and an unknown blank margin are gone on the right side. As we proceed to the left, the damage becomes worse. The left part of the papyrus consists of loose fragments, namely 7857C and 7845, fragments 6–7, and a large unnumbered fragment. Fortunately, the full witness copy still contains many of the passages lost at the beginning of the main contract, so that we are able to provide a running translation (more or less).

P. Louvre E 7858 has been lying in the Louvre—unread and almost forgotten—ever since it was acquired by Eugène Revillout in 1885. This is not to say that Revillout did not try to read it. He actually published 'translations' of the text on more than one occasion, for instance in his *Corpus Papyrorum Aegypti* (1885–1902).

In Revillout's day, however, it was not yet known that the left part of the papyrus could be partly reconstructed from the loose fragments he had himself bought in Heidelberg in 1885, so that he only published a photo of the right part—with some fragments wrongly placed—and a consecutive translation of the main contract, the full witness copy, and some of the witness signatures as if this were a single contract.

In table 11, we only reproduce his version of the main contract and our own translation on the right.

From some parts of Revillout's translation it becomes clear that every now and then he did see something in the papyrus that modern Egyptologists see today, but 90 percent of his work on this papyrus was made up on the spot.

This is, in fact, a very straightforward and brief contract. Even the mandatory abnormal hieratic oath invoking the king and Amun is missing. Revillout's translation "prêtre d'Amon, prêtre du roi à qui Amon a donné la puissance" is nowhere in the papyrus, but it suggests that he was also looking for this oath: "As Amun lives, as the King lives, may Amun grant him victory, etc."

The only scholar who did some really serious work on P. Louvre E 7858 was the undisputed master of hieratic, Jaroslav Černý, whose famous *Notebooks* are now kept in the Griffith Institute in Oxford, including a transcription into hieroglyphs of the right half of P. Louvre E 7858 (Černý MSS 3.502). This suggests that he made his transcription from the plate in Revillout's *Corpus Papyrorum Aegypti*, which would explain why he did not transcribe some of the more obscure passages. P. Louvre E 7858 was only published recently. It took more than two hundred hours of hard work, and even then only a fraction of the problems were solved. Still, we now—more than 2,600 years after the contract was written—at least have an idea of what happened to Mrs. Ituru daughter of Peteamunip on 21 May 609 BCE, the female choachyte who received five *aruras* of land to look after the needs of the donor's mother in the hereafter, about 112 years before Tsenhor's daughter did almost the exact same thing.

Since P. Louvre E 7858 is a contract proving that the ownership of the field had been transferred to Ituru, it is tempting to suggest that Mrs. Ituru may perhaps have been the mother of Djekhy's father Tesmont, who would have been born around the time this contract was concluded, and that this is actually how the papyrus ended up in the archive of

Table 11. Parallel translation of P. Louvre E 7858

Revillout	Modern translation
L'an 2, choiak 30, du roi Niku—à qui vie, santé, force! Pnekhtosor, le prophète . . . dit à la femme choachyte Ntsusu, fille du choachyte . . . fils d'Épi, le choachyte:	[Regnal year 2, first month of *peret*, last day under Pharaoh l.p.h.] Nekau l.p.h. Has said [Pe-] tiese <son of Pa>ystjenef to the choachyte Mrs. Ituru daughter of the choa[chyte Pete]amunip:
"Je t'ai donné la part de fils formant le terrain de 3 mesures sur 15 que j'ai reçu dans le sanctuaire de Tashen au lieu dit Pmanmoounkeftah (le lieu de l'eau du dromos).	"[I have given you these/my five *arura*s of land] . . . in the high land [on] the Domain of Amun in Tashetresy . . . the Canal of Khefty (?) [true of voice] as an endowment
"Je vous ai donné cela en part pour (en échange du) domaine de Nekhta, fille du prophète d'Amon Pentubnneteru—en dehors de ma part que m'avait établie en main, comme apport, le prophète Hotep.	"[for Mrs. N.N. daughter of the god's servant of Amunras]onter Patjenef, my mother, which the god's servant of Horus . . . Patjenef established for me. South of them: the dike of
"J'ai donné en mains à cette choachyte, en transmission, cette domaine; par aliénation, (mot à mot: en dehors). C'est l'apport apporté en part depuis ce jour, à jamais, en équivalence de ces choses (indiquées plus haut). Dans le sanctuaire de'Hermonthis est le terrain de ces mesures, terrain que j'ai reçu moi-même.	"[. . . the (?) Quarter (?) of the Crocodile (?)], north of them: The Tomb of Osorkon . . . , the west of them being the . . . (?) [. . .] (and) the east of them being [. . . the children . . . (?) of Iufau].
"J'ai dit (fait la déclaration) au prêtre d'Amon, prêtre du roi à qui Amon a donné la puissance: J'ai donné cela depuis le jour ci-dessus. Personne au monde ne peut écarter ces choses de toi: ni fils, ni fille, ni frère, ni soeur, ni personne au monde agissant en maître *(hir)*."	"I have given them to you from today onward. No man on earth can exercise authority over it except you (?)." [In the writing of N.N. son of N.N.] . . . .

Djekhy & Son. *Si non è vero, è ben trovato*. But the vaults of the Louvre actually house many more hidden treasures besides P. Louvre E 7858, such as some missing items from the papers of Tsenhor.

The Missing Tsenhor Papyri

Two documents never made it into the scientific publication of the Tsenhor papers, namely P. Louvre E 3231B and C. This is very strange. P. Louvre E 3231A—which definitely belongs to Tsenhor's papers—was acquired by the Louvre in 1857 at a sale of the Anastasi collection on 23–27 June in Paris. It received the inventory number E 3231 when it was entered in the *Livre d'Entrées* by Théodule Deveria, whose brilliant career as an Egyptologist was cut short by his sudden death in 1871 at the age of thirty-nine. In 1858 or 1859 the staff of the Louvre unrolled the papyrus for conservation and found that it contained two other papyri ("plus deux petits papyrus dans le même rouleau"). By now the inventory numbers 3232 and up had been assigned to other antiquities, so that the decision was made to add the letters 'A,' 'B,' and 'C,' instead.

If we look at the dates of P. Louvre E 3231A–C, we see what is laid out in table 12.

Table 12. The dates of P. Louvre E 3231A–C

P. Louvre E 3231A	Regnal year 25, second month of the *shemu* season	21 September–20 October 497 BCE
P. Louvre E 3231B	Regnal year 25, second month of the *shemu* season, day 10	30 September 497 BCE
P. Louvre E 3231C	Regnal year 25, first month of the *shemu* season, day 29	19 September 497 BCE

This is, of course, no coincidence. These papyri were kept together in antiquity. So the question becomes: if P. Louvre E 3231A belongs to the Tsenhor papers, why not include P. Louvre E 3231B and C as well? They seem to belong together. At least the ancient Egyptian who rolled them into P. Louvre E 3231A thought they did.

But who was this ancient Egyptian? Was it Ruru's father Psenese, as was proposed by American demotist Eugene Cruz-Uribe, who published

P. Louvre E 3231B and C? Above, we saw that Psenese fell ill and probably died somewhere between 498 and 494 BCE. In that case he would
have made a most remarkable recovery in 497 BCE when P. Louvre E
3231A, B, and C were written.

P. Louvre E 3231B and C deal with the cultivation of farmland and a
man who *could be* our Psenese. But even if he was still alive, he was fifty-
six, which was very old by ancient Egyptian standards, and much too old
to work the fields himself. Or was he managing things for Ruru and Ituru?

But there is a problem with P. Louvre E 3231B and C. Each time
the name of Psenese seems to be written, the ink is partly erased, which
renders a reading of 'Psenese' uncertain—or, to be more precise, highly
attractive, perhaps likely, but still uncertain—which was, of course, also
noted by Cruz-Uribe. P. Louvre E 3231C predates B. It is a small papyrus
of 11 x 11.5 cm containing four and a half lines. The text was written by
a professional scribe who left a number of his inky fingerprints on the
papyrus. This is a memo rather than an official letter. Psenese is referred
to as "this choachyte," probably because he was given the memo to hand
over to another official in charge of the fields involved.

(To) Payiramun son of Peteamunip. Let Psen[ese], this choachyte,
work in the fields. He has paid today. Do not cause (any) delay for him
in working in them. In the writing of Peteret (?) in regnal year 25, first
month of the *shemu* season, day 29.

This is not a very polite official letter. This is an order. In an official
early demotic administrative letter, one would at least expect something
like, "Oh, may Ra give that his life be long" (even if the sender did not
mean it). This scribe bluntly states what has to be done. This could be an
email written yesterday. Remember, this was 19 September 497 BCE.

Eleven days later, the same official, Peteret (we still have some trouble reading his name), wrote P. Louvre E 3231B. This was once again
addressed to Payiramun, but this time Peteret had thought of a more
appropriate introduction. The text—as happens so often with early
demotic sources—is fraught with difficulties:

Peteret (?) greets Payiramun son of Peteamunip before Amun King
of the Two Lands. The choachyte Psen[ese] son of Herer has
brought another document in the name of Ankhsematawy son of N.N.

concerning thirty-three *aruras* of land, these lands in the name of god's father N.N., the ones that were made into the … of the place of Hor son of Wennefer, this priest of Montu, Lord of Hermonthis, whose lands were allotted to N.N. son of N.N. from regnal year 41 to regnal year 42. Let him work them. Do not cause (any) delay for him in them. In writing in regnal year 25, second month of the *shemu* season, day 10.

The obvious weak spots in the above translation are the names Psenese, which is—again—partly in a lacuna, and Heryrem, which was spelled Herer, forcing the modern editor to supplement the final 'em,' which one mostly should only do as a last resort. But even if the readings are wrong and the connection between P. Louvre E 3231B and C and the Tsenhor papers eludes us, someone in antiquity thought they belonged together because he or she rolled them up with P. Louvre E 3231A. And if the reading of these names is correct, we will have to find an explanation for the fact that Psenese, a man well into his fifties and ill enough to have his final will written, was still doing business—and no mean business, because this apparent lease-related memo was about thirty-three *aruras*, which would be more than eight hectares—at a time when his son and daughter had probably taken over the family business.

The Bread of the Choachyte
20 September–19 October 491 BCE (P. Turin 2127)

In 491 BCE Tsenhor and her eldest brother Nesamunhotep—here called Amunhotep—divided the income from the mummies of a former police officer called Nespaser son of Teos and his children. Tsenhor received a quarter of the income. Since they had at least two other (half-)brothers, any shared income had to be divided into four parts, as had been done when they divided the house of their father Nesmin in 506 BCE (P. Turin 2125). Part of Nesmin's inheritance may already have been divided fifteen years earlier.[1] The mummies of Nespaser and his children were probably therefore a new acquisition by Nesamunhotep, suggesting that the funerary services provided by him, Tsenhor, Burekhef, and Inaros and the income from these mummies were shared among them. So Nesamunhotep probably had to draw up similar contracts for his (half-)brothers as well on this day.

P. Turin 2127 was not signed by the scribe or by any witnesses. Apparently Nesamunhotep and Tsenhor decided that this was good enough (and this type of contract was seen more often as time went on in ancient Egypt, as well as today).

Regnal year 31, second month of the *shemu* season under Pharaoh l.p.h. Darius l.p.h. The choachyte of the valley Amunhotep son of Petemin, whose mother is Tays, has said to Tsenhor daughter of Nesmin, whose mother is Ituru:

"To you belongs a quarter of the bread of the choachyte and any other things that will be given to us as an offering for the mouth of the *kalasirian* of the nome Nespaser son of Teos and his children. You will perform the service of a choachyte for its quarter in accordance with their needs at any time."

There is no way Tsenhor would have been physically able to perform services in the necropolis herself. She was now sixty years old or so, and the same applied to Nesamunhotep, who was her senior by several years. One supposes they arranged this deal as the representatives of the separate branches of the family and that the work was done by their children and perhaps their grandchildren.

Even if time had been very gracious to Tsenhor's health—which is doubtful—our guess is that when she put this contract with the rest of her papers, she knew well that her days were numbered. And if Pieter Willem Pestman—who did the scientific publication of her papers—was right, both her son Peteamunhotep from her first marriage and her daughter Ruru from the second were no longer alive, along with all the other children who had not survived childhood.

But here Tsenhor was, still proud and independent, minding her own business. Maybe she was living with her one remaining son Ituru—or they had moved in with her—and on one fateful day she died peacefully, surrounded by her loved ones, who promised her that they would take care of her soul and eternal well-being. Sure, mum!

After a few generations the libations would inevitably stop, and in time Tsenhor would be—and indeed was—forgotten. After all, she was just another ordinary woman from ancient Egypt. Or was she? One would very much like to believe that she was not. I do. So let this book be her own little monument, to make sure that she will never be forgotten again. *Adishatz. A la gràcia de Diou!*

Notes

Notes to Chapter 1

1   So far, the editor of the demotic papyri from Elephantine, the German demotist Karl-Theodor Zauzich, has published two catalogs of demotic Elephantine papyri. P. Berlin 23584 is unpublished, but the author also prepared a preliminary catalog describing the characteristics of the Berlin papyri, presenting samples of the writing.

2   The best general introduction to the Aramaic, demotic, hieratic, and other papyri found at Elephantine is *The Elephantine Papyri in English: Three Millennia of Cross-Cultural Continuity and Change* (Leiden: Brill, 1996), edited by the Israeli scholar Bezalel Porten, with major contributions by Cary Martin and Günter Vittmann, which was recently published in a new edition.

Notes to Chapter 2

1   P. Rylands 1 and 2 (644 BCE) are from the reign of Psamtik I. They are in early demotic, but their provenance is al-Hiba, which was to the north of Thebes.

Notes to Chapter 3

1   Reference courtesy of Damien Agut.

2   *Ma'at* was personified as a goddess wearing a feather on her head. Before people could enjoy a happy time in the afterlife, their heart—the seat of righteousness—was weighed against this feather.

3   Eugene Cruz-Uribe, "A New Look at the Adoption Papyrus," *Journal of Egyptian Archaeology* 74 (1988): 220–23.

4   Schafik Allam, "A New Look at the Adoption Papyrus (Reconsidered)," *Journal of Egyptian Archaeology* 76 (1990): 189–91.

5   P. Bibl. Nat. 216 and 217 (517 BCE), P. Bibl. Nat. 223 (516 BCE), P. Turin
     2123 (512 BCE), P. Louvre E 7128 (510 BCE), P. Turin 2124 (507 BCE), P.
     Turin 2126 (498 BCE), and P. Louvre E 3231A (497 BCE).

Notes to Chapter 4

1   This was suggested to me by Cary Martin.
2   The analogy between self-dedication as *bak* and health insurance con-
     tracts was pointed out to me by Janet Johnson.
3   The verso of the contract is inaccessible, but in his *Quelques textes démo-
     tiques archaïques* (1895), the French pioneer demotist Eugène Revillout
     wrote that there were eight witnesses to this contract.

Notes to Chapter 5

1   See Donker van Heel, *Djekhy & Son* (Cairo: American University in
     Cairo Press, 2012), pp. 7–8.
2   Robert J. Demarée, "A House Is Not a Home—What Exactly Is a Hut?"
     in *Living and Writing in Deir el-Medine: Social-Historical Embodiment of
     Deir el-Medine Texts*, edited by Andreas Dorn and Tobias Hofman (Basel:
     Schwabe Verlag, 2006), 57–66.
3   Reference courtesy of Cary Martin.
4   Schafik Allam, "On the Right of Way in Ancient Egypt (Entry to and Exit
     from an Estate: ΕΙΣΟΔΟΣ ΚΑΙ ΕΞΟΔΟΣ)," *Journal of Egyptian Archaeology*
     97 (2011): 203–206.
5   Reference courtesy of Cary Martin.

Notes to Chapter 7

1   Janet Johnson pointed out to me that this space was probably used for
     these specific moments, and probably not for a whole week.
2   Terry Wilfong, "Menstrual Synchrony and the 'Place of Women' in
     Ancient Egypt (OIM 13512)," in *Gold of Praise: Studies on Ancient Egypt in
     Honor of Edward F. Wente*, edited by E. Teeter and J.A. Larson, Studies in
     Ancient Oriental Civilization 58 (Chicago: The Oriental Institute, 1999),
     419–34.
3   Deborah Sweeney, "Women Growing Older in Deir el-Medina," in
     *Living and Writing in Deir el-Medine: Socio-Historical Embodiment of Deir
     el-Medine*, edited by Andreas Dorn and Tobias Hofman (Basel: Schwabe
     Verlag, 2006), 135.

Notes to Chapter 8

1   The Tsenhor papers do not include any contract dealing with the division of the eleven *arura*s acquired by Nesmin in 556 BCE (P. Louvre E 10935). On the question of who owned this field after Nesmin died, just Tsenhor or the four siblings together, see "Was There a Rent-a-Cow in Thebes?" above.

Indexes

Deities
Rulers and officials
Private persons
Professions, titles, and occupations
Place names
Sources
General

Bibl. Nat. = Bibliothèque Nationale
BM EA = British Museum Egyptian
   Antiquities
CG = Catalogue Général
DB = Deir al-Bahari
DeM = Deir al-Medina
G = Giza
JdE = Journal d'Entrée
KM = Kunsthistorisches Museum
KRU = Koptische Rechtsurkunden
KV = Valley of the Kings
l.p.h. = life, prosperity, health
MH = Medinet Habu
MK = Middle Kingdom
MMA = Metropolitan Museum of Art
NK = New Kingdom
O. = Ostracon
OIM = Oriental Institute Museum
OK = Old Kingdom
P. = Papyrus
Sta. = Statue
Ste. = Stela
T. = Tablet
TT = Theban Tomb
UC = University College (London)
VOK = Valley of the Kings

Please note that the General index
includes synonyms, meaning that the
entry 'afterlife' also covers terms such
as 'hereafter' and 'netherworld.'

Deities

Amenophis 64
Amun 2, 11, 13, 23, 32, 33, 34, 35, 36, 37,
   39, 40, 41, 51, 52, 53, 81, 83, 94, 111,
   112, 123, 124, 131, 132, 133, 134,
   135, 136, 138, 139, 141, 142, 143,
   144, 147, 163, 164, 165, 166, 168,
   169, 171, 192, 197, 198, 200, 201;
   Amun of the Holy Eight 68; Amun-
   emope 88; Amunnestytawy of the
   Mansion of the Benben 170; Amun-
   Ra 139; Amunrasonter (Amun-Ra
   King of Gods) 39, 169, 170, 198,
   201; Great God 169, 170; Great One
   168; King of the Two Lands 203
Amunhotep I 108, 109
Amunhotep son of Hapu 43, 146, 165
Anty 84
Anubis 16, 101, 136, 137, 197
Apis 13, 46, 47, 48, 49; Apis-Osiris 49
Atum 16
Harsaphes 54, 94, 95, 123
Horus 4, 39, 49, 101, 163, 169, 196, 201;
   Great One of the Sacred Place 168
Isis 39, 123, 196, 197; Mistress of the
   West and Mistress of Burial 197
Khnum 24, 25, 26, 27, 30; Great God
   25; Lord of Elephantine 25
Khonsu 139

Ma'at 139, 207
Min 3
Montu 61, 62, 67, 72, 88, 89, 91, 92,
   96, 97, 124, 139, 141, 155, 158;
   Lord of Hermonthis 204; Lord of
   Thebes 62, 88, 99, 124, 125, 126,
   135, 141, 157, 175, 198
Mut 139
Neith 46, 58, 59, 61; Neith the Great,
   the Mother of God 57
Nephthys 196, 197
Nut 16
Osiris 19, 39, 40, 42, 45, 53, 55, 107,
   112, 136, 140, 165, 167, 168, 175,
   176, 196, 197; Lord of Abydos 40;
   Lord of Eternity 55
Osiris-Buchis 21
Osiris-Wennefer 196, 197
Ptah 54, 62, 72, 112, 157, 164, 168,
   169, 184
Ra 24, 49, 82, 203
Seth 15, 81, 82, 84
Sobek 120, 121; Lord of Tebtynis, the
   Great God 120
Wepwawet 74, 77, 78
Yahweh 30

Rulers and officials

Akhenaten 60, 167
Alexander Duke of Hamilton 41
Alexander the Great 28, 64
Amasis I (Ahmose I) 113
Amasis II 22, 23, 27, 29, 32, 33, 43, 44,
   45, 46, 47, 49, 50, 51, 53, 54, 55,
   58, 60, 90, 167
Amasis son of Amasis II 50, 51, 53
Amenemhat III 114
Amenmesse 181
Amunhotep I 108, 109
Amunhotep III 119, 137
Amunirdis 165, 166, 171
Ankhkara (Psamtik III) 58
Ankhnesneferibra daughter of Psamtik
   II 34, 184
Ankhu (MK) 115
Apries 28, 29, 33, 35, 46, 50
Besmut family 171
Cambyses II 23, 29, 45, 46, 47, 48, 49,
   50, 51, 53, 54, 58, 59, 60, 65

Cleopatra II 120
Cleopatra III 120
Cyrus the Great 46
Darius I 22, 23, 24, 25, 26, 27, 28, 51,
   54, 55, 60, 61, 88, 98, 112, 123,
   124, 133, 140, 147, 157, 163, 164,
   175, 183, 195, 198, 205
Djoser 168
Hadrian 57
Hakoris 165
Hatshepsut 41
Hekaemsaf 167, 168
Hippias 140
Hor son of Besmut 94, 95
Horemheb 14
Horiraâ 167
Horkheby 168
Horus, Uniter of the Two Lands,
   King of Upper and Lower Egypt
   Mesutyra, Son of Ra, Cambyses 49
Iby son of Wepemnefret (OK) 101,
   103, 104, 105
Karomama II 138
Khababash 64
Khafra 123
Khefren 123
Kheops 100
Khnumibra (Amasis II) 58
Khufu 100
Lucius Tarquinius Superbus 140
Mehywesekhy daughter of Pabasa 34,
   35
Menmaatra Setepenptah l.p.h., Son
   of Ra, Lord of Appearances,
   Ramesses Khaemwaset Meryamun,
   the God, Ruler of Heliopolis 82
Mesutyra (Cambyses II) 49, 58
Montuemhat 171
Nakhtbasteru queen of Amasis II 50,
   51, 53
Napoleon 122, 158, 159, 160
Necho II 199
Neithiyty daughter of Apries 46, 50
Nekau 199, 201
Nelson, Horatio 159
Neskhonsu daughter of Tahendjehuty
   169, 170
Nesptah son of Montuemhat 171
Nimlot 138

Nitocris daughter of Petosiris 33, 34,
    35, 36, 37, 40
Nitocris I daughter of Psamtik I 34
Nitocris II daughter of Amasis II 23
Noumenios 77
Osorkon 137, 138, 139
Osorkon II 138
Osorkon III 131, 133, 137, 138, 139,
    140, 141, 201
Pabasa son of Petebastet 34, 35, 41,
    42, 171, 195
Padineith 168
Pepy II 136, 139
Petebastet (Pedubast, Pedubastis) 138
Petiese son of Ankhsheshonq 52, 137
Petiese son of Ituru (Petiese I) 51, 52, 53
Petosiris son of Wenamun and
    Mutirdis 33, 35, 36, 39, 40, 41
Pherendates 24, 25, 26, 27
Piankhy 121, 122
Pinodjem II 169
Psamtik 122, 164
Psamtik I 28, 29, 30, 33, 34, 35, 52,
    142, 164, 207
Psamtik II 30, 34
Psamtik III 45, 46, 47, 50, 53, 54, 58,
    90, 164
Psamtik IV 164
Ptolemy I 64
Ptolemy II 15, 21
Ptolemy V 18
Ptolemy VI 80
Ptolemy VIII 120
Ptolemy Lagides 64
Pye 121, 122, 123
Ramesses Khaemwaset l.p.h.
    Meryamun, the God, Lord of
    Heliopolis l.p.h. 81, 82
Ramesses II 122, 139, 177, 192
Ramesses III 165, 189
Ramesses V 186, 187
Ramesses VI 108
Ramesses IX 192
Ramesses XI 80, 82, 86
Ravaka 26
Resseneb (MK) 115
Sety I 122
Shepenupet I 139
Shepenupet II 184

Sheshonq 138
Sheshonq III 138
Sheshonq IV 138
Sheshonq V 138
Sheshonq VI 138
Smerdis brother of Cambyses II 47
Sobekhotep III 114, 115
Taharqa 35
Takelot 138
Takelot I 138
Takelot II 138, 139
Takelot III 139
Tefnakht 122
Theomnestes 76, 77
Timarchos 77
Tjaynahebu 168
Unas 167, 168
Wedjahorresne 46, 47, 50, 52, 53, 54,
    55, 56, 57, 58, 59, 60, 61, 65
Wepemnefret (Wep) son of Khufu
    (OK) 100, 101, 102, 103, 104, 105
Xerxes I 164

Private Persons
Abigaia daughter of Samuel and
    Tshenoute 145, 150, 151, 152, 153
Adjedaâ (NK) 82
Amasis son of Psamtik 111, 112, 124
Ammonios 13
Amunhotep (builder) 13
Amunhotep (smith) 13
Amunhotep *aka* Nesamunhotep *see*
    Nesamunhotep son of Petemin *aka*
    Nesmin
Amunhotep son of Parety 21
Amunhotep son of Thotirtais 13
Amunnakhte 109
Amunnakhte (NK scribe) 189, 190,
    193
Amunnakhte son of Khaemnun and
    Naunakhte (NK) 186, 188, 190,
    191, 192, 193
Ananiah son of Azaria 30
Ananias son of Abraham 151
Andromachos 78
Ankhamunirdis 166
Ankhefenamun 136
Ankhefenkhonsu son of Nespayutawy
    197, 198, 199

Satameniu (NK) 82
Satibar 25
Sawadjy (NK) 109, 110
Sen son of Iufau and Kepeshaese 32, 35, 36, 37
Senebtisy (MK) 114, 115, 121
Setairetbint (Thabis) daughter of Petehorpakhrat and Tsenmin 64
Setyemheb (NK) 84
Shakhepery daughter of Amunhotep and Tahedja 12, 13, 14
Sheshonq 198
Suawyamun (NK) 84
Taamunniut 83
Tabastet daughter of Tasua 197
Tadyipwer 2, 107, 197, 198
Taese daughter of Psenamun and Taese 12
Tagemy (NK) 108
Tamin daughter of Kallias (Gelya) 68, 69
Tamut 30
Tanefershy daughter of Hor and Nebetwedja 20, 21, 22
Tanephthys (NK) 84
Taous 120
Tapanebtynis daughter of Sobekmen and Isiswery 120, 121
Tawa daughter of Panakhetu 22
Tawa mother of Tufhapy 74, 76, 78
Taydy (maternal grandmother of Tsenhor) 2, 98
Taymutnefer (NK) 84
Taynehsy (NK) 109, 110
Tays mother of Nesamunhotep *aka* Amunhotep 2, 3, 4, 147, 205
Tayuhery (NK) 84
Telptah (NK) 118
Teos son of Ip 61, 62, 63, 87, 88, 89, 91, 92, 93, 99, 124, 125, 126, 135, 141, 173
Teos son of Iufau and Neshorpakhrat 64
Teos son of Psamtikmenekh 31, 32, 37
Tesmont father of Djekhy 200
Tetimuthes daughter of Imuthes and Djedherbastet 15, 16, 106, 107, 126
Tetimuthes daughter of Peteatum 75
Thaues 120
Tipaâ son of Psengay 95

Tjauheser son of Neskhonsu and Neskhonsu 111, 112, 123, 124, 156
Tjaynahebu son of Bay 94
Tjayutayudeny son of Peteamunip and Setairetbint 134, 140, 141, 143, 144
Tsenamun 13
Tsenbastet 67, 68, 128
Tsenese mother of Tutu 74, 78
Tsenhor (client) 4, 10, 31, 32, 36, 37, 107, 146, 156
Tsenhor daughter of Petemin *aka* Nesmin and Ituru *aka* Ruru *passim*
Tufhapy son of Peteatum and Tawa 74, 75, 76, 77, 78, 79, 80, 89, 148
Tutu son of Imuthes 19, 21
Tutu son of Peteatum and Tsenese 74, 75, 76, 77, 78, 79, 80
Wah (NK) 109, 110
Wasetnakhte daughter of Khaemnun and Naunakhte (NK) 186, 188, 190
Wedjarenes 13
Wedjasematawy 52, 53
Wennefer (NK) 119
Wennefer son of Hor 12
Wennefer son of Horwedja and Khonsupaysarebty and grandson of Wennefer 33, 35, 36, 37, 90
Wennefer son of Petebastet 90
Wennefer son of Wesirten 90
Wesirptah 13
Wesirweris son of Nespameter 164

Professions, Titles, and Occupations

administrator 33, 58
admiral 58
agent 37
army commander 18, 30; commander of the foreign mercenaries 56; garrison commander 26; general 14, 29; *generalissimo* 138; overseer of the army 50; soldier 16, 29, 116, 117, 118
bak 113, 120, 121, 208
beekeeper 13, 140
bishop 70
bread baker 77
brewer 16, 114
builder 13, 145, 146
business partner 91, 106, 131, 164, 183

carpenter 13
cattle-keeper 3, 11, 91, 155, 157, 158, 163
cavalryman 77
chief manufacturer of amulets 168
chief of the palace 101
choachyte *passim;* female choachyte 13, 14, 97, 98, 106, 124, 126, 133, 134, 143, 144, 195, 196, 198, 199, 200, 201; libationer 15; water-pourer 12
controller of the palace 167
cook 114
courtier 47, 103, 166, 171
dancer 16
deacon 151
divine adoratrice 23, 34, 35, 37, 41, 139, 165, 166, 171, 184
doctor (physician) 13, 50, 60; chief doctor (physician, overseer of doctors) 55, 56, 58; eye doctor 50
domain manager 101
doorkeeper 88
draftsman 187
dyer 13
economic director 166
eisagogeus 78
embalmer 19, 134, 136
emperor 57
envoy 6, 29
epistates 19
faience-maker 170
farmer 14, 16, 80, 84
fashioner of amulets 169
fieldworker 114
financial manager 24, 30, 151
first chief 25
first prophet 166
fisherman 13
fourth prophet 39, 171
funerary service provider 1, 15, 16, 19, 131
gardener 114
giver of prayers 17
goatherd 94
god's father 31, 35, 36, 37, 39, 198, 204; of Amun-Ra King of Gods 198; of Montu 61, 62, 88, 99, 124, 125, 126, 135, 141, 157, 175, 198

god's seal-bearer *(khetemu-netjer)* 16, 57, 136
governor 18; of Egypt 23; of Thebes 34, 35, 40, 41
graniteworker 52
grave-digger 17
great harbormaster 52, 137
guerrilla fighter 30
gum-maker 17
hairdresser 114, 198
hem 113, 121
herdsman 114, 119
hereditary nobleman 57
inspector of the scribal council 58
intercessor 17
isionomos 13
judge 78, 79, 116, 118, 145
judicial authority 23, 145
king *passim;* King of Lower Egypt 58, 167; King of Upper Egypt 138; King of Upper and Lower Egypt 49, 58, 59, 81, 82
land-measurer 13, 77
lashane 151
lawyer 18, 67, 78
lesonis 24, 25, 26
manager 115, 167, 168, 169, 187, 190; of the palace 58; of the secret 21
master of funeral ceremonies 17
master of secrets (mysteries) 22, 32, 36, 37, 101, 136
mayor of Thebes 116
medium 17
men of Anubis 16
men of Nut 16
mer khasut haunebu 56
merchant 16, 116, 117, 118
monk 70, 151
mourner 21, 185
official 19, 23, 46, 56, 108, 109, 136, 203; district official (officer) 19, 187, 190; temple official 2, 11, 17, 24, 59, 120; town official 17
overseer: of doctors *see* doctor; of horses 168; of sacred clothing 26; of the army *see* army commander; of the double treasury of the residence 167; of the necropolis (Thebes) 17, 21, 22, 90, 93, 134, 140, 143; of the

royal *kebenut* ships 58; of the royal ships 167, 168; of the scribes of the Great Hall 58; of the storehouse of refreshments 167

pharaoh *passim*

policeman 1, 3, 9, 11, 107, 148, 204; chief of police 18, 116; *kalasirian* 1, 205

priest 16, 46, 47, 48, 49, 55, 58, 65, 105, 117, 119, 138, 139, 155, 158, 166, 168, 196; of Amun(rasonter) 39, 41, 51, 52, 53, 139, 198; of Anubis 101; of Horus 101; of Khnum 24, 25, 26, 27; of Montu 89, 204; of Osiris 40; of Sobek 121; of Wepwawet 74, 78; chief priest 39, 61, 62, 88, 99, 124, 125, 126, 141; high priest of Amun 138, 139, 169; high priestess of Amun 23, 34, 184; *ka* priest 105; lector-priest 74, 79, 101, 103, 136, 196; monthly priest (of Montu) 61, 62, 88, 99, 125, 166; priest-king 137; *wab* priest 25, 40, 119

prince 50, 53, 57, 100, 138, 167

princess 34, 46

queen 50

representative 121, 152, 205; of the king 78, 142; of Thebes 141, 142

sacred book reciter 17

satrap 23, 24, 25, 26, 27, 51, 64

scribe *passim*; chief of scribes of the royal cattle 168; of the Divine Book 101, 197, 198; of the Domain of Amun 32, 33, 35, 36; of the House of Life 60; village scribe 79; witness scribe 123

seal-bearer of the King of Lower Egypt 167

servant 17, 25, 82, 114, 120, 168, 187; domestic 114; of the divine adoratrice 34, 41; of the entrance of the palace of the divine adoratrice 166; of the falcons 16; of the ibises 16; of the royal palace 35, 37

shrine-bearer 13, 88; *pastophoros* 13, 16, 64, 88, 111, 112, 124

singer 81, 82, 84; of the interior of Amun 34, 35, 36, 37, 40, 147, 166

slave 2, 10, 14, 30, 45, 70, 81, 82, 83, 84, 85, 86, 88, 98, 106, 107, 111–21, 123, 124–29, 156, 170, 175, 176

slave trader 117

smith 13

sole (unique) friend 58, 101, 103, 167

spin doctor 50

stablemaster 81, 82, 83, 84

steward 6

stonemason 52

strategos 18, 76, 77

superintendent of the district 116

tomb watcher 17

true acquaintance of the King 58

undertaker 17

vizier 52, 115

water-carrier 17

wise woman 185

workman 107–10, 177–78, 188, 189, 190, 191, 192

Place Names

Abu Simbel 30, 122

Abusir 55, 56, 57

Abydos 39, 40, 55, 60, 197

Aegean 56, 58

Africa 28, 123

Alexandria 158

Amarna 60, 167

Armant 151

Assasif 3, 34, 41, 42, 108, 132, 171

Aswan 26, 29, 182

Asyut 73, 74, 77, 79, 80

Babylonia 48

Berenike 123

Bubastis 195

Buto 64, 101

Cairo 40, 116, 122, 136, 171

Coptos 32, 33, 35, 36, 70

Daphnai 28

Deir al-Bahari 41, 132, 169

Deir al-Medina 6, 54, 65, 70, 107–10, 132, 133, 177–82, 185, 186, 187, 189, 190, 191, 196

Delta 46, 122, 195

Dendara 136

Djeme 3, 18, 65, 68, 70, 71, 147, 150, 151, 153, 163, 165

Egypt *passim*

TT 279 41
TT 320 169
Turin Strike Papyrus 189
VOK Demotic Ostracon 2 22
Wenamun 51
Will of Naunakhte 65, 186, 190

General

Aâmu 114, 121
account 70, 119, 177, 183
administration 23, 27, 29, 90, 115,
    163; Arab rule 151; Egyptian
    administration 47, 54, 77, 107,
    119, 145, 180, 195; Persian
    administration 22, 23, 24, 26, 27, 47,
    48, 51, 53, 60, 140, 195; Ptolemaic
    administration 13, 18, 19, 78
adoption 30, 34, 35, 40, 65, 80–86,
    113, 190, 207
adultery 5, 6, 7, 66, 68, 69, 70
afterlife 12, 22, 41, 51, 53, 55, 57, 103,
    136, 139, 167, 168, 170, 197, 200,
    207; *duat* 197
Agut, Damien 207
altar 40, 41, 42, 139, 197
American University in Cairo Press
    1, 208
amulet 48, 168, 169, 197
Anastasi, Giovanni 158, 160, 161;
    Anastasi collection 93, 159, 161, 202
*Annales du Service d'Antiquités
    Égyptiennes* 48–49
annuity 66; annuity contract *see* contract
Arabs 28
Aramaic 24, 25, 27, 29, 30, 54, 207
archive 74, 79, 97, 151, 160, 161, 162,
    183, 192, 193, 198, 199; of Djekhy
    & Son 13, 33, 38, 39, 44, 89, 91,
    106, 133, 134, 140, 155, 158, 163,
    171, 197, 199, 200–202; of Tsenhor
    3, 8, 87, 93, 97, 112, 156, 160, 165;
    Tsenhor papers 1, 3, 4, 8, 9, 13, 23,
    54, 89, 99, 106, 111, 112, 131, 158,
    161, 183, 184, 198, 202, 204, 205,
    209; royal archive 60
L'archivio demotico da Deir el-Medineh
    (1967) 32
Ark of the Covenant 30
army 18, 28, 29, 30, 46, 47, 50, 58, 139

arson 52
Asiatics 114, 121
Association of Theban Choachytes 7,
    14, 17, 43, 123, 134, 137, 146, 175,
    196
Assyrians 28
d'Athanasi, Giovanni 41
aunt 76, 108, 140
autobiography 46, 54, 57, 58, 59, 60,
    65
ba 19, 197
Babylonians 30
Barsanti, Alessandro 167, 168
barter 54, 117
Belzoni, Giovanni Battista 122, 123,
    158
Berlin Museum 12, 23, 24, 158
Bibliothèque Nationale (Paris) 1, 97, 161
birth 4, 7, 10, 43, 48, 61, 62, 63, 74, 82,
    83, 87, 91, 92, 96, 162, 163, 174,
    178, 179, 185
Bolshakov, Andrey 51
Botti, Guiseppe 32
Bouchard, Pierre-François 160
brand (cattle) 32, 113, 161, 163, 164,
    165
British Museum (London) 1, 73, 93,
    122, 158, 160, 168
Brooklyn Museum (New York) 114
brother *passim*
brother-in-law 74, 117, 118
Brugsch Bey, Heinrich 96
Bubastite Gate 138
burial 21, 22, 49, 108, 110, 136, 167,
    197; intrusive burial 14
Byzantine Egypt 182
Caminos, Ricardo 138
capital 54, 127, 128, 134
Carians 30
cattle 32, 113, 142, 155, 158, 163, 164,
    168; cow (ox) 2, 3, 11, 32, 67, 80, 88,
    98, 111, 112, 155, 156, 157, 158, 161,
    163, 164, 165, 175, 176; donkey 2,
    14, 15, 83, 88, 98, 109, 112, 175, 176
Černý, Jaroslav 191, 200
cession 12, 145
chapel 53, 55, 137; mortuary chapel
    100, 103, 104, 105, 165
Chauveau, Michel 26

mummy 12, 13, 14, 16, 17, 18, 19, 21, 22, 46, 55, 106, 107, 122, 123, 134, 137, 157, 164, 166, 169, 196, 197, 204; mummification 12, 17, 50, 167; mummy label 19, 20
murder 47, 48, 49, 52, 123
Musée Auguste Grasset (Varzy) 164
Musée du Cinquantenaire (Brussels) 38
Museo Egizio (Turin) 1, 156, 158, 160
Museo Gregoriano Egizio (Vatican) 55
Museum of Fine Arts (Boston) 100
mutilation (of monument) 51, 52, 53, 56, 57
necropolis 21, 107, 137, 169; Abusir 56; Abydos 40; Asyut 74; Djeme 3, 70, 147, 163, 165; Giza 100, 103, 105; Land of Mooring 16; Memphis 15, 16, 56; Thebes 1, 2, 8, 9, 12, 15, 17, 18, 21, 22, 45, 61, 88, 107, 111, 112, 115, 124, 127, 131, 133, 135, 137, 140, 146, 147, 175, 176, 195, 205; see also overseer (of the necropolis)
Negative Confession 41
New Kingdom 54, 60, 65, 70, 80, 85, 107, 113, 115–17, 119, 132, 133, 139, 164, 171, 185, 186, 196
New Year 22, 43, 123, 134, 146
Ny Carlsberg Glyptothek (Copenhagen) 165
oath 6, 7, 65, 69, 85, 86, 117, 118, 119, 148, 149, 152, 190, 192, 20; temple oath 68, 106, 149
offering formula 40
offerings 1, 2, 12, 14, 25, 30, 31, 39, 40, 55, 57, 59, 60, 81, 103, 139, 166, 178, 196, 197, 205
Old Kingdom 27, 56, 100, 139, 196
one-third (of conjugal property) 7, 8, 61, 62, 64, 67, 69, 72, 73, 127, 134, 188
'opening of the mouth' 21, 170
oracle 108–10
Oriental Institute (Chicago) 166, 208
owner(ship) passim; co-owner(ship) 3, 11, 135, 157, 181–83
The Palace of Apries (1909) 28
Papandriopoulos, Demetrio 41
Papyrologisch Instituut (Leiden) 19, 20

Les papyrus démotiques de Tsenhor (1994) 44, 198
A Papyrus of the Late Middle Kingdom in the Brooklyn Museum (1955) 114
parents-in-law 17
Passover 30
paterfamilias 73, 74
patron deity 43, 108, 146
payment passim
pension 191, 192
peret (er) kheru 103, 196
Pernigotti, Sergio 44
Persian 23, 27, 28, 29, 45, 46, 47, 50; Persian conquest 22, 34, 50, 51, 53, 57, 59, 70, 140; Persian Empire 23, 46; Persian occupation 23, 27, 28, 64; Persian period 12, 13, 29; Persians 22, 48, 50, 51, 53, 54, 57, 64, 70, 140, 184; see also administration
Pestman, Pieter Willem 44, 87, 106, 108, 131, 198, 205
petition 18, 19, 51, 59, 76–80, 115, 120
Petrie, William Flinders 28, 136
Petrie Museum of Egyptian Archaeology (London) 113
Phoebe A. Hearst Museum of Anthropology (Berkeley) 100
Phoenicians 30
phyle 61, 62, 88, 99, 124, 125, 126, 141
plow 3, 11, 12, 39, 77, 80, 114, 155–58, 199, 203, 204
Posener, Georges 48
prayer 9, 17, 25, 41, 195, 197
pregnancy 14, 61, 63, 87, 91, 162, 176
La première domination perse en Égypte (1936) 48
Processional Way of Amun 133–36, 141–44, 147
property passim; conjugal 5, 7, 8, 67, 69, 72, 73, 127, 145; property transfer 36, 81, 86, 100, 103, 106, 115, 200; see also marital property arrangement
Ptolemaic period (Egypt) 12, 13, 18, 32, 54, 66–69, 88, 111, 113, 126, 137, 142, 147, 164
Ptolemies 58, 64
public protest 75, 76

pyramid 100, 103, 123, 167, 168; Step
  Pyramid 167–68
Quaegebeur, Jan 39
Quelques textes démotiques archaïques
  (1895) 208
Ramesside scribal tradition 34
al-Rasul family 169
Ray, John 120
receipt 21, 24, 33, 70, 94, 95, 142, 155,
  157
*Reflections of Osiris: Lives from Ancient
  Egypt* (2002) 120
Rent-a-Cow 155, 158, 209
Rhodians 30
right of way (*eisodos* and *exodos*) 5, 144,
  145, 208
Roman period 27; Roman king 140;
  Roman Republic 140
royal family 23, 53, 137–38; Tanite
  kings 138
royal titulary 23, 49, 58
saint 55, 70, 146
Saite period 12, 13, 34, 137
Saite Restoration 52, 90
Saites 90
sale *passim*
Salt, Henry 122, 158
sanctuary 55, 58, 201
satrapy 23
security 37, 66, 74, 75, 112, 113, 128,
  152
Serapeum 48, 49, 120
sex 30, 71, 72, 119, 162, 177
Shabbat 30
Sherden 82
sibling 3, 5, 17, 30, 81, 83, 84, 145,
  148, 149, 150, 181, 187, 195, 209
silver 2, 12, 21, 24, 37, 45, 61, 62, 64, 66,
  67, 68, 72, 88, 94, 98, 111, 112, 117,
  118, 123, 124, 128, 134, 139, 141,
  157, 164, 168, 170, 175, 176, 184
sister *passim*
sister-in-law 89, 148
son *passim*; stepson 123
son-in-law 65
Spiegelberg, Wilhelm 26, 38, 179
Stable of the Milk Can of Amun 32,
  132, 163, 164, 165, 197, 198; as
  cattle brand 32, 161, 163, 164, 165

Star of Horus 101
strike 169, 189
Sweeney, Deborah 184, 185, 208
Syrian 111, 116, 118
taboo 176, 180, 181
Taheri, Amir 17
tax 23, 33, 142; cattle tax 142; dike tax
  142; donation tax 142; harvest tax
  31, 39, 80; mummy transfer tax
  17, 21, 22, 134; poll tax 142; sales
  tax 141, 142; sheep tax 142; tax
  exemption 139; tax reduction 58;
  tax reform 142; tax revenues 142
Teeter, Emily 208
Tel Aviv University 184
temple 2, 8, 12, 17, 24, 45, 46, 47, 48,
  52, 57, 58, 59, 60, 61, 68, 87, 88,
  98, 107, 112, 120, 149, 165, 168,
  170, 175, 176, 182; of Abu Simbel
  122; of Amun (al-Hiba) 51, 52,
  53; of Amun (Karnak) 2, 111,
  112, 124, 131, 138, 139, 140, 166,
  197; of Amunhotep son of Hapu
  165; of Buto 64; of Djeme 68; of
  Hatshepsut 41; of Jerusalem 30; of
  Khnum (Elephantine) 24, 26, 30;
  of Land of Mooring 16; of Montu
  (Karnak) 61, 62, 63, 67, 72, 88, 89,
  91, 92, 96, 97, 99, 124, 125, 141; of
  Neith (Sais) 46, 59, 61; of Osiris
  (Karnak) 140; of Osiris (Sais) 55;
  of Sobek (Tebtynis) 120, 121; of
  Wepwawet (Asyut) 77; of Yahweh
  (Elephantine) 30
Theban rebellion 18, 138, 139, 140
title deed 4, 33, 34, 35, 36, 74, 135, 156
Toivari, Jaana 186
tomb 2, 9, 12, 13, 14, 15, 16, 17, 21, 22,
  34, 41, 42, 45, 50, 51, 56, 57, 70, 98,
  106, 107, 109, 112, 115, 118, 136,
  137, 147, 166, 167, 168, 169, 170,
  171, 175, 176, 196, 197; Belzoni's
  Tomb 122; cenotaph 55, 57; cult
  room 42, 100, 103; foundation
  deposit 55; house of eternity 103;
  ka tomb 16; *mastaba* 56, 100; royal
  tomb 22, 107, 122, 133; shaft tomb
  42, 56, 57; sun court 42; tomb of
  Akhenaten 167; tomb of Amasis